PRIMARY
POLITICS

PRIMARY POLITICS

*How Presidential Candidates Have Shaped
the Modern Nominating System*

ELAINE C. KAMARCK

BROOKINGS INSTITUTION PRESS
Washington, D.C.

Copyright © 2009
THE BROOKINGS INSTITUTION
1775 Massachusetts Avenue, N.W., Washington, D.C. 20036
www.brookings.edu

Library of Congress Cataloging-in-Publication data

Kamarck, Elaine Ciulla.
  Primary politics : how presidential candidates have shaped the modern nominating
system / Elaine C. Kamarck.
      p.   cm.
  Includes bibliographical references and index.
  Summary: "Explores one of the most important questions in American politics—how
we narrow the list of presidential candidates every four years. Focuses on how presidential
candidates have sought to alter the rules in their favor and how their failures and successes
have led to even more change"—Provided by publisher.
  ISBN 978-0-8157-0291-7 (cloth : alk. paper)— ISBN 978-0-8157-0292-4 (pbk. : alk.
paper)
  1. Presidents—United States—Nomination. 2. Presidential candidates—United States.
I. Title.

  JK521.K36 2009
  324.273'15—dc22   2009020914

9 8 7 6 5 4 3 2 1

Typeset in Minion

Composition by Cynthia Stock
Silver Spring, Maryland

Printed by R. R. Donnelley
Harrisonburg, Virginia

To Nelson W. Polsby

1934–2007

A scholar who loved politics.

CONTENTS

PREFACE   ix

INTRODUCTION   1

1 THE GOOD OLD DAYS?
   When Parties Controlled Nominations and Primaries
   Were to Be Avoided at All Costs   6

2 SEQUENCE AS STRATEGY
   How Jimmy Carter "Got It" and Taught Subsequent
   Presidential Candidates the New Rules of the Road   27

3 THE FIGHT TO BE FIRST
   Why Iowa and New Hampshire Dominate
   Presidential Nominating Politics   51

4 PROPORTIONAL REPRESENTATION
   Why Democrats Use It and Republicans Don't   81

5 DEVIL IN THE DETAILS
   How the Delegate Count Shapes Modern
   Nominating Campaigns   119

6 DO CONVENTIONS MATTER ANYMORE?
*Superdelegates, the Robot Rule, and the Modern
Nominating Convention* 147

7 THE PROBLEM OF "THE DECIDER" 174

NOTES 187

INDEX 207

PREFACE

The field of political science includes many wonderful books that trace the evolution of the modern presidential nomination system and describe how it works today. This book owes a great deal to all of them. Some, such as Byron Shafer's classic *Quiet Revolution: The Struggle for the Democratic Party and the Shaping of Post-Reform Politics*, tell the story of the last major transformation of the system that took place in and around the tumultuous political year of 1972 and changed the balance of power within American political parties. Others, such as Austin Ranney's *Curing the Mischiefs of Faction: Party Reform in America*, place the most recent changes in the nomination system in the context of Americans' historic ambivalence toward political parties. Nelson Polsby's *Consequences of Party Reform* clearly delineates the values at stake as the country moved from one nomination system to another. Larry Bartels's work in *Presidential Primaries and the Dynamics of Public Choice* focuses on the key role that voters have in the creation of momentum in the new system. Andrew Busch and William Mayer have published a variety of important works on the modern nominating system, including *The Front-Loading Problem in Presidential Nominations*, which traces the growth of the modern primary system. These books have been augmented over the years by many journalistic accounts in the Theodore White tradition that tell the human and inside story of presidential nominations and general elections.

So where does this book fit? This book focuses on a more or less untold part of the presidential nomination story, the interaction between presidential candidates and the modern nominating system. It began life as a doctoral dissertation, written under the late Nelson Polsby and submitted by the author to the University of California, Berkeley, in 1986. The title, "Structure as Strategy: Presidential Nominations in the Post-Reform Era," reflected not only my academic training under Polsby, but also a considerable amount of direct experience in presidential politics.

Although I finished writing the doctoral dissertation, it was years before I took a full-time academic job. I had gotten hooked on practical politics and spent the years after the dissertation in a variety of political and policy jobs, ending up in Bill Clinton's White House where I created and managed the National Performance Review for Vice President Al Gore. I went to Harvard in the fall of 1997 to teach management, not politics. Thanks to Al Gore I'd become a member of the Democratic National Committee and its Rules and By-Laws Committee in 1997. So, with the exception of those meetings, where on occasion I would show off by explaining some piece of ancient history relating to the rules, I moved on from the dissertation topic and wrote a book about the future of government instead.

And then came the long and fascinating 2008 primary election. Both the Democratic and the Republican nomination contests went on longer than any contests had in either party since the 1980s. And instead of getting bored, the public became fascinated, if also somewhat appalled, by the process of nominating presidential candidates. By that time I'd been a "superdelegate" for eight years, and no one I knew had ever cared. But suddenly, in 2008, my grown children looked at me with new respect; my Harvard colleagues introduced me at meetings as a superdelegate; and the whole country began to discuss what had heretofore been a boring piece of inside baseball—how delegates to the national conventions were elected. I knew something had changed when a student from Greece, who was taking my course in presidential elections, reported that when he had called home and spoken to his father, a grocer in Athens, before he could show off even a bit of his new-found knowledge his father asked him what the superdelegate count was!

It was time to dust off the dissertation. I had to retype the portion on superdelegates in order to post it on the Harvard Kennedy School website. (The first-generation Apple it had been written on was at the bottom of a trash heap somewhere.) When the posting got thousands of hits, I figured that the time had come to dust off the whole thing, update it, and tell the story of why we nominate presidents the way we do.

Over the years, presidential candidates have affected the shape and structure of the current system in two ways. First, changes in the rules of the game are almost always made in the context of the preceding presidential elections. Democrats, in particular, have been obsessed with thinking that they could solve their late-twentieth-century losing streak with the "right" rules. But while the Democrats have been the most frenetic tinkerers, the Republicans too have fallen prey to the desire to "fix" the system. Second, presidential candidates, especially those with some sort of political clout within their party (usually front-runners), have tried to modify the rules in ways that will enhance their prospect of gaining momentum and winning delegates.

The role of presidential candidates in creating the modern nomination system is often left out of books on the topic. In American culture it is considered "unseemly" to attempt to "fix" the rules in your favor. Thus there are few public records or paper trails for the historian or political scientist to follow. Basically you had to be there, early on and inside a political campaign, to watch the maneuvering unfold. I was on the inside of some of the campaigns discussed in this book, but not all. If you aren't on the inside but suspect something is up, you have to know whom to ask and what to ask them. As this book will show, once a respectable amount of time has passed, your ordinary political insider is more than happy to talk about his or her strategic manipulations—but figuring out whom to ask in the first place can confound even the most intrepid scholar.

If in this book there seems to be a slightly more robust storyline on the Democratic side than on the Republican side, it is for good reason. First, I am a lifelong Democrat and as such have been on the inside of some of the elections in this book. In 1980 I served as director of the Democratic National Committee's Compliance Review Commission; in 1984 I was Walter Mondale's director of delegate selection; and in 1988 I was the deputy campaign manager for the short-lived [Bruce] Babbitt for President Campaign. In 1992 I was on the staff of the Democratic Leadership Council and got to watch the early days of the Clinton for President campaign. Ironically, since I was serving in the White House and busy "reinventing government" in 1996, I had little to do with that campaign, but Clinton was an incumbent without a challenger, so it didn't matter much. And in 2000 I was senior policy adviser to Al Gore's presidential campaign. That campaign was enough to cure even a hardcore campaign junkie like myself of campaigns, and so in 2004 and in 2008 the closest I got to a campaign was serving as a superdelegate and as an at-large member of the Democratic National Committee and member of the Rules and By-Laws Committee.

The second reason why this book contains more of a Democratic than a Republican story is that it was the Democrats who created the modern presidential nominating system. The Republicans have not spent the past thirty-six years discussing rules. Compared to the Democrats, they have had very few rules commissions or committees; and because they have, until recently, believed firmly in passing the rules for the next nominating season at their nominating convention, there have been relatively few opportunities for Republican presidential candidates to try to "adjust" the system to their advantage. This doesn't mean that they are not subject to the same incentive structures as Democratic candidates. It simply means that at the national level they are loath to try to change the system. They also believe seriously in states' rights, and their actions match their rhetoric; they are reluctant to impose national mandates on the state parties. Finally, this book covers ten presidential elections, of which Republicans won six and Democrats won four. In general, winners are much less likely than losers to see problems in a system that nominated them and got them to the White House.

I wish to express my gratitude to three Harvard students who at various times have served as research assistants on this book: Johnson Elugbadebo, Jacqueline Palumbo, and Alec Barrett. I also wish to express my gratitude for support from the Institute of Politics at Harvard University, which provided research assistance and which sponsored two important conferences that were critical to some of the insights in this book. I also wish to thank the Shorenstein Center at Harvard's Kennedy School of Government for its support in allowing me to explore some of the dimensions of momentum in presidential campaigns. Also, many thanks to those who shared their insights with me back in the 1980s when this book began life as a doctoral dissertation and to those who talked to me about more recent campaigns.

PRIMARY
POLITICS

INTRODUCTION

Senator Hillary Clinton walked into the small conference room at the Park Phoenix Hotel on Capitol Hill wearing one of her signature pantsuits, this one navy blue silk with white piping. It was May 22, 2008, and she was in the home stretch of what had been a very long race for the Democratic nomination for president. Along the way her once-surefire quest had run into a phenomenon, a first-term senator from Illinois, half-white, half-African, named Barack Obama. Her husband, former president Bill Clinton, famously called "the first black president" by the author Toni Morrison, had watched the black community reject his call to support his wife and rally to Obama. Hillary and Bill had seen old friends like New Mexico governor Bill Richardson endorse Obama. Yet despite many setbacks, Clinton's delegate count was tantalizingly close to Obama's. She had had a strong finish, winning a series of important states, including Ohio and Pennsylvania. She had a good argument for why she was a stronger general election candidate. And yet in the end, she needed delegates.

Hence the meeting at the Park Phoenix.

Around the table sat seven of her most loyal supporters. Some had been with her for decades; some were currently serving on the staff of her presidential campaign; and all were members of the Democratic National Committee's Rules and By-Laws Committee. I was one of them. Nine months earlier every single member of the Rules Committee in the room had joined the majority of their colleagues on the committee in a vote that stripped

Michigan and Florida of 100 percent of their delegates. Those two states had, in violation of Democratic Party rules, attempted to hold their primaries too early in the primary season. In the summer of 2007, when the decision to punish Michigan and Florida had been made, there had been chaos in the nomination calendar, with New Hampshire threatening to hold its primary before the end of the year. In the summer of 2007, Clinton had fully expected to knock Barack Obama out of the race early and to deal with the two upstart states, Florida and Michigan, as the party's anointed nominee.

But history played out differently. By the time Clinton sat down with her seven supporters on the Rules and By-Laws Committee, she needed the delegates from Florida and Michigan. She was trying to do something that presidential hopefuls before her had tried to do. She was trying to reverse Barack Obama's momentum and catch him in the delegate count. Seating the full delegations and awarding Clinton the proportion of the vote she had won in each state would close the gap between her and Obama considerably. It wouldn't put her over the top, but it might, just might, change the assumption that had dominated political circles for months—that Obama had this thing locked up.

The merits of the issue on the table were fairly clear. Yes, voters in Florida had voted in good faith and they felt betrayed that their votes would not count. As Clinton, fresh from campaigning in Florida, pointed out, being stripped of their delegates opened up old wounds from the 2000 general election when the Supreme Court had cut off the vote count, thereby giving Florida, and the election, to the Republicans. On the other hand, the Obama campaign had taken the Democratic Party at its word, not campaigning in those two states and going so far as to take his name off the ballot in Michigan.

At stake in the upcoming meeting of the Rules and By-Laws Committee was the Democratic Party's authority to make and enforce rules, an authority that had, miraculously, survived repeated challenges over nearly four decades. If Senator Clinton had really pushed hard, most of those gathered at the Park Phoenix would have gone back on their August 2007 votes and voted to seat the full delegations. But she did not push hard. For one thing, it would not be an easy vote. Moreover, it would take fourteen votes, not seven, to seat the full delegations; and as became evident more than a week later, when the Democratic Party's Rules and By-Laws Committee met in a circus-like atmosphere at the Marriott Wardman Park Hotel in Washington, Barack Obama, not Hillary Clinton, had a narrow majority of the votes on the committee.

Perhaps this was why Hillary Clinton, usually a force to be reckoned with in any meeting, seemed unusually quiet, as if she knew that this was the end game and that it would not end well. Her only hope of changing the outcome was to ask the seven people in the room to torch a system that most of them had spent decades creating. But she could only ask them to play that kind of political hardball if she knew they had the votes to win.

When the Rules Committee met nine days later on May 31, it took nearly nine hours of private meetings for each member to show his or her hand. It didn't happen until about 5:00 p.m. on May 31 when, in a dingy conference room, surrounded by trays of petrifying Mexican food left over from lunch, the committee took a straw vote. Clinton's preferred proposal, to seat all the delegates from both states with full votes, had only eleven votes—three short of the needed majority. When the public vote was taken an hour later, several Clinton supporters voted—as did I—for a compromise solution, at the request of the committee co-chairs, James Roosevelt and Alexis Herman. The compromise reinstated half of the Michigan and Florida delegations, punishing them for their violation of party rules without altogether disenfranchising primary voters, and it gave Clinton four fewer votes in Michigan than she would have received if the delegates had been distributed in proportion to the popular vote, thereby rewarding the Obama campaign for respecting the committee's rules and staying out of Michigan.

One week later, Hillary Clinton ended her presidential race in a gracious speech in front of hundreds of supporters in Washington, D.C. Hers was not the first presidential campaign, and it would not be the last, whose fate would be entangled with party nominating rules—the topic of this book.

In contrast to the general election, where, like it or not, the Electoral College, enshrined in the U.S. Constitution, has ruled since the days of John Adams, the rules of the game for party nominations for president have changed dramatically over the course of American history. The process has undergone many transformations; from the days of "King Caucus" when candidates for president were nominated in the House of Representatives, to the convention system when candidates were nominated in large, raucous gatherings of party bosses, to the current system where primaries dominate but party rules still mystify the public.

This book weaves the presidential candidates into the story of the modern nomination system by showing how they regard structure strategically, how they attempt to shape the system to their advantage, and how their failures and successes have contributed, after the fact, to even more change. It is organized around the primary characteristics of the modern nominating system. Each chapter shows where those features come from, how they have influenced candidate strategy, and how these actions have, in turn, caused further evolution in the system.

Chapter 1, "The Good Old Days? When Parties Controlled Nominations and Primaries Were to Be Avoided at All Costs," describes and contrasts the old and new presidential nominating systems.

Chapter 2, "Sequence as Strategy: How Jimmy Carter 'Got It' and Taught Subsequent Presidential Candidates the New Rules of the Road," describes the fundamental strategic imperative of the modern system: sequence. It shows how some presidential candidates have attempted to manipulate sequence for their own strategic purposes and how others have adapted or failed to adapt to the sequence as strategy imperative.

Chapter 3, "The Fight to Be First: Why Iowa and New Hampshire Dominate Presidential Nominating Politics," describes why those two states came to play the dominant role in the system that they do today and the role that presidential candidates have had in reinforcing their primacy.

Chapter 4, "Proportional Representation: Why Democrats Use It and Republicans Don't," traces a twenty-year fight over proportional representation that took place in the Democratic Party but not in the Republican Party. Along the way, candidates had strong feelings about the kinds of rules that would help them or hinder them in the race for the nomination and attempted to change the system accordingly.

Chapter 5, "Devil in the Details: How the Delegate Count Shapes Modern Nominating Campaigns," describes how candidates have tried to use the delegate count and the allocation rules that determine it to create momentum and even change the course of the nomination.

Chapter 6, "Do Conventions Matter Anymore? Superdelegates, the Robot Rule, and the Modern Nominating Convention," takes on the question of the modern nominating convention, which still is, in spite of all the changes that have happened, the final, legal end of the process.

Chapter 7, "The Problem of the Decider," is perhaps an unusual end to a book on the nomination system. Rather than advocate one or more of the many more rational nomination systems that have been put forward over the years, I explain why none of them has ever seen the light of day and argue for smaller, more incremental steps.

1

THE GOOD OLD DAYS?

*When Parties Controlled Nominations and
Primaries Were to Be Avoided at All Costs*

Imagine for a moment that Franklin Delano Roosevelt, Dwight D. Eisenhower, and John F. Kennedy were among us once again. Then imagine that they found themselves in the middle of a presidential campaign. Despite all the new technologies now in use, especially the Internet, the campaign strategy for the general election campaign would look quite familiar to them. The goal would be to win the majority of electoral votes. States would be categorized as safe for one party or the other, hopeless for one party or the other, and battleground. Candidates would move around the country giving speeches and holding rallies in an attempt to win the electoral votes of the crucial battleground states. The goal of winning a majority of electoral votes and the strategy of winning a critical combination of states would be very much the same as it had been in their day.

Suppose, however, that our three returned presidents found themselves in the midst of a campaign for a party's nomination. The object today would be the same as it had been in their day, to accumulate a majority of the delegates at the party's nominating convention. There, however, the similarities would end. The strategy for winning the nomination today bears little resemblance to the strategy of days gone by because the system is so different.

For example, imagine FDR's confusion to hear people talking about momentum in February of the year before the convention. In his day *momentum* was a term used to describe behavior at the convention itself. Imagine Eisenhower's reaction to the news that Senator Howard Baker had given up his job as majority leader of the Senate as well as his Senate seat *four years before* the presidential election in order to campaign full-time. Eisenhower spent the years before the 1952 convention in Europe with NATO, arriving home in June to campaign for his nomination at the convention in July. Imagine JFK's reaction to the fact that Walter Mondale, a former vice president and favorite of the Democratic Party establishment, had to enter every single primary election held in 1984. Kennedy had to run in primaries, but only because he was viewed as a young upstart by party leaders and needed to prove his vote-getting ability before he could deal seriously for delegates. And imagine how all three men would react to a Democratic primary race in which two senior Democratic senators, Joseph Biden and Christopher Dodd, who between them had logged seventy years in the United States Congress, were never seriously considered for their party's nomination because all the attention and energy were consumed by a former first lady and a first-term African American senator!

What our three returned presidents would soon realize is that winning the presidential nomination of one of America's major political parties in the twenty-first century is a whole new ballgame. Changes in the structure of the nominating system have driven fundamental changes in strategy. The structural changes originated with a reform movement that began in the Democratic Party in 1968 in response to its failure to deal with and incorporate the movement against the war in Vietnam into party politics. This reform movement had the effect of changing not only the Democratic nomination process, but (mostly inadvertently) the Republican nomination process as well. But before we look at the current nomination process and its evolution since the late 1960s, it might make sense to look back at the process it replaced.

The Pre-Reform Nominating System

For much of American history, beginning in the Jacksonian era and up until the catalytic turmoil of 1968, the presidential nominating system was controlled almost exclusively by political parties. The system had some public features, but it was primarily a private, intraparty affair. For most of this time, getting the nomination meant winning the allegiance of enough major party leaders—who controlled delegates—to accumulate a majority of the delegates at the nominating convention. Presidential primaries, the most visible and public part of the campaign, were not an important part of this process. The real race for the nomination was conducted either totally in private or in the semi-public arena of local caucuses and state conventions.

While the process differed from state to state and from party to party, the outlines of the nominating system were similar. Every four years, local party officials, precinct leaders, ward leaders, county chairmen, and others would participate in a series of meetings throughout their state that usually culminated in a state convention. At that point the assembled party leaders would choose a group of (mostly) men to attend the national nominating convention. If the state party happened to be controlled by a particularly powerful party "boss," often a big-city mayor, a governor, or a senator, he would have sole discretion in the selection of delegates. If there was no dominant party leader, the selection of delegates would be privately negotiated by party officials and elected officials.

Presidential primaries were invented as part of the Progressive Era reforms that took place in the early decades of the twentieth century. They were meant to bring the nomination process at all levels, not just presidential, out of the backrooms of political parties. It was the invention of primaries that caused, for the first time ever, state legislatures and state laws to be involved in the process of nominating candidates for office, since some states enacted legislation requiring primaries and then provided public money to pay for them.

Thus from the Progressive Era through 1968 the presidential nominating process had two stages. The first stage involved competition in a small number of presidential primaries. However, such common practices as electing delegates pledged to favorite-son candidates (whose only goal was to wield influence at the convention) and electing delegates who were pledged to no candidate at all, meant that party leaders maintained firm control over the convention delegates. More often than not, presidential candidates didn't even put their name on the ballots of primaries. The primaries were thus largely irrelevant to the outcome of the old-fashioned nominating contest. They were sometimes used strategically—to demonstrate a presidential hopeful's vote-getting ability, for instance; but as two famous scholars of presidential elections point out, this meant that in the pre-reform era, running in presidential primaries was often a sign of weakness, not strength. Writing in the 1971 edition of *Presidential Elections,* Nelson Polsby and

Aaron Wildavsky sum up the role of primary elections in the pre-reform era as follows: "Primary activity is often (although by no means always) a sign that a candidate has great obstacles to overcome and must win many primaries in order to be considered for the nomination at all."[1]

The second, and more important, stage of the old-fashioned nomination system involved intense negotiation between the serious national candidates and powerful party leaders. Decisionmaking power rested firmly with the party leaders in stage two. In 1960, W. H. Lawrence, a political reporter for the *New York Times*, used the image of the proverbial smoke-filled room to describe the nomination race: "With the end of the contested presidential preference primaries, the struggle for the nomination has moved from Main Street to the back rooms of individual party leaders and state conventions dense with the smoke of cheap cigars."[2] Eight years later, in the last of the old-fashioned nomination races, James Reston described the fight for the nomination as follows: "This presidential election is being fought out on several levels. The most important of these, so far as nominating candidates is concerned, is the least obvious . . . the underground battle for delegates."[3]

To understand just how different the modern nomination system is, consider the case of Senator Estes Kefauver of Tennessee. Kefauver was an unusual senator for the 1950s. A liberal from Tennessee, he defeated the famous political machine of sometime U.S. representative and Memphis mayor Edward Crump—an achievement few Tennessee Democrats could claim—to win his 1948 bid for the United States Senate. In 1951, just as thousands of Americans were buying their first televisions, Senator Kefauver conducted a series of hearings on organized crime. The Kefauver hearings made for gripping television. They introduced midcentury Americans to the Italian mafia and a world of colorful and violent gangsters, the real ancestors of the fictional Tony Soprano. The hearings turned Kefauver into a household name. In 1952 he decided to run for the Democratic nomination for president.

Kefauver beat the sitting Democratic president, Harry Truman, in the New Hampshire primary. All in all, he entered and won twelve of the fifteen primaries held that year, campaigning across the country in a coonskin cap. By the time the Democratic convention began in July 1952, Kefauver had received over 3 million votes, compared to about 78,000 votes for his chief opponent, Adlai Stevenson.

But Kefauver's national fame did not translate into the affection of his peers, and in the old-fashioned nominating process, that was what mattered. Delegates were controlled by powerful politicians, not primary voters. Kefauver's hearings had ended up taking down some fellow Democrats, such as the Senate majority leader from Illinois, Scott Lucas; former governor Harold G. Hoffman of New Jersey; and Mayor William O'Dwyer of New York City. In addition Kefauver was one of only three senators who refused to sign the so-called Southern Manifesto in 1956.[4] (The others were Senate Majority Leader Lyndon B. Johnson of Texas and fellow Tennessee senator Albert Gore Sr.) Despite his national fame, Estes Kefauver was too much of a maverick for the party. Blocked by party bosses and opposed by President Truman (who did not run), Kefauver lost the nomination to Adlai Stevenson on the third ballot. Four years later, he failed in his second bid to become the Democrats' nominee, but was awarded the second spot on the ticket as a consolation prize.

In 1960, by contrast, Senator John Kennedy of Massachusetts used stage one of the nominating system, the presidential primaries, to convince the party bosses who ruled stage two that he could win a general election despite his Catholic faith. This was his sole purpose in filing for a series of primaries, and the investment took time to pay off. The "Political Notes" columns in *Congressional Quarterly* for the summer of 1959 report on a very active John Kennedy and his lieutenants traveling from state to state trying to block favorite-son candidacies that could deprive Kennedy of his chance to prove his vote-getting ability in the primaries.[5]

On April 5, 1960, Kennedy won the Wisconsin primary, but not in a way that would convince the people who mattered that he could overcome anti-Catholic prejudice. As Theodore White tells it in his famous book, *The Making of the President, 1960,* "The break of the popular vote would convince none of the bosses who controlled the delegates of the East that he was a winner. He had lost all four predominantly Protestant districts. . . . His popular margin had come entirely from four heavily Catholic areas. . . . They would be read, he knew, wherever men read politics, as a Catholic-Protestant split."[6] Kennedy's loss in Wisconsin's Protestant districts meant he had to look for another opportunity to put the Catholic question behind him and convince the powerful bosses who could deny him the nomination that it would not be a problem in November. A month later he found his opportunity in West

Virginia, where his decisive victory over Hubert Humphrey effectively ended Humphrey's presidential ambitions and gave Kennedy and his people the ammunition they needed to convince party leaders that a Catholic could win in a non-Catholic state. Thus for Kennedy the primaries were important to his negotiations in stage two.

Yet four years later, the success of Barry Goldwater's insurgent campaign for the Republican nomination demonstrated once again the irrelevance of primaries. Rather than appeal to primary voters, Goldwater's campaign focused on capturing the party machinery from the grass roots on up. In his book on Goldwater, Stephen Shadegg points out that Goldwater had been effectively cultivating the loyalties of the precinct committeemen and county chairmen who chose delegates for more than six years before 1964.[7] Similarly, John Kessel recounts an October 1961 meeting in Chicago at which a group of conservatives, led by Republican strategist Cliff White, decided to encourage other conservatives to "run for precinct, county and state party positions of little visibility which would allow them to select conservative delegates in 1964."[8] As journalist Robert Novak pointed out, "The new Goldwater style of pre-convention politics did not waste time on winning over county and state organizations, but concentrated on actually taking over the county and state organizations by an inundation of Goldwater volunteers."[9]

In contrast to today's highly visible process of electing delegates in primaries and open caucus systems, Barry Goldwater's chief strategist, Cliff White, pursued a nearly invisible nomination strategy aimed at the low- and mid-level party elites who would eventually control the delegate selection process. This process largely escaped the scrutiny of the press, and what was observed was anecdotal and sketchy at best. Theodore White's comments about Goldwater's nomination are most instructive in retrospect: "All over the country, in the spring and summer months, such precinct, county and state conventions gathered without national notice. . . . Like the Kerensky government, they [the Republican establishment] were unaware of revolution until the Red Guards were already ringing the Winter Palace."[10]

In circumstances almost impossible to imagine today, Barry Goldwater was able to wrap up a delegate victory by early May 1964 while losing primaries and sliding downhill in the polls. The May 18, 1964, issue of *Newsweek* concluded that the fight for the Republican nomination was all but over because Goldwater already had the delegates he needed—even though his support among Republican voters was down to 14 percent and he had just suffered his second major loss in a primary.[11]

Fast Forward to 2008

Twenty-first-century voters, accustomed to the importance of presidential primaries, find the old-fashioned nomination system very undemocratic. The strength of this sentiment was dramatically illustrated in the spring of 2008, when the public discovered the existence of superdelegates—that is, unpledged party leaders and elected officials. New voters, especially, were appalled to discover that superdelegates could potentially overturn the will of the voters. Fearing that Hillary Clinton's institutional advantages and early lead among these delegates could lead her to victory at the convention, Barack Obama's campaign fed the notion that superdelegates should reflect the will of the voters. "The superdelegate spin," recalled Obama campaign manager David Plouffe, "was directed at superdelegates," in an effort to make sure that as Obama held a lead among district-level delegates, the superdelegates would follow suit.[12]

It wasn't a hard sell. In the modern nomination system the notion that party leaders would exercise their judgment, independent of the preferences of primary voters, was so abhorrent that many superdelegates found themselves rejecting their own role. Donna Brazile, a superdelegate and party strategist, told the *Los Angeles Times,* "My one vote shouldn't matter more than a voter who stood in a long line in the rain in St. Louis to vote," and threatened to quit her post at the Democratic National Committee if superdelegates decided the nomination race.[13] U.S. Representative Ron Kind of Wisconsin called for scrapping the entire superdelegate system, saying that perplexed constituents had been asking him about the process: "I've always believed you've got to make participatory democracy as simple as possible. . . . The whole concept of superdelegate leaves people scratching their heads. It smacks them as possibly going against the wishes of the voters."[14] Other superdelegates sat tight and hoped that the primaries would produce a clear winner so that they wouldn't have to choose.

As we will see in chapter 6, the creation of superdelegates was an attempt to restore a role for party leaders following the reforms of the early 1970s, which some felt put too much power in the voters' hands. But for the first six nomination contests following their reinstatement, party leaders played no independent role in stage two; instead they merely ratified the results of the primaries. And when it looked as if they might play such a role in the close nomination race of 2008, large parts of the public screamed in protest and treated the very existence of superdelegates as illegitimate, insisting that they follow the will of the voters.

Explaining the Reforms

How did this happen? What accounts for the transformation of the presidential nomination system? The story starts with the Vietnam War and the protest movement it sparked. That movement found a forum in the 1968 presidential primaries when protest candidate Senator Eugene McCarthy of Minnesota challenged President Lyndon Johnson in the New Hampshire primary and nearly beat him. (This was not the first time that the actual "winner" of the New Hampshire primary was deemed the "loser," owing to his failure to meet public expectations; nor would it be the last.) McCarthy's run prompted Robert Kennedy, the slain president's brother, to enter the race for the Democratic nomination. President Johnson saw the writing on the wall and on March 31, 1968, just over three weeks after the New Hampshire primary, went on national television to declare that he would not seek reelection.

Johnson's decision not to run opened the door for his vice president, Hubert Humphrey, to declare his candidacy. Thus began a tumultuous nomination race run against the backdrop of an unpopular war, the assassination of Martin Luther King Jr., riots in the streets of major American cities, and the eventual assassination of Robert Kennedy. By the time the 1968 Democratic Convention met in Chicago, anger was boiling over inside and outside the hall. Mayor Richard Daley's police force clubbed the youthful protesters who had gathered outside the hall to protest Lyndon Johnson's war in Vietnam while antiwar activists inside the hall cried foul as Hubert Humphrey (who did not enter and thus did not win *one single primary*) coasted to the nomination.

Humphrey was the last candidate to be nominated in the old-fashioned way. As the sitting vice president and therefore heir apparent, he inherited delegates that had been chosen as far back as 1967 to support Lyndon Johnson. Humphrey's attitude toward primaries was shaped in part by his own losing experience in 1960, but it also represented the view held by most party leaders at the time: "Any man who goes into a primary isn't fit to be president. You have to be crazy to go into a primary. A primary now is worse than the torture of the rack."[15] As the vice president, Humphrey saw no reason to enter *any* 1968 primaries. Despite the chaos in and around the convention, he easily won the nomination on the first ballot.

Antiwar sentiment, to the extent that it had been expressed in primary voting for both McCarthy and Kennedy, had little impact on the distribution of power inside the convention hall. In fact, 25 percent of the delegates to the 1968 Democratic convention had been chosen in 1967—long before the New Hampshire primary crystallized antiwar sentiment against President Johnson. And of the nine primaries that even listed the presidential candidates on the ballot, only three had been in states where the primary results were binding when it came to delegate selection.

To the young antiwar activists inside and outside the hall, the deck seemed stacked against them. On Tuesday of convention week, the party regulars who were in charge sought to buy a modicum of peace by promising that a reform commission would look at the nomination process. That reform commission, formally known as the Commission on Party Structure and Delegate Selection, but called the McGovern-Fraser Commission for its two chairmen, Senator George McGovern of South Dakota and Mayor Donald Fraser of Minneapolis, would ultimately transform the presidential nomination system for Democrats and Republicans alike. Political scientist Byron Shafer tells the story of this commission in great detail in *Quiet Revolution: The Struggle for the Democratic Party and the Shaping of Post-Reform Politics.* He concludes that the reforms enacted in the years between 1968 and 1972 resulted in "the diminution, the constriction, at times the elimination, of the regular party in the politics of presidential selection."[16]

The McGovern-Fraser Commission, which set out the basic parameters of the modern nominating system, was heavily dominated by antiwar party reformers. It conducted hearings and meetings throughout 1969, and its recommendations were adopted by the Democratic National Committee in time to affect the 1972 nomination contest. The cumulative effect of the McGovern-Fraser reforms was to transform the modern nominating system into a system where mass persuasion replaced elite persuasion.[17] Two developments played a central role in this process: the transformation of party caucuses from closed to open events and the related increase in the number of binding presidential primaries.[18] Along the way, the traditional closed-party caucus essentially disappeared. According to Shafer, this outcome was largely unanticipated by the Democratic National Committee: "Despite its status as the device by which the largest share of delegates to national party conventions in all of American history had been selected, the party caucus was abolished by rules which were not assembled in any one guideline, which were not presented in the order in which they had to be assembled, and which did not at any point claim to be making their actual, aggregate, institutional impact."[19]

The extent of this change is frequently misunderstood since many caucuses still have old-fashioned trappings and continue to conduct routine party business.[20] In most states, however, caucuses have become the "functional equivalent of a primary," in Senator Howard Baker's words.[21] Three new requirements bear primary responsibility for this shift: first, that first-tier caucuses (usually party meetings held at the precinct level) be open to anyone who wished to be known as a Democrat (implicit in the McGovern-Fraser Commission's Guidelines A-2, A-5, and C-5); second, that every participant as well as every candidate delegate declare his or her presidential preference (Guidelines B-2 and C-1); and third, that first-tier caucuses be held at the same time on the same day (Guideline A-5). Together these reforms transformed a semi-public process into a completely public and transparent system.

The post-reform history of caucus systems shows just how friendly the reformed caucuses have been to nonestablishment candidates and how far caucuses have moved from control by the regular party. In the pre-reform era caucuses were often closed to those who did not hold party office, and if they weren't formally closed the lack of publicity surrounding them made it difficult for all but the most intrepid and well organized to attend them, let alone dominate their business. In 1972 most states still had some form of party-run caucus and convention, but by then the caucuses were open and publicized. In many of these states McGovern activists turning out for their first caucus upset and dominated the party regulars, who remained faithful to the 1968 nominee, Hubert Humphrey. Over the weekend of June 17–18, McGovern won a majority or a plurality of delegates in party conventions in Colorado, Montana, Utah, Idaho, Connecticut, North Dakota, and Puerto

Rico. His wins were substantial enough that aides to rivals Humphrey and Senator Edmund Muskie admitted that the race for the nomination was all but over.[22]

In 1984 the Mondale campaign spent over $500,000 organizing for caucuses in Maine and had the endorsement of every major Democratic politician in the state. Yet Senator Gary Hart of Colorado, a young challenger with momentum coming off his surprise victory in New Hampshire, but no organization, beat Mondale as hundreds of new participants turned out for the party caucuses. When Maine governor Joseph Brennan accompanied Vice President Mondale to several Portland caucuses, he remarked to a friend that he could tell that Mondale was in trouble the moment he walked into the room and saw it filled with people he had never seen at a party function before.[23]

And most recently, in 2008, the new kid on the block, Senator Barack Obama, beat the establishment candidate, Senator Hillary Clinton, in the all-important Iowa caucuses and in every subsequent caucus state with the exception of Nevada.

Growing turnout among first-time caucus-goers has played an important part in the success of outsider candidates. Turnout for the Iowa caucuses, for example, has increased over its previous level in almost every year in which there has been a competitive contest for the nomination (see table 1-1). (Although 1992 was a competitive year for the Democrats, the presence of favorite son Senator Tom Harkin in the race made that year's Iowa caucuses all but irrelevant.) By 2008 turnout had increased by a factor of 11 for the Democrats since 1972 and by a factor of 6 for the Republicans since 1976, and the Iowa caucuses were a far cry from the informal living room affairs they had been just a few decades earlier.

A dramatic increase in press coverage—amounting to a frenzy at times—both reflected and helped bring about this change. This development was jump-started by the requirement that all of a state's caucuses take place simultaneously. This measure had the intended effect of making it impossible for one group of candidate supporters to pack several caucuses on several different days. It had the unintended effect of transforming first-tier caucuses into a discrete, newsworthy event. Traditionally, precinct caucuses, county conventions, and other party meetings had been scheduled by local party leaders, sometimes within a period of time mandated by state statute

Table 1-1. *Turnout in the Iowa Caucuses, 1972–2008*

Year	Democrats	Republicans
1972	20,000	No data, incumbent
1976	38,500	20,000
1980	100,000	106,051
1984	75,000	No data, incumbent
1988	126,000	108,838
1992	30,000	No data, incumbent
1996	50,000	96,451
2000	60,800	87,000
2004	124,000	No data, incumbent
2008	227,000	120,000

Source: Rhodes Cook, *United States Presidential Primary Elections 1968–1996* (Washington: Congressional Quarterly, 2000), p. 258. Mark Blumenthal, "Iowa Caucus: Only the Beginning" (www.pollster.com/blogs/iowa_caucus_polling_only_the_b.php [April 28, 2009]). "Iowa Caucus Turnout Shatters Record," CNN, January 3, 2008 (http://politicalticker.blogs.cnn.com/2008/01/03/democratic-caucus-turnout-shatters-record/ [November 25, 2008]).

or party rule and sometimes at a convenient time before the next-level convention. Unless the state statute or party rules mandated a uniform starting date, party meetings could be spread out over a period of weeks or even months. Once the caucuses were required to be held on the same day (and once participants were required to state a presidential preference), it became possible for the press to observe and report the outcome of first-tier caucuses in much the same way they would report the outcome of a statewide primary.

In 1972 most of the press misunderstood the importance of the Iowa caucuses and therefore missed the early signals of McGovern's strength and Muskie's weakness in the new system. In his book on that campaign, Jules Witcover explains the explosion in press coverage of the 1976 Iowa caucuses as follows: "For their romance with Muskie the press and television paid heavy alimony after 1972 in terms of their reputation for clairvoyance, let alone clear thinking and evidence at hand. In 1976, if there were going to be early signals, the fourth estate was going to be on the scene en masse to catch them."[24]

Since then, interest in the Iowa caucuses has only increased. Yet the importance of caucuses as a whole has declined as the number of primaries

Table 1-2. *Number of Presidential Primaries: Pre-Reform Era and Post-Reform Era*

Year	Number of primaries
1932	17
1936	14
1940	14
1944	15
1948	14
1952	16
1956	19
1960	16
1964	17
1968	15
Reform Movement	Reform Movement
1972	21
1976	27
1980	37
1984	31
1988	35
1992	35
1996	33
2000	35
2004	32
2008	42

Source: Congressional Quarterly, *Presidential Elections since 1789*, 4th ed. (Washington: Congressional Quarterly, 1987); and Office of the Secretary, Democratic National Committee, Washington, D.C.

Notes: In many of the pre-reform years, a presidential primary was held to elect delegates, but this did not necessarily mean that the presidential candidate's name appeared on the ballot; often it was only the names of those running for convention delegate. Texas is counted as a primary even though it has a caucus attached to it as well. In some years one party uses a primary to select delegates and the other party does not; thus these numbers may differ slightly from one party to the other. In 2008, Florida and Michigan were initially beauty contests; eventually the Democratic Rules Committee seated those delegations with half votes.

has grown (table 1-2). This trend can also be traced in part to the McGovern-Fraser Commission. Guidelines issued by the commission were intended to make caucuses not only more open but also more representative of the electorate. Representativeness in those days had two meanings: the reformers wanted convention delegates to represent minorities and women; but they also wanted delegates to represent the presidential preferences of those who turned out. Hence the mandate that participants in first-tier caucuses declare a presidential preference. This forced local politicos to jump into presidential politics much earlier than they had been accustomed to doing and made the new caucus procedures complicated to administer and even more complicated to control. Thus many party leaders decided that holding a primary was safer than trying to comply with the complex new caucus procedures. Burned by the record number of credentials challenges brought in 1972 as a result of rules that were new and not fully understood, in the following years some state party chairmen turned to the presidential primary as a system that would be easier to implement.[25] Other states adopted a primary because they believed it would generate more media attention than a caucus. Still others adopted primaries in order to become part of a de facto regional primary. Two state chairs encouraged their states to adopt a presidential primary because George McGovern's people had taken over their states' caucuses in 1972 and they did not want that to happen again.[26]

Primaries have not only grown numerous, but they have also seen a sharp increase in their importance as a result of McGovern-Fraser reforms that made primaries binding on the selection of delegates. The few "beauty contests" (primaries that don't count for purposes of delegate selection) that took place in recent elections took that form because the states in question tried to move early and were denied permission by the Democratic National Committee (see table 1-3).

Reluctant Reformers

While Democrats were transforming their nomination system into a public system easily observed and covered by the press and others, the Republicans were undergoing their own less comprehensive transformation. However, theirs was far more inadvertent. Republican politics in the 1960s did not lead to internal calls for reform. First, as we have seen, the insurgent element in the Republican Party, the Goldwater conservatives who captured the party in 1964, were able to accomplish this takeover within the framework of the rules as they existed at the time, unlike the antiwar insurgents who were foiled at the 1968 Democratic Convention. Second, the Republicans won the 1968 and 1972 presidential elections, and winning always reduces a party's inclination to change the rules. But finally and perhaps most important, until 2008 the Republicans retained a system that preserves final

Table 1-3. *Number of Binding versus "Beauty Contest" Primaries:*
Pre-Reform and Post-Reform Era

Year	Presidential preference poll is binding	Presidential preference poll is advisory only (a beauty contest)
1952	3	7
1956	3	7
1960	3	8
1964	3	9
1968	3	6
Reform Movement	Reform Movement	Reform Movement
1972	12	6
1976	17	8
1980	33	2
1984	19	6
1988	34	1
1992	35	0
1996	32	1
2000	30	5
2004	31	1
2008	40	2[a]

Notes: The presidential preference poll is a fairly recent innovation in American elections. Thus many primaries in the pre-reform era and some primaries in the post-reform era took place without a separate preference poll on the ballot. This accounts for the disparities between this table and the previous table.

a. In 2008, the Michigan and Florida primaries on the Democratic side were initially beauty contests only; eventually those delegates were seated with half votes.

authority over the nomination system to the quadrennial nominating system itself. This means that changes in the Republican rules could not happen as a result of party actions *between* nominating conventions; they could only happen once every four years at the nominating convention. This system has made it impossible for Republicans to appoint the kinds of commissions and committees that the Democrats have used to adjust their rules after every presidential election.

Nonetheless, the Republican National Committee did appoint, in 1968, a sixteen-member Committee on Delegates and Organization, the "DO" committee, which banned automatic delegates (people who became convention delegates as a result of their party or elected office) and required that the meetings at the first stage of the delegate selection process (usually the caucuses held at the precinct level) be open to all party members.[27] These provisions, adopted by the 1972 convention, initiated a transformation in the Republican Party that paralleled the changes taking place in the Democratic Party. The party caucus and convention system, long a private or at most semi-public process, became, by law in both parties, a fully public system. While the Republican Party rejected other attempts to mimic the Democratic reforms, especially efforts by the so-called Rule 29 Committee to adopt a system similar to the affirmative action recommendations of the Democrats, the opening up of the caucus/convention system effectively transformed the nominating system.[28] The end of the old-fashioned caucus/ convention system led many Republican state parties to decide that a primary was the easiest path to follow. In many states where Democrats controlled the legislature, they passed legislation that created a primary for *both* political parties. In addition, as the process became public it attracted the kind of attention and voter interest that was unheard of in prior days. Republican Party leaders envied the attention that the Democrats were receiving and began a competition for attention in the nomination process that continues to this day.

Consider the case of Iowa in 1976. On caucus night in Iowa that year, traditionally the same night for both parties, Democrats, as a result of the reform rules, were required to state their presidential or uncommitted preference upon attendance at the caucus; Republicans were not. The preferences of those Democrats elected to county conventions were reported, along with their names, to the Iowa Democratic State Committee that very night, making it possible for the press to report on the outcome of the night's events almost as if a primary had been held. No such reports were made on the Republican side; thus their contest went unnoticed. For example, in Jules Witcover's 656-page book on the 1976 presidential campaign, the Republican precinct caucuses in Iowa are never mentioned, while the Democratic caucuses receive a full chapter, even though the nomination race between Governor Ronald Reagan and President Gerald Ford was every bit as interesting and close as the race on the Democratic side.[29]

Between 1976 and 1980 Iowa's Republican State Committee, eager to share in the media limelight and to increase caucus attendance, decided to hold a nonbinding straw poll at each precinct caucus and to have the results reported to the Republican State Central Committee at a central location in Des Moines. In the words of Marge Askew, a national committeewoman active in Republican politics at the time: "People kind of realized that we had to do something. We decided to go along with the media and poll delegates at the caucuses and use it as a real media affair because they (the media) were going to do their own polling if we didn't."[30]

FRONTLOADING AND MANDATORY ATTENDANCE

The transformation of the nomination process from a semi-public to a public process dramatically increased the ability of the press to cover and interpret the early stages of the nomination race. As a result, the early Iowa precinct caucuses and the first-in-the-nation New Hampshire primary assumed disproportionate importance in the nomination race. As presidential candidates poured resources into early states, attracting the lion's share of media attention, other states, envious of the attention, began to look for ways to hold delegate selection contests earlier.[31] This interaction or vicious circle created the phenomenon known as "frontloading," the move by more and more states to schedule their nominating contests earlier in the year of the convention.[32] Table 1-4 looks at the timing of presidential primaries in recent presidential elections.

Victory (however defined), or at least a decent showing in these early, highly influential contests, is increasingly critical for would-be nominees. A former mayor of New York City, Rudy Giuliani, learned this lesson the hard way in 2008. As we will see in chapter 2, Giuliani's decision to skip the early contests and start his campaign in Florida left him on the sidelines of the race. By the time he got to Florida he had spent nearly a month out of the story and out of the limelight. He did poorly in the Florida primary and was out of the race shortly thereafter.

But it's not just the early caucuses and primaries that matter. In the old-fashioned system primaries were, by and large, not binding. In contrast, in the modern nomination system serious candidates for president cannot pick and choose which contests they will and will not enter. If they do, they risk being left out of the delegate count, and equally important, out of the very public chronicle of the race. To some analysts' surprise, Hillary Clinton failed to understand this dynamic in 2008. Unlike Giuliani, Hillary Clinton was not a rookie. She had, after all, been through two nomination races with her husband. However, she and her advisers were spooked by their loss in the

Table 1-4. *Frontloading of the Presidential Nomination Process: Percentage of Convention Delegates Elected by Month for Contested Nomination Years, 1964–2008*

Percent

Year and party	Pre–calendar year of the convention	Before March	March	April	May	June
1964 Republicans	9	9	13	22	21	16
1968 Democrats	25	2	6	12	23	26
1972 Democrats	0	7	14	18	33	24
1976 Democrats	0	9	17	25	29	20
1980 Democrats	0	5	35	19	20	21
1980 Republicans	2	13	25	14	24	21
1984 Democrats	0	6	26	17	21	13
1988 Republicans	0	2	51	15	14	17
1988 Democrats	0	5	53	19	10	13
1992 Democrats	0	3	47	19	11	20
1996 Republicans	0	6	57	7	20	9
2000 Democrats		2	72	9	10	6
2000 Republicans	0	17	54	6	16	8
2004 Democrats		25	52	8	7	7
2008 Republicans	0	80	6	4	6	4
2008 Democrats	0	70	13	5	10	3

Sources: Republican data from Rhodes Cook, *United States Presidential Primary Elections 1968–1996*, chaps. entitled "Race for the Presidency: Winning the 2000 Nomination," "Winning the 2004 Nomination," and "Winning the 2008 Nomination" (Washington: Congressional Quarterly Press, 2000, 2004, 2008). Democratic data from Office of the Secretary, Democratic National Committee.

Note: The data do not include Democratic superdelegates; they do include Republican National Committee members.

first caucus state, Iowa, and the campaign, short on money, decided to devote less time and resources to the remaining caucus states. Barack Obama ended up accumulating large delegate leads in those states, and the ability of caucus states to report first-tier results as if they had held primaries meant that Clinton suffered serious momentum losses as well.

Critiquing the Reforms

One might have expected changes in the nomination system as fundamental as those that occurred between 1968 and 1976 to cause a considerable amount of grief among the party leaders who abruptly lost so much power. In fact, that did not happen. While the Democrats and occasionally the Republicans have continued to create reform commissions to try to solve this or another real or perceived problem with the nomination system, the fundamental premise of the modern nominating system—that voters, not political elites, should choose party nominees—has never been fundamentally challenged. Having made a very public show of their party's superior virtue due to its more open processes, the Democrats have not dared, in more than a quarter of a century, to retreat from their widely promoted participatory ethics.

It has fallen to academics to assert the virtues of the old-fashioned nomination system. Perhaps the most comprehensive critique can be found in *Consequences of Party Reform* by Nelson Polsby.[33] Polsby looked not only at the ways in which the reforms have weakened political parties, but more important, at the consequences of weakened parties for governance. Polsby maintained that the ascendance of numerical participation as the chief value by which a nominating system should be judged was flawed. He argued that it displaced the values of peer review and peer deliberation in the process. This was not simply an old-fashioned point of view. Today most parliamentary democracies in the world—democracies that are every bit as healthy as our own—nominate their major party leaders through a party-run process in which peer review is a major consideration.

Peer review loomed so large in Polsby's analysis because *Consequences of Party Reform* was written in the aftermath of Jimmy Carter's failed presidency. Polsby was clearly concerned that the reformed system produced inadequate presidents by encouraging and rewarding candidates who employed strategies geared toward mobilizing factions of primary voters, rather than forming coalitions of governing elites. For Polsby, the Carter administration was a case in point of a strategy that succeeded in the nominating system but was a massive failure in the governing process.

The defense of the old system was not without merit. And as we shall see, more recent party reform commissions have sought to enhance, albeit modestly, the role of elected and party officials. As late as 1992, scholars such as Andrew E. Busch defended the merits of the old-fashioned "mixed system," arguing that it successfully accommodated both insider expertise and, contrary to the conventional wisdom, radical grass-roots change.[34] Nonetheless, by the last decade of the twentieth century the debate over the nominating process had fizzled, even among academics.

To explain this quiescence, we reach back to the long history of American ambivalence toward political parties, an ambivalence that originates with James Madison's warning in *Federalist* No. 10 that we must "cure the mischiefs of faction." After all, as Austin Ranney pointed out, Americans have always regarded political parties as, at best, unavoidable evils whose propensities for "divisiveness, oligarchy and corruption must be closely watched and sternly controlled."[35] Since choice in the general election has been limited, for all practical purposes, to two major parties for most of American history, there has been periodic pressure to make the nominating system more "fair" and to allow for changes in the balance of political power within parties. As Ranney and others trace the history of the presidential nominating process, one is struck by the ever-widening circle of participation produced by successions of reformers.[36] The shift in nominating power from congressional caucuses to national conventions and from local party elites to primary electorates is all part of a process in which direct participation in presidential nomination has been extended to larger and larger numbers of people.

The culmination of this pattern would be the adoption of a national primary, the ultimate in public participation. The fact that for the past thirty years polls have shown substantially more than 50 percent of the American public in favor of a national primary is in keeping with the strain in American political thought that favors the simplest and most direct form of democracy and that distrusts the role of parties as intermediaries in public choice. Most recently, Ken Baer, writing in the journal *Democracy,* has suggested that it is about time to get rid of delegates altogether and proceed to direct election of the presidential nominees.[37]

Conclusion

Thus, by the turn of the twenty-first century, the old-fashioned nomination system had been relegated to history, with large numbers of voters, young and old, believing that even the last remnants of the old system—the superdelegates—were somehow illegitimate. But while some political scientists have, from time to time, tried to keep alive the values inherent in the old-fashioned peer review system, politicians have looked at this very differently. What they understood was that once participation was broadened to include the voters there could be no turning back the clock. As the passions aroused by the Vietnam War and the other protests of the 1960s faded, the party reform movement came to be dominated by the interaction of presidential candidates and their interests with political parties. A series of rules, governing such issues as the timing of contests, the allocation of delegates, and the conduct of the delegates, became the fodder of intricate negotiations among presidential candidates, party leaders, and sometimes the party's rank and file. These negotiations have fundamentally changed the political strategy of candidates for each party's presidential nomination. It is to that story that we now turn.

2

SEQUENCE AS STRATEGY

How Jimmy Carter "Got It" and
Taught Subsequent Presidential Candidates
the New Rules of the Road

Of all the people who wanted to become president in 1976 it was Jimmy Carter, a former Democratic governor from Georgia, unknown on the national stage, who best understood the new nomination system. As the first post-reform Democratic candidate to make it all the way to the White House, Carter's impact on the shape and structure of the modern nomination system cannot be overstated. His two campaigns for the Democratic nomination taught subsequent generations of candidates the new rules of the road. The most important of these was: sequence mattered. From then on, presidential candidates of national standing would attempt to manipulate the sequence of contests as best they could, and presidential candidates without that clout would have to build their campaign strategies around the sequence for any given year.

What Carter and his strategist Hamilton Jordan understood better than anyone else was that, for an unknown candidate, an early win in the first delegate selection contest of the year—the Iowa caucus—would be critical. They realized that in a fully public and transparent system a sequence of wins would generate momentum, and momentum would generate traditional campaign resources, such as money and endorsements. Momentum in a fully public nominating system means that simply winning in one primary (or caucus) can have a powerful impact on a candidate's odds of victory in the next primary or caucus. These insights were incorporated into a campaign plan written by Jordan. The Carter team realized that in the reformed system *sequence was strategy,* a lesson other candidates would ignore at their peril.

While Jordan understood the fundamentals of sequence, Carter's other close ally, Jody Powell, understood the press. He knew that "if they [the press] missed it once, they damn sure weren't going to miss it twice" and thus anticipated that the 1976 Iowa caucuses would be so heavily covered that they would generate the momentum Carter needed.[1] While Jimmy Carter was completing his Iowa precinct organization, Mo Udall's campaign advisers were still arguing about whether they should seriously contest the Iowa caucuses, an oversight from which the Arizona representative's candidacy never recovered.[2]

Not only was Jimmy Carter the first modern candidate to fully understand the importance of the first contest, but he was also the first to understand the importance of the sequence of contests that followed. Although the ability of an underdog former southern governor to move the dates of presidential primaries around was minimal, Carter tried in 1975 to create the best possible calendar for his candidacy. Important to the overall Carter strategy was an early southern contest in which Carter could defeat George Wallace, thereby removing any competition for delegates from his southern base. When the Florida legislature took up a bill to move its primary from early March to later in the spring, the Carter campaign acted quickly. Carter himself, his close friend and lawyer Charles Kirbo, and his campaign manager, Hamilton Jordan, made a trip to Tallahassee in March 1975. There, with the help of House Speaker Don Tucker and Governor Reubin Askew, they succeeded in keeping the Florida primary in early March.[3]

President Carter Creates the Southern Super Tuesday

Jimmy Carter went on to run in 30 presidential primaries, the most any candidate had ever competed in. He then went on to win the presidency against the incumbent Gerald Ford, a candidate hobbled by the scandals of his party and wounded by the fact that he had pardoned former President Richard Nixon for his role in Watergate. But considering the poor state of the Republican Party in 1976, Carter's win was a narrow one, and Jimmy Carter took office an outsider in his own party. Thus almost from the very beginning, Carter was aware of the dangers he would face in his quest for the 1980 nomination.

By the time Carter was preparing for his reelection campaign in 1980, he had resources far beyond his own powers of persuasion and his friendship with a fellow southern governor to use in influencing the sequence of nomination contests. The power of the presidency could cause state legislators to pay serious attention to the wishes of White House political aides. The White House also controlled the Democratic National Committee and the DNC's Compliance Review Commission.[4] The latter body approved state delegate selection plans and offered advice to state parties on how to comply with the latest series of delegate selection rules, including the newly adopted "window rule," which named the second Tuesday in March as the start date of the primary season and the second Tuesday in June as its end.

At the time that the initial planning for the president's renomination was going on, Carter was facing the possibility of a nomination challenge from Governor Jerry Brown of California. Three things were important to the Carter campaign as it looked toward renomination, and they all revolved around creating the best possible sequence. First, the season should begin no earlier than it had to in order to avoid providing a challenger with a chance to acquire an early win and resources with which to challenge the president. In other words, Carter did not want another upstart like he himself had been in 1976, coming out of nowhere and amassing the resources for a serious challenge. Second, numerous simultaneous contests should be held soon after the first two, making it difficult for a challenger with relatively limited resources to compete. Third, the early contests should be primarily in southern states, allowing Carter to build up a delegate lead early. Hamilton Jordan, Carter's chief strategist, sent the president a memo that emphasized the importance of thus structuring the nomination season to Carter's advantage.[5]

The new DNC window rule forced the 11 states that had held a primary or first-tier caucus before the second Tuesday in March 1976 to look for a date inside the new window. But the rule also permitted the DNC to give exemptions to certain states. The possibility of exemptions allowed the White House political operatives, led by a young man named Rick Hutcheson, who was Carter's staff secretary, to try to make the sequence as favorable as possible to the president. Iowa and New Hampshire received assurances from the White House that they would receive exemptions from the rule, as it had promised when the rule was enacted. Not only did Carter owe Iowa especially, big time, but he was genuinely fond of the Democrats in that state. Minnesota, Vice President Mondale's home state, was also an easy call for the White House, and they encouraged an exemption for Minnesota so that it too could go early.

However, by the time the Maine and Massachusetts requests to move their events to earlier dates were considered by the Democratic Party's Compliance Review Commission, Massachusetts senator Ted Kennedy had replaced Jerry Brown as Carter's most serious rival for the nomination. By then Carter's presidency was in serious trouble. The economy was terrible, suffering from both high unemployment *and* high inflation; there was an energy crisis, long gas lines, and a presidential retreat at Camp David that ended up increasing the nation's anxiety and calling Carter's leadership into question. Senator Kennedy and President Carter had never gotten along, and as Carter's presidency progressed, Kennedy's overt criticism increased. It became clear that Kennedy would challenge Carter.

It would have been easy to conclude that allowing Massachusetts and Maine to go early would help Kennedy since Massachusetts was his home state and Maine a neighboring state, and he would naturally be expected to do well in both. For all their problems governing, Carter's strategists understood not just the role of sequence, but also the role of expectations in the new nominating system. Because expectations for a candidate are high in his home and neighboring states, the White House political strategists decided that permitting these two states to go early would not disadvantage Carter. John Rendon, a DNC official with strong Massachusetts ties, arranged for an early primary with the speaker of the House, the top official in Massachusetts supporting President Carter. The reasoning was simple. If Carter lost there it would be discounted; if he won it would be a huge blow to Kennedy.

The White House also encouraged Mississippi, South Carolina, and Oklahoma (all good states for President Carter) to move to the earliest dates possible within the window. Together with the Georgia and Alabama primaries, which moved to the second Tuesday in March, they joined the Florida primary to create an early nomination calendar in southern territory favorable to the president. These moves, along with some successful, some unsuccessful, attempts at damage control, such as placing the Missouri caucuses on the same day as the Pennsylvania primary (to offset an antici- pated northern loss with a southern win) and convincing Washington State to remain a caucus, not a primary, state so as to deprive Brown of an early western primary, gave Carter the best shot possible at establishing momen- tum early in the season.

When the 1980 primary season opened, the maneuvering over dates quickly paid off. Carter started off with a significant victory in Iowa, followed closely by a win in the Maine caucuses, right in Ted Kennedy's backyard, and a substantial win in the New Hampshire primary, again in Kennedy's back- yard. Although the early manipulations of the calendar could not prevent a challenge to Carter's nomination, they were enormously helpful to Carter in establishing an early series of wins and an early delegate lead. According to Polsby: "It took the president only a short period of time to establish a lead in the delegate count. By St. Patrick's Day, Carter had begun to pull sharply away from Kennedy. The rate of his progress toward the nomination in 1980 was much faster than in 1976."[6]

Front-Runners and the Frontloading Strategy

In the end, Carter's primary manipulations could not save his presidency, but they clearly contributed to his ability to withstand one of the strongest pri- mary challenges in recent Democratic Party politics. These lessons were not lost on former vice president Mondale as his campaign conducted, in early 1983, its first assessment of the 1984 nomination calendar. Like Carter, Mon- dale looked for ways to create early momentum and early delegate strength. When Ted Kennedy dropped out of the nomination race in late 1982, it was clear that Mondale would have a substantial financial and organizational lead over his rivals. This lead would be worth much less in a nomination sys- tem that was spread out over a long period of time, allowing candidates to compete in one small state after another. Hence "frontloading" the calendar as a political strategy was born.

Frontloading had begun to happen on its own in 1980 as states caught on to the fact that in the new nomination system early was better. Carter added to the trend, but Mondale took frontloading to new heights. His campaign even encouraged the creation of party "straw polls"—meaningless beauty contests conducted in the year before the nomination contest as a means of forcing the less-well-financed candidates to spend their money early. The frontloading theory rested on two assumptions: that Mondale would win Iowa and New Hampshire and that no other candidate would have the time to muster enough resources to run in many contests simultaneously. Both assumptions turned out to be wrong. Mondale lost the New Hampshire primary and found out that Gary Hart's momentum was nearly enough of a resource in and of itself to obviate the need for more standard resources such as money and organization. But none of this could have been foreseen in early 1983.

Although the emerging 1984 calendar was definitely front-loaded, as the Mondale campaign desired, it was front-loaded with predominantly southern states. This was partially a result of Carter's efforts in 1979 to put many of the southern states up front and partially the result of the desire of southern Democratic parties to play a major role in the process. Bert Lance, the former Carter administration Office of Management and Budget official who had had to resign after a banking scandal, made a political comeback in 1982 when he was elected chairman of the Georgia Democratic Party. From that perch he encouraged southern states to move early in the nomination season in order to have a major impact on the choice of the Democratic nominee. In 1983, Arkansas switched from a presidential primary to an early caucus system and set the date of its first-tier caucuses for March 17, the first Saturday within the window, making it the seventh southern state to schedule its vote for the first week of the window. Kentucky's draft delegate selection plan called for first-tier caucuses on that Saturday as well. In Tennessee a bill was in the legislature to move the primary up to March 13.

As long as Kennedy was Mondale's chief rival, this emerging southern calendar was not a problem. While the South had been solidly Democratic when John F. Kennedy ran for president, it was becoming more and more conservative, and Ted Kennedy had become, in some parts, the poster boy for everything wrong with the liberal North. He was unlikely to draw southern support away from Mondale. But when Senator John Glenn of Ohio replaced Kennedy as Mondale's biggest threat in the late spring and summer of 1983, it looked as if Glenn could be the beneficiary of southern frontloading. Glenn's military background and his fame as the young astronaut who had, in 1962, piloted the first manned orbital mission for the United States, made him exceptionally popular in the South. In a 1983 poll that was widely reported in the media, Glenn was shown leading Mondale by nine points in the South. And national polls that summer showed Glenn in a virtual tie with Mondale.[7] Faced with the possibility that nine southern states would hold caucuses or primaries in the first week of the primary season, following Iowa and New Hampshire, the Mondale campaign adopted a strategy of trying to move nonsouthern states into that week, in order to protect Mondale from the threat of an emerging "southern candidate."

As Mondale discovered and others have since learned, the process of moving states' primaries and caucus dates is much more difficult for a candidate who is not an incumbent president. With encouragement from the Mondale campaign, Rhode Island and Massachusetts moved their primaries to March 13, 1984. After much prodding and a special trip to Michigan by campaign chair Jim Johnson and campaign manager Bob Beckel, Michigan moved its first-tier caucuses to March 17, creating a much-needed counterpoint to the list of southern caucuses already on that day. Ironically, the campaign was unsuccessful in convincing Mondale's home state of Minnesota to move to March 13, largely because of a conflict with state law. New Jersey, another state thought to be good for Mondale, had under consideration a bill to move its primary into March, but this failed in the legislature once it became clear that the primaries for all other offices in the state would have to be moved up as well. Wisconsin, another good Mondale state, especially in its newly adopted caucus form, decided against moving its caucuses into the first week in March and in favor of holding them as close as possible to the state's popular open primary.[8]

By the time the 1984 calendar was final, slightly fewer than half of the delegates elected in the first week of the window were from southern states. Nevertheless, by the time election year came around, Mondale's problem was not Glenn, who faded early, a casualty of the Iowa caucuses, where he came in fifth, but a young Colorado senator named Gary Hart who had first burst onto the national political scene as campaign manager for George McGovern in 1972. In the kind of serendipity that thwarts even the most well thought out attempts to manage sequence, because John Glenn's campaign collapsed in Iowa, Gary Hart's distant second-place finish in Iowa catapulted him into a victory over Mondale in New Hampshire. Hart then beat Mondale in Massachusetts and Rhode Island, two states Mondale had moved up in the expectation that he would win.

Hart's victory illustrated a fundamental change in Democratic Party politics. Mondale, for all of his understanding of the new rules, was, at heart, an old-fashioned party machine candidate, the candidate of the AFL-CIO and many other interest groups that, by 1984, were beginning to be viewed not as the backbone of the party but as "special interests." In the old nomination system no one could have beaten a candidate so beloved by these groups; in the new nomination system someone almost did.

It was another 16 years before the Democrats had an open nomination race with a clear front-runner. In 2000 a sitting vice president, Al Gore, was planning a run for the presidency and, unlike the Democratic candidates in 1988 (including himself) and 1992, he had the political clout to influence the sequence of primaries in which he would run. Like Jimmy Carter and Walter Mondale before him, he knew that a crowded, frontloaded calendar would benefit an establishment candidate who could raise the money to run in many contests at the same time. In the days before the Internet, getting money into the bank, even by playing off an early win, took weeks. Thus front-runners were advantaged by a crowded calendar.

The Gore campaign faced two sequencing decisions. First was California. In previous years, California had toyed with the idea of moving its primary up to the first date party rules would allow, but for a variety of reasons it had not.[9] But in 1999, Gore's political operatives let it be known in California that they thought moving that state's primary early was a pretty good idea. California moved its primary up from the end of March, where it had been in 1996, to March 7, 2000.

A second sequencing issue arose when South Carolina and Michigan, at the insistence of their statewide political leadership, attempted to move their primaries before the opening of the window. On the Republican side, the South Carolina primary had been set for February 19 and the Michigan primary for February 22. Super Tuesday that year fell on March 7.[10] Once the Republican parties in each state decided to move their primaries into February, the Democrats, led by former National Party Chairman Don Fowler in South Carolina and Senator Carl Levin in Michigan, began lobbying to get permission from the Democratic National Committee's Rules and By-Laws

Committee to move the Democratic contests as well. But strategists for the Gore campaign were worried about former senator Bill Bradley's challenge to Gore. Throughout the fall of 1999, Bradley had been mounting a stiff challenge to Vice President Gore in New Hampshire, and some polls showed him within striking distance of Gore.

The Gore campaign consulted Democratic strategist Tad Devine, veteran of many delegate fights. Devine's thinking was as follows: "If Gore loses New Hampshire, it leaves Bradley with five weeks and no place to go. . . . But if Gore wins New Hampshire, Bradley will wither on the vine."[11] To create enough momentum to defeat a sitting vice president for the nomination, Bradley needed not only a win in New Hampshire but also wins in other contests soon after New Hampshire, where his momentum could translate into votes and money. The Gore campaign, nervous about the situation in New Hampshire, lobbied the Rules and By-Laws Committee against a change in the calendar. The committee members, ever sensitive to the desires of the White House and a sitting vice president, denied South Carolina and Michigan permission to go early, and those two states ended up having their primaries on March 9 and March 11, respectively. In this instance, manipulation of the sequence paid off. Gore won the New Hampshire primary, and as predicted, Bradley "withered on the vine" and was soon out of the race.

Trying to manipulate sequence as part of a presidential strategy requires luck as well as political skill and clout. There are three major problems faced by a candidate trying to create the best possible nomination calendar. The first is that dates need to be set by legislatures or state parties more than a full year before the election year. (Typically, if the legislature pays for the primary, it sets the date. Otherwise, the state party sets the date and pays for either a party-run primary or a series of caucuses.) Calculations about who will do well where and who the opposition will be are extraordinarily difficult to make and are often wrong that far in advance. Second, few states are able to overcome the dictates of their own local politics and customs just for the glory of holding a quadrennial event. This is especially true in the case of presidential primaries, which must be financed, in most cases, by the states. Accommodating the preferred date for the presidential primary requires that the legislature either move all primary elections to the same date or face the expensive proposition of holding a presidential preference primary and the state's regular primaries on separate dates. And finally, most presidential candidates, unless they are incumbent presidents or have been incumbent vice presidents, don't have the national clout necessary to move too many states around.

Ronald Reagan, Lee Atwater, and the Creation of the "Firewall"

Republicans are subject to the same dynamics of the post-reform nominating system as Democrats. They need to win early in order to establish enough momentum to influence subsequent electorates. In 1979, former California governor Ronald Reagan's campaign was initially pleased with the emerging southern calendar that the Carter White House was putting together. (When state legislatures moved the dates of primaries they usually moved them for both political parties.) After all, in his 1976 bid for the nomination, Reagan had consistently beaten Ford in the South, and with any luck he expected to win those states again. As the Republican field took shape, however, former governor John B. Connally of Texas emerged as a potential rival to Reagan in the South. With the southern contests concentrated in one week, Reagan needed an early southern test against Connally in order to establish himself as the dominant southern candidate, much as Carter had needed an early southern contest in 1976 in order to get rid of George Wallace.

South Carolina's Republican political establishment was divided. Strom Thurmond, the senior senator who had long dominated South Carolina politics, was backing John Connally. But a first-term U.S. representative, Carroll Campbell, was Ronald Reagan's campaign chairman, and he had working with him a brash young political consultant named Lee Atwater. Together the two Reagan supporters began to put in place the mechanics needed to get an early date for the South Carolina Republican contest. With the support of state Republican Party chairman Dan Ross, a special state convention was called for October 1979. At that special convention, the South Carolina Republican Party decided to hold its first presidential primary ever on the Saturday before the Tuesday on which the other, larger, southern primaries would be held. (South Carolina law allows each party to schedule its own caucus or primary.) The new primary was opposed by John Connally's supporters in the state, who knew that he lagged behind Reagan in polls of likely Republican voters; it was favored by Reagan supporters, who worked hard to secure the best possible date for their candidate. According to Dan Ross, the choice of the Saturday before Super Tuesday, "wasn't just luck. . . . I think they anticipated knocking Connally out of the race. Reagan campaigned real hard here, going from little town to little town—working the state."[12]

Both candidates ended up mounting intense and expensive campaigns in South Carolina.[13] But in the end, Connally's defeat in South Carolina (54 percent voted for Reagan, 30 percent for Connally) took him out of the race, and as Reagan backers had predicted, the Reagan campaign went on to a series of decisive and important victories in the South. These victories turned out to be especially important to Reagan, who by then needed to reestablish his momentum following his surprise loss to George H. W. Bush in Iowa.

This experience landed the young Lee Atwater a job in the Reagan White House and taught him an important lesson: build a safety net or firewall into your sequence. The South Carolina Republican primary that Atwater helped create became a fixture in the Republican sequence, the place where unexpected problems up north could be fixed. As political reporter Michael Kramer wrote in 2000:

> It's called the South Carolina Firewall because it's meant to do what its name implies: stop an insurgent candidate, fresh from romps in Iowa or New Hampshire, from toppling the Republican establishment's preferred horse. And it's worked for 12 years and three presidential campaign cycles. In 1988, Vice President George Bush used it to send Pat Robertson packing. Four years later, it worked for President Bush against Pat Buchanan—who was its victim again in 1996, when the state's GOP machine backed Bob Dole. Now, according to President Bush's son, the Firewall is set to do the same for him on February 19— assuming John McCain needs killing after a New Hampshire primary victory this Tuesday.[14]

The Republican establishment feared that the Iowa caucuses could be controlled by candidates with narrow but fervent bases of support. Thus South Carolina became the place where candidates such as Pat Buchanan and Pat Robertson (who were seen as too radical to win a general election) or John McCain (seen, in 2000, as too much of a maverick to win the Republican base) could be stopped early on. And in 2000, true to form, George W. Bush ran an exceptionally nasty race in South Carolina that put an end to the McCain candidacy that year.

When Candidates Can't Shape the Sequence, the Sequence Must Shape the Campaign

In 1988, none of the Democrats in the nomination race had the political clout to influence sequence. In fact, they were collectively dubbed "the seven dwarves" for their lack of stature. Most of the candidates prepared to slug it out in state after state, starting with Iowa and New Hampshire. But Al Gore, then a young and relatively unknown senator from Tennessee, bet that he could win the nomination by skipping the early contests in the Midwest (Iowa and Minnesota) and in the Northeast (New Hampshire and Maine) and holding out for the delegate-rich states that would vote on March 8, 1988. Certainly the math seemed favorable. Of the 22 Super Tuesday states, 12 were in the South, including Gore's home state of Tennessee. The southern states represented 67 percent of the 1,363 delegates at stake that day, far more than the 199 delegates at stake in the early contests. So Senator Gore decided to skip the early states of Iowa and New Hampshire and concentrate his race on southern Super Tuesday.

The other candidate who saw an opportunity in Super Tuesday was Massachusetts governor Michael Dukakis. As Dukakis campaign manager John Sasso recalled years later, "We watched the southern Super Tuesday and realized that because of Florida and Texas it was pretty good for us. Florida had a lot of northern Jews, and Texas had Hispanics and Mike spoke Spanish. So we agreed not to say anything to anyone about this in order to keep expectations low."[15] South Carolina Democratic chairman Don Fowler, an opponent of the southern strategy, agreed with the Dukakis campaign's assessment and also saw promise in Super Tuesday for another northern candidate: "If this turns out the way I think it's going to, Jesse Jackson and Mike Dukakis are going to get more delegates than anyone else out of Super Tuesday. And I'm going to call a news conference on March 9 and say 'I told you so.'"[16]

As Fowler predicted, the winners of the 1988 Super Tuesday contests were the Reverend Jesse Jackson, a black minister from Chicago who had never held public office and who was running very much as a protest candidate, and Governor Dukakis, the very embodiment of a Harvard-educated northeastern ethnic liberal. Dukakis won the two big prizes that day, Florida and Texas. Jackson, meanwhile, won Alabama, Georgia, Louisiana, Mississippi,

Virginia, and South Carolina. Al Gore, the self-proclaimed "southern candidate," won only four states, and though he remained in the race for another two months, Gore's candidacy effectively ended that day.

Two lessons stand out from the Gore campaign's 1988 miscalculations. First, sequence drives everything. It is possible, as George H. W. Bush showed that year, to recover from losses early in the season (in his case, to Pat Robertson), but it is not possible to skip the early season altogether. In the modern nominating system, candidates cannot pick and choose because the early contests can radically reshape the competitive landscape. Second, winning on what is perceived to be your "home turf" is simply not as important as winning on more neutral territory.

Senator Al Gore may have been the first candidate to try to skip the early contests, but he wasn't the last. Twenty years later, in the 2008 Republican presidential primary, former New York City mayor Rudy Giuliani pursued his own version of Al Gore's dream. But instead of counting on the South as a whole, Giuliani pinned his hopes on Florida.

Rudy Giuliani's leadership following the terrorist attacks in New York City on September 11, 2001, catapulted him to national prominence. He became known as "America's mayor," and his toughness on terrorism put him at or near the top of every 2007 poll for the Republican nomination. Many Republicans reasoned that, in what was shaping up to be a Democratic year because of the unpopularity of President George W. Bush, a nontraditional Republican with strong antiterrorist credentials could be just the ticket to stave off a Democratic presidential victory.

But Giuliani's campaign had trouble answering one big important question. How could a cultural liberal expect to win in two early Republican contests—Iowa and South Carolina—where cultural conservatives dominated the Republican electorate? Giuliani was, after all, a former Democrat, a New Yorker to his bones, an admitted adulterer and refugee from a messy divorce, and a candidate whose previous record included tolerance of gay rights and abortion. Giuliani and his advisers understood that this side of the candidate would not play well in the early Republican states. As campaign manager Brent Seaborn explained, "I think he [Giuliani] knew that he had taken a number of positions over the years not in line with the Republican electorate—at least not the early electorate. With Florida moving forward we saw a shot. . . . With [Mitt] Romney in New Hampshire we saw a good shot going away. South Carolina and Iowa are states that Rudy was not going to win. . . . A traditional campaign calendar would not allow him to make it through."[17]

Therefore Giuliani placed all his bets on a win in Florida. Florida was a pretty good state for a former New York City mayor since a large part of its population consisted of New Yorkers and other northeasterners who had moved there to retire. With Florida's primary scheduled for January 29, 2008, Giuliani's campaign reasoned that a win there would catapult Giuliani into the lead in the February 5 (Super Tuesday) contests, which offered a bonanza of delegates. Internal Giuliani campaign memorandums from April 2007 reported that Giuliani held a lead in 11 of the 17 February 5 states that had conducted polling and that he led "in the February 5 primary states with the largest number of delegates."[18]

There were plenty of doubts about Giuliani's big-state strategy. New York–based pollster John Zogby pointed out that that absence of coverage in the month before the primary was "risky, and the worst thing you can say is that it was foolish."[19] Larry Sabato, an expert on presidential politics from the University of Virginia, concurred: "As long as Giuliani can stay afloat through January 29, he should do well on February 5 and beyond, emerging with the overall delegate lead. That's a big 'if' though."[20] Another seasoned observer of presidential politics, Georgetown University's Stephen Wayne, said, "You just can't skip all those states and expect voters in later states to take you seriously."[21]

While Giuliani backers acknowledged the risk, they built their campaign on the assumption that the earlier contests—Iowa, New Hampshire, Michigan, and South Carolina—would deliver a split verdict and allow room for Giuliani to emerge in Florida. Attorney General Bill McCollum, Giuliani's Florida state chairman, acknowledged that Giuliani would be threatened if a single challenger won enough early primaries to build momentum going into Florida, but he denied that something like that could happen.

What McCollum and the rest of the Giuliani campaign did not foresee is that the pre-Florida contests would revive John McCain's candidacy and introduce a new factor into the equation—former Arkansas governor Mike Huckabee, who turned out to be a favorite of the evangelical base. Of the seven Republican contests before Super Tuesday, Huckabee won the Iowa caucuses, McCain won New Hampshire and the South Carolina "firewall," and former Massachusetts governor Mitt Romney won Wyoming, Nevada, and Michigan. Meanwhile, Giuliani was missing in action, never even getting out of single digits in the contests leading up to Florida. Media and voter fascination with the other candidates contributed to Giuliani's meager third-place finish in Florida, which put him out of the race before he even got to his strongholds on Super Tuesday.

In contrast to Gore in 1988 and Giuliani in 2008, Massachusetts senator Paul Tsongas, an early front-runner in 1992, understood the demands that sequence placed on his campaign, but what looked like a sound strategy was undermined by a tactical mistake. In 1992, once New York governor Mario Cuomo had bowed out of the race, no one in the Democratic field had the political clout to change the sequence of primaries and caucuses. Instead, they had to do their best to exploit the opportunities and avoid the pitfalls of the existing calendar. With the Iowa caucuses sewn up in advance by favorite son Senator Tom Harkin, most candidates avoided the state. So the race began in New Hampshire, where Tsongas finished first, followed in second place by Arkansas governor Bill Clinton.

Clinton had taken a beating before the New Hampshire primary. First, a nightclub singer named Gennifer Flowers went to the tabloids and then on television to assert that she had had an affair with Bill Clinton, the first of what his former chief of staff had predicted would be "bimbo eruptions." That was followed quickly by assertions that Clinton had used political pull to get out of being drafted into the Vietnam-era army. Doubts about Clinton as the front-runner began to circulate. In light of these revelations, his second-place finish in New Hampshire was astounding, earning him the moniker "the comeback kid" and a new rush of media attention in the period leading up to the opening of the primary window.

Seven states held Democratic primaries or caucuses on March 3, and eleven chose their delegates on March 10, Super Tuesday.[22] Of the March 3 contests, only two were primaries—Maryland and Georgia—and the others were caucuses. Thus the press watched the two primary states carefully for signs of whether Clinton could be stopped by Tsongas, who had won the New Hampshire primary. March 3 turned out to be a draw; Tsongas won Maryland handily, but Clinton was the victor in Georgia, thanks to an enormous African American vote. Georgia proved that Clinton, in spite of his problems, was not going to be stopped easily. The next significant set of contests occurred on March 10—a mixture of New England states favorable to Tsongas and southern states favorable to Clinton. Of the states that held primaries that day, Florida was the most diverse; consisting of parts that were southern in culture and politics and parts that were northern. And thus Florida became the place where Clinton would be stopped—if at all. If Tsongas, like Dukakis before him, could win Florida—a big, complex state that was part North and part South—he would be able to survive what remained of the southern Super Tuesday, win in his home state of Massachusetts and in his neighboring state of Rhode Island (which voted on the same day as Florida), and move on to the next set of primary states, Illinois and Michigan, which would be more hospitable to a northern politician.

Outgunned on the ground in Florida, the Tsongas campaign made the tactical decision to try to create momentum for the Florida primary with an earlier win. Thus Tsongas decided to spend the Thursday before the crucial Florida primary campaigning in Arizona, in the hope that a first-place finish there would create enough momentum to bring large numbers of Florida voters to his side.[23] The detour to Arizona, however, turned out to be a waste of time. The Arizona caucuses (held on Saturday) reported their results too late for the Sunday papers, and Tsongas's win there, instead of creating momentum going into the Tuesday primary in Florida, ended up having little impact at all. Clinton scored a solid win in the Florida primary. The lesson was clear: for a contest to generate momentum, it needed to be at least "the functional equivalent of a primary" and make sufficient news to influence subsequent voters. Tsongas's day in Phoenix was not the only reason he lost Florida, but it surely didn't help.

Although the 1992 nomination contest ended for all practical purposes with Clinton's win in Florida, the rapid end to the season caused considerable angst among Democratic insiders. The frontloaded primary calendar had delivered a Democratic nominee who was, as more than one Republican liked to remind people, a "dope-smoking, draft-dodging, womanizer," leading some to wonder if frontloading was such a good idea after all. And as Clinton limped through the spring of 1992, Democratic activists began to wonder about a process in which there was no opportunity for buyer's remorse. In an April 1992 poll, Clinton was losing to Bush by eleven points; in May Bush was beating both Clinton and Texas billionaire Ross Perot; and in June, Clinton was polling a paltry 24 percent of the vote.[24]

As political analyst William Schneider wrote, "Democrats have tried to speed up the primary calendar. This year, almost 50 percent of the pledged delegates will be chosen by the end of the fourth week of primaries. But the troubles of Arkansas Gov. Bill Clinton have given party leaders a new worry, not that the party will take too long to make a decision, but that the decision will be made too quickly."[25] But the moment passed. Clinton, ever the comeback kid, won the presidency despite allegations about his personal life, and the modern system chugged on.

The Rookie and the Pro

Most races for the nomination of a major political party consist of two kinds of candidates—the front-runners and the rookies. Front-runners, as we have seen, often have both the experience and the national political clout to use sequence as strategy; rookies often misunderstand how sequencing works or think that they can reverse the laws of sequencing. In the 2008 race for the Democratic nomination these two roles were reversed. From early 2007 on, Barack Obama, in his forties and in his first term in the Senate and first presidential campaign, was the rookie who understood the system like a pro; and Hillary Clinton, veteran of two of her husband's presidential runs, made the kinds of mistakes usually associated with a rookie.

Obama's success in winning the nomination from a powerful candidate like Hillary Clinton had every bit as much to do with his campaign's capacity to understand the modern nomination system as it did with his extraordinary political gifts and the revolutionary nature of his high-tech Internet campaign. The Obama campaign understood both sequence and the importance of the delegate count (discussed in chapter 5). Most of the credit for this achievement goes to his political team of David Plouffe, manager of the Obama campaign, and Jeff Berman, who became Obama's national director of delegate selection in the spring of 2007.

Jeff Berman is a certifiable rules junkie, a gray-haired lawyer whose first job hunting delegates was for John Glenn in 1984. He learned the game the hard way. The Glenn campaign had no national field organization, and it was forced to play in a frontloaded calendar created by Walter Mondale's campaign for the express purpose of wearing down less-well-financed candidates. So Berman cut his teeth flying around the country cajoling local politicians into helping him fill slates and collect petitions to get his candidate and his candidate's delegates on the ballot. Twenty-four years later he is still proud of the fact that he filed complete delegate slates for John Glenn in every state in the country. (As we'll see later, had Gary Hart had a Jeff Berman working for him in 1984 he might well have won the nomination from Mondale.) Berman went on to hunt delegates for Missouri representative and House Speaker Dick Gephardt in his two presidential runs, and by the time he joined the Obama campaign in February 2007 he was as experienced a person as could be found.

"The way the system works," Berman explains, "requires candidates to carry out many complex operations before they can emerge [from obscurity to prominence through the primaries]."[26] So Berman and Plouffe started planning for the 2008 primaries in the spring of 2007. Berman had no illusions that Obama could skip either of the two early contests, and he hoped to win both Iowa and New Hampshire. But he was experienced enough to know that would be tough and that unless Obama won both those states the likelihood of knocking Clinton, the "inevitable" front-runner, out of the race in Nevada or South Carolina was slim.

So Berman developed a "Plan B," which revolved around Super Tuesday, February 5, 2008. In 2007, Clinton led in almost every February 5 state. "February 5th for us—22 primaries—we were terribly frightened," Plouffe told an audience at Harvard's Kennedy School of Government one month after the general election. "So the only way we could do it was maximum velocity out of South Carolina [January 26, 2008]. If the Florida primary had come three days after South Carolina we could have been stopped. When the Clinton campaign agreed not to campaign in Florida [following the DNC's decision to take away Florida's delegates after the state party refused to move back its primary], I was very surprised. If we hadn't had that moment of velocity coming out of South Carolina, we may not have survived."[27] That strategic insight was echoed by Guy Cecil, who joined the Clinton campaign in October 2007: "There's no doubt that Florida would have been very helpful [for Clinton] in stemming the tide in terms of lowering the South Carolina repercussions and adding to the delegate count."[28]

Plouffe and Berman understood not only the need to go into Super Tuesday with momentum, but also the need to add to that day some states that they could win and some states where their wins could translate into a larger delegate count. "We viewed February 5 not as a political race but as a delegate race," said Plouffe.[29] The Obama campaign acted to maximize its delegate count on that day. Six states moved from late in the season to Super Tuesday 2008. In January 2007, Illinois House Speaker Michael Madigan and the Illinois Democrats moved their primary to February 5, 2008, so that Illinois could help build Obama's delegate count should he get into the race.[30] In Alabama, a young black U.S. representative and Obama ally, Arturo Davis, was instrumental in moving Alabama's primary to February 5. In Kansas, supporters of Governor Kathleen Sebelius helped move Kansas's caucuses to an earlier date since the Obama campaign felt confident that they would do well in caucus states. Colorado moved its caucuses to February 5 without any prompting from the Obama campaign.[31] The movement of these four states was critical to Obama's surprising success on Super Tuesday. He won lopsided victories in the Colorado and Kansas caucuses and in the Alabama and Illinois primaries. "We won a lot of landslides," said Plouffe, reflecting on that day; "she [Clinton] won less and that's how you win delegates."[32] The other two states that moved up in 2008—Arkansas and New Jersey—were good for Hillary Clinton, but there is no evidence that anyone tried to move those states on her behalf.

Once the calendar was set, Berman focused on allocating resources for maximum effect, working together with Plouffe, deputy campaign manager Steve Hildebrand, and the campaign's political and field departments. Berman explained: "I identified early on which Super Tuesday states we could win, and how many we could get second place in, such as New York and New Jersey. . . . Then you have the third category of states we can't win but [where] we need to win delegates."[33] By Labor Day 2007, the Obama campaign had begun to move people into high-priority states, with special concentration on caucus states. According to Berman, "I went to all the caucus states myself, and then the field people came in. I felt that Barack's candidacy did well in activist settings because of a strong grassroots movement and [support from] antiwar activists."[34] In addition, Berman concentrated on western states, where there is little or no tradition of party regulars and where activists could control the open caucuses.

But Berman's planning didn't stop at Super Tuesday. He had worked out a "Plan C" in case Super Tuesday produced no obvious winner. "I had identified that February 9–19 was potentially our territory, especially Louisiana and Washington State—Louisiana because of the large black population and Washington State because of the large activist population. I predicted that we could win all of them. . . . Plouffe had a separate [campaign spending] account for post–Super Tuesday. It meant that we could go up on the air in Louisiana *before* Super Tuesday. . . . We won the nomination in that period."[35]

In stark contrast, the Clinton campaign failed to plan ahead for the sequence and spent almost all its money on the first two contests. Harold Ickes, a Clinton adviser with even more history in the nomination process than Jeff Berman, had emphasized the need for a reserve fund, but the Clinton campaign did not have the discipline to plan for the long haul. Patti Solis Doyle, the campaign manager, and Mike Henry, her deputy, had never been in a presidential nomination fight before. According to the *Atlantic Monthly*, "Fatefully, Ickes cited the need to maintain a $25 million reserve fund for use after Iowa—but following Clinton's loss, he confessed to colleagues, 'The cupboard is empty.'"[36]

The Clinton campaign was convinced that it would score an early knockout and spent accordingly—meaning that by the end of January 2008, days before Super Tuesday, Hillary Clinton had to loan her campaign $5 million. No planning or polling had been done for the series of states that followed Super Tuesday, as one of the internal Clinton campaign memos released by the *Atlantic Monthly* after the campaign revealed.[37] In addition, according to insiders, Clinton's campaign had a strong bias against competing in small caucus states following its decisive defeat in Iowa. Another Clinton campaign memo characterizes caucuses as "flawed, uncontrolled and low turnout," in comparison to primaries.[38]

Thus, unlike the Obama campaign, the Clinton campaign had no "Plan C." In late January and early February, experienced observers were shocked to learn that the Clinton campaign was rushing organizers into states at the last minute and scrambling for money. All this while Berman's Plan C was not only in place, but funded! Of the 22 primaries and caucuses held on Super Tuesday 2008, Obama won 13 and Clinton won 9, including the two big states of California and New York. But the peculiar characteristics of proportional representation in the Democratic Party meant that Clinton's big-state wins didn't give her a substantial delegate lead. (More on that in chapter 5.) Thus the race went on to encompass the contests in Berman's

Plan C.[39] Obama won every single one of the contests in Berman's Plan C, creating a delegate lead that Hillary Clinton could never catch and a momentum going into the big states of Texas and Ohio (March 4, 2008) that helped him keep Clinton's victories in those states small.

By the end of February the Clinton campaign was having to reassure donors that their candidate could raise enough money to continue in the race and that the superdelegates who had been pledged to Clinton were holding firm. With the conclusion of Berman's Plan C the Clinton campaign realized, belatedly, that it was in a race for delegates (also addressed in more detail in chapter 5). The Obama campaign had to resort to a Plan D and a Plan E before they could convince Clinton to get out of the race, but he'd won the nomination in those crucial ten days, proving once again the importance of sequence.

The Death of Public Financing

These examples demonstrate the powerful impact that sequence has had on post-reform candidates and their campaigns. Because in the modern nomination process sequence is strategy, the post-reform candidate who chooses that strategy has a much tougher task and many more uncertainties to deal with than her pre-reform counterpart, who simply had to decide which, if any, primaries to enter. Successful efforts to rework the calendar may suggest that in compensation, post-reform candidates have greater control over the nomination process. Yet this control is largely illusory. The effort devoted to fine-tuning the calendar only drives home the point that in the post-reform era, presidential candidates have no option but to contest all the early primaries and caucuses in the hope of establishing momentum.

The impact of sequence as strategy does not stop there. It is also the cause, in no small measure, of the death of the public financing system for presidential primaries. Sequence means that small states, depending on their place in the calendar, can be vastly more important than large states. However, federal election law limits the amount that a candidate can spend in each state based on the size of the state, as well as the overall amount that he can spend seeking the nomination—if, that is, the candidate accepts federal matching funds for his campaign.

In the context of a nomination system governed by sequence, the state expenditure limits have been especially vexing to presidential candidates. State expenditure limits are based on voting-age population. Yet in the modern nominating system the small early states of Iowa and New Hampshire have an importance in the nomination race that is out of all proportion to the size of their populations. These limits have traditionally been the impetus for some creative bookkeeping on the part of presidential campaigns. In New Hampshire, for example, schedulers regularly drove the candidate and his or her entourage across the border to Vermont or Massachusetts so that the costs could be allotted to that state's limits rather than to New Hampshire's.[40]

Moreover, as frontloading pushed the bulk of the nomination season earlier and earlier in the year, some candidates, such as Senator Bob Dole, the Republican nominee in 1996, and Vice President Al Gore, the Democratic nominee in 2000, found that, having won their party's nomination, they were left with months before their convention and limitations on the money they could spend in what had become the de facto beginning of the general election campaign. Dole's experience led the George W. Bush campaign in 2000 to forgo participating in the federal matching fund program. This decision allowed the campaign to spend heavily in critical early states like New Hampshire and South Carolina. The state expenditure limit in South Carolina in 2000 was $1,583,606, but Bush (unlike McCain, who had accepted federal funds) was not required to stay under the limits, and estimates are that he spent as much as $5 million in the state to get a win that was critical in allowing him to recover from his loss in New Hampshire.[41] In addition, once he had beaten McCain and secured the nomination, Bush could raise and spend as he pleased in the long months before the conventions. Bush had raised more than $91 million by the end of July 2000, whereas Gore, who was bound by Federal Election Commission (FEC) limits, raised a fraction of that, about $34 million.

By 2004 it was clear that voters did not care whether a candidate opted into or out of the federal financing system. To no one's surprise, President Bush once again chose not to accept federal financing for the nomination campaign. On the Democratic side, neither did Howard Dean, a former Vermont governor with very little national exposure, who stunned the political establishment by raising an unprecedented $40 million—most of it over the Internet. In late 2003 he conducted a poll of his supporters, again over the Internet, to ask whether he should forgo federal matching funds. His supporters voted yes, and Dean opted out of the system. Dean's decision was the death knell for the federal financing system. It was one thing for a wealthy Republican to opt out of a system Republicans had never liked in the first place; it was quite another for a liberal reformer to opt out. Several months later, John Kerry followed Dean's lead, making it possible for him to lend his campaign money and spend heavily in Iowa. This decision is credited with enabling Kerry to overtake Dean in Iowa and eventually win the nomination.

The desire to spend without limit in the all-important early states, the enormous impact of the Internet on fundraising, and the fact that, when push came to shove, voters didn't care much at all about whether a candidate used the public financing system meant that by 2008 the major candidates had opted out of the system. Both Hillary Clinton and Barack Obama declined to participate in the public funding program. Having each raised about $100 million in 2007, they had no need for federal matching funds and the restrictions on strategy that came with them, especially the overall cap of about $42 million on primary expenditures.[42] On the Republican side, former mayor Rudy Giuliani and former governor Mitt Romney opted out early, while Senator John McCain, faced with unexpected money problems, went back and forth on the issue before ultimately deciding to opt out of the system. Most observers felt that from then on the public financing system would have to be completely redesigned or it would be used only by second-tier candidates.

In the absence of federal funding, which requires campaigns to report expenditures by state, there is no exact way to know how much more candidates spent on the early states. But media spending in each state is knowable, and the Democratic and Republican candidates were reported as spending more than $23 million dollars in television ads alone in Manchester, New Hampshire, and Boston, Massachusetts—the two major media markets for New Hampshire.[43] The 2008 FEC expenditure limit for New Hampshire was $841,000. Thus had the six top candidates from each party stayed within the federal limits, they would have been able to spend only $5,046,000, less than a quarter of what was actually spent.

Conclusion

Jimmy Carter's successful race for the presidency established that, in the modern, reformed nominating system, sequence defines strategy. As we have seen, subsequent presidential candidates of both parties have had to cope with the tyranny of sequence, sometimes attempting to create a favorable sequence and sometimes failing to understand just how powerful it is. In a system dominated by sequence, being first is all-important, hence the topic of the next chapter.

3

THE FIGHT TO
BE FIRST

*Why Iowa and New Hampshire
Dominate Presidential Nominating Politics*

By 1976 the transformation of the nomination system, from one dominated by party elites to one dominated by primary voters, was largely complete. In this new system, sequence dictated outcomes and primary voters replaced party leaders as the most important players. To be first was to have a hefty impact on the whole system and to inspire the envy of other less fortunate states. Thus as the modern nomination system entered its second decade, the proper role of the early contests in the nomination system emerged as a leading source of controversy, replacing earlier battles over representation and affirmative action. And this meant that attention centered disproportionately on two states, Iowa and New Hampshire.

There is nothing new about the New Hampshire primary's being first. New Hampshire has held the first-in-the-nation primary since 1920. However, from 1920 to 1948 the New Hampshire primary ballot listed only the names of those seeking to become convention delegates, a system common to presidential primaries in the pre-reform era. If the presidential preferences of the delegate candidates were known, they were known only to other party insiders. Then in 1949, Richard F. Upton, speaker of the New Hampshire House of Representatives, decided to make the primary "more interesting and meaningful . . . so there would be a greater turnout at the polls."[1] He amended the law to enable citizens to vote directly for any presidential candidate who had submitted fifty supporting petitions from each of the two congressional districts. The new legislation also allowed potential delegates to run, with the permission of a presidential candidate, as favorable to that candidate or as uncommitted. Upton had created one of the earliest presidential preference primaries, and the revisions he engineered received immediate and favorable national attention, although it was to be more than two decades before other states followed suit.

Then came Ike. From the time General Dwight D. Eisenhower arrived home from the Second World War, politicians from both parties tried to convince him to run for president. He had been, after all, commander of Allied Forces in Europe, he had organized the Normandy invasion, and he had defeated the Nazis. Not a bad résumé for a presidential candidate. But he was a reluctant candidate, and initially people didn't even know whether he was a Democrat or a Republican. He was courted by both Democrats and Republicans in 1948 but refused to run. Then in 1952, a group of Eisenhower supporters in New Hampshire took advantage of the new law and put his name on the Republican primary ballot. That did the trick. Eisenhower beat longtime Republican Party leader Robert Taft—without ever going to the state! He told the *New York Times* that he was "astounded" and "moved" by the results. "Any American who would have that many other Americans pay him that compliment would be proud or he would not be an American," said Eisenhower.[2] He went on to win the nomination and the presidency.

Over the following years, the New Hampshire primary functioned primarily as an early warning system for party elders. In 1952 and again in 1968, two unpopular presidents, Harry S. Truman and Lyndon B. Johnson, decided not to seek reelection after unfavorable showings in the New Hampshire primary. Thus while the New Hampshire primary occasionally played an important role, in the pre-reform system its role was usually not big enough to make other states envy its position.

But in the post-reform system, where the creation of momentum in one primary affected the actions of voters in subsequent primaries, New Hampshire (and the first caucus state, Iowa) took on enormous importance. From Mo Udall in 1976 to Al Gore in 1988 to Howard Dean in 2004 to Hillary Clinton and Rudy Giuliani in 2008, the political landscape of both parties is littered with the political corpses of plausible presidents who failed to win or skipped one or both of the all-important early tests. It is therefore not surprising that, as the modern nominating system matured, the two earliest contests, the Iowa caucuses and the New Hampshire primary, began to attract animosity from other states and other players in the system. Nor is it surprising that, as their power and influence grew, the two early states became more and more sophisticated at protecting their privileged position.

Mo Udall's Revenge

By the time Jimmy Carter emerged triumphant from the 1976 presidential campaign, it was clear to many Democratic Party insiders that presidential nominating politics had changed in fundamental ways, not all of which they liked—even though the new process had elected a Democratic president. Initial criticism of the new process focused on the increase in the number of presidential primaries from 21 in 1972 to 30 in 1976. To a political generation reared on the old-fashioned, semi-public nomination system described in chapter 1, the new dominance of primaries made the system long, expensive, and unmanageable. In January 1977 the Democratic National Committee established the Commission on the Role and Future of Presidential Primaries, led by Michigan Democratic Party chairman Morley Winograd.[3] The commission's mandate was to look at the proliferation of primaries, their effects, their costs, and reform proposals, including plans for regional primaries or a national primary.

This was no easy task. The proliferation of primaries could not be traced to one rule that could be amended or repealed. The reform rules in their entirety had caused the increase in the number of primaries, but no one had the nerve to propose undoing the entire reform movement—especially when the new rules had just elected a Democratic president and when the reformers themselves were still active and on guard to protect the progress they had made. So the Winograd Commission proceeded to concentrate on problems with individual parts of the system, leaving the overall reforms in place.

One of the problems identified in 1976 was the unprecedented amount of attention that the early Iowa caucuses had received. January precinct caucuses were not a new phenomenon in either the Democratic or the Republican Party. What was new was the transformation of these events into the "functional equivalents" of primaries—a fact that Carter operatives Hamilton Jordan and Jody Powell had understood. It *seemed* as if the delegate selection process was beginning earlier than ever because the process had become completely transparent under the new rules.

This perception was particularly acute for those who had watched the Carter bandwagon roll from victory to victory in 1976. The "early start" of the process surprised the favorite candidate of the left-wing establishment—Representative Mo Udall of Arizona—whose campaign was torn by arguments over whether to contest the Iowa precinct caucuses until it was too late. The "early start" also surprised the favorite candidate of the Democrats' labor wing—Senator Henry S. ("Scoop") Jackson of Washington—whose decision to make Massachusetts his first contest left him trying in vain to catch up with the momentum Carter gained from his New Hampshire victory.

The attention lavished on Iowa and New Hampshire was not lost on other states. Having realized, belatedly, that early was better, in 1977 several states were considering proposals to move their primaries to the same day as the New Hampshire primary, or even earlier. Maine and Puerto Rico were the first to have bills introduced that would move their primaries up to or before the date of the New Hampshire primary. Discussions were also taking place in legislatures in Kansas, Missouri, North Carolina, and Texas about adopting early primaries. Testifying before the Winograd Commission on behalf of the Democratic Conference (an arm of the Americans for Democratic Action formed to promote and protect the original reform agenda), Louis Maisel expressed the sentiments of many when he said: "It seems to me that it is not a rational process to have states competing against each other for the economic benefit of having early primaries."[4]

Seeing no way to limit the number of presidential primaries, the commission focused on ways to shorten the length of the primary season and dilute the impact of the early contests—the major source of candidate displeasure with the 1976 process. Not surprisingly, the most vehement attack on the early contests, especially New Hampshire's, came from the man who had suffered the most as a result of Jimmy Carter's successes there, Representative Mo Udall. Testifying before the full commission he said:

These early primaries really have become media events and there's a momentum which develops out of them that, to a considerable degree, does not equalize the power of Democrats in each of the different states. In my judgment, the voters of New Hampshire, an unrepresentative state, were probably more important in '76 in both parties, probably than all of the voters of California. I do think that we've got to find some way to lessen the impact of these early primaries.[5]

Others on the commission echoed Udall's sentiments. "I think the real problem in '76 and '72 was that full, meaningful opportunity to participate under our rules is fulfilled, but by the time the media gets done with it, especially at a very early stage, they are able to limit their interpretation of the results. . . . I just think we've got to attempt to have the Democrats around this country make decisions on their candidates rather than having the press tell them after one percent or two percent of the electorate speaks that the following person is the overwhelming choice."[6]

Fueled by complaints from candidates who had failed to anticipate the importance of sequence and momentum in the new system, the preliminary report of the commission included what was known as the "window rule," the brainchild of commissioner Scott Lang. The window rule sought to condense the delegate selection process into a 13-week window: it mandated that primaries and first-tier caucuses occur no earlier than the second Tuesday in March of the presidential election year, and no later than the second Tuesday in June.[7]

The outcry from New Hampshire and Iowa was predictable. At fall hearings in those two states, almost every person testifying spoke against the proposed new rule. The state chairman of Iowa called the proposal devastating to the Iowa system. In New Hampshire every statewide-elected Democrat turned out to oppose the proposed rule or to argue that New Hampshire should be given a special exemption. The New Hampshire state chairman argued that the adoption of this rule, without provision for exemptions, would severely hurt the New Hampshire Democratic Party.[8]

President Carter's White House, which supported the window proposal, soon found itself under enormous criticism. The irony of the White House position was lost on no one. The early contests in Iowa and New Hampshire had allowed President Carter, who was at 1 percent in the January 1976 Gallup Poll, to become the nominee of the Democratic Party by the spring. Commissioner Ken Bode, former research director of the McGovern-Fraser Commission, was one of the earliest to call attention to this fact. Speaking before the commission in August, he said: "In 1976 Jimmy Carter probably would not have been able to get the kind of start that he got and run the kind of race that he did if he didn't have places like Iowa and New Hampshire."[9] Commissioner Tom Whitney from Iowa complained that by creating a narrower window: "We really stifle the opportunity in many ways for unknown candidates to become known in this country."[10]

As other proposals became public, including the proposal to raise the percentage of the vote a presidential candidate needed in order to win a delegate, criticism of President Carter intensified. In short, the proposals looked like an attempt by Carter's political operatives to rewrite the rules for 1980 so that he, the incumbent and front-runner, could not be upset by the 1980 version of himself! The *New York Times* characterized the package of recommendations "as intended to hinder any Democratic challenge to Mr. Carter's nomination in 1980."[11] Ken Bode wrote a piece along similar lines in the *New Republic* titled "Restacking the Deck"; the *Des Moines Register* ran an article titled "Primary 'Reforms' That Keep the 'Ins' In"; and David Broder wrote an article for the *Washington Post* called "Changing the Rules—Or Stacking the Deck?"[12]

Ultimately, the White House, which controlled a slim majority on the commission, bowed to pressure from its friends in Iowa and New Hampshire. President Carter and his advisers realized what most candidates in both parties have since grasped: voters in these two early states care deeply about being early. The White House agreed to grant the DNC's Compliance Review Commission (the body charged with enforcing the rules) the power to grant exemptions from the requirement that no primaries or caucuses be held before the second Tuesday in March. They also offered private assurances to party leaders in both Iowa and New Hampshire that their requests for exemptions would be viewed favorably. The measure passed over strong objections from the original proponents of the window, who saw this move as institutionalizing the early contests in Iowa and New Hampshire. Scott Lang, author of the window concept, protested in vain: "If we have exemptions to the window then there's no sense in having a window."[13]

The final window rule, as adopted by the commission and eventually the full Democratic National Committee, read as follows:

No meetings, caucuses, conventions or primaries which constitute the first determining stage in the presidential nominating process (the date of the primary in primary states, and the date of the first tier caucus in caucus states), may be held prior to the second Tuesday in March in the calendar year of the Convention. In no instance may a state which scheduled delegate selection procedures on or between the second Tuesday in March and the second Tuesday in June, 1976 move out of compliance with the provisions of this rule.[14]

The rule effectively "grandfathered" Iowa and New Hampshire and created the privileged place in the presidential nomination system that they have held ever since.

For 1980, the White House, through the DNC, granted five states exemptions from the window rule: New Hampshire, Iowa, Maine, Minnesota, and Massachusetts. Iowa and New Hampshire Democrats went through the somewhat comical process of introducing bills into their legislatures to prove that they had tried, in conformity with Rule 20C (passed with the window rule), to change the date of the primary. To be granted an exemption from national party rules, state parties were required to take "provable positive steps" that they had tried to change the conflicting statute and failed. In the New Hampshire legislature, no Democrat even voted for the Democratic proposal; it was shouted down.[15]

Thus the first major assault on Iowa and New Hampshire and their disproportionate influence on the nomination race did not succeed in reducing the number of early contests significantly; nor did it succeed in reducing the impact of those contests on the rest of the season. Probably the most important effect of the window rule was to prevent states from trying to move their primaries or caucuses earlier than Iowa's or New Hampshire's. Instead, several states moved their primaries or caucuses into the first week of the window, causing the number of delegates at stake in March to jump 50 percent from 1976 and 1980. This created the frontloading problem illustrated in table 1-4.

What's So Good about Unknown, Inexperienced Presidents Anyway?

Despite the relative ease with which Iowa and New Hampshire retained their positions of preeminence in 1980, after the election Democrats in both states knew that they would have to fight hard to protect their privileged positions in 1984. In the minds of contemporary politicians, the prominence of the two early states was tied to the success of Jimmy Carter, who lost to Ronald Reagan in a landslide in 1980 and took the Democratic Senate with him. Iowa and New Hampshire had given the Democrats Carter, and the Democrats were not so sure that that had been a good thing. Four years earlier, the Winograd Commission had praised the existing rules for having produced a nominee who won the election. In contrast, some members of the next party rules commission, the Hunt Commission, faulted those same rules for having produced a failed president.

The Commission on Presidential Nominations, headed by North Carolina governor Jim Hunt, began meeting in August 1981 and issued its final report to the DNC in February 1982. In its very first meeting, commissioner Justin Ostro, a labor union activist who had supported Ted Kennedy in 1980, drew the contrast between Carter's success in winning the Democratic nomination twice and his failure as a president. "What has happened to our nominating and our governing system where a person who is enormously skilled at getting a nomination, is nothing like so skilled at being a candidate in a general election to say nothing of governing?" he asked.[16] Carter's failed presidency was not always referred to so directly, but it was on the minds of many. Doug Fraser, president of the United Auto Workers, told the commission: "I believe that we can bring about changes so that when we select the standard bearer of the Party, we will be proud that he or she is carrying the banner, and, more importantly, if elected they can govern this nation."[17]

It had taken a decade, but party activists were finally confronting the impact of the party transformation that had occurred as a result of the 1968 election. The majority of the Hunt Commission believed that party reform had gone too far in allowing influence over the nomination process to be taken away from party professionals. Members talked about writing rules that would nominate "winners," meaning no more outsiders like George McGovern and Jimmy Carter. The labor movement had a very strong influence on this commission and very definite ideas about what had gone wrong in the past. AFL-CIO president Lane Kirkland was quoted as saying that he would put "the bosses back in charge" because they would "pick winners."[18]

The dominant philosophy of the labor leaders and many other Democratic Party activists meshed well with the strategic objectives of the front-runner for the 1984 nomination, former vice president Walter Mondale.

With the active prodding of Mondale's partisans, the Hunt Commission took action on a number of fronts designed to put the party pros back in the nomination process. After lively debate, the commissioners voted to permit party leaders and elected officials—House and Senate members in particular—to automatically become uncommitted voting delegates to the 1984 convention. These were the first superdelegates. A second major change allowed states to adopt formulas for allocating delegates among candidates that deviated from strict proportional representation, the standard that had been applied in the past. (See chapters 4 and 6 for detailed discussion of these changes.)

In addition, the Hunt Commission attempted, once again, to decrease the impact of the early contests on the remainder of the nomination process. The practice of holding the first Democratic primaries in Iowa and New Hampshire was criticized because, at the time, those states were largely Republican and unrepresentative of the national Democratic electorate. According to critics, media attention to those two states was so intense that it overwhelmed the coverage given to other states, making the later contests in larger states insignificant. Commissioners from large states, especially California, argued against allowing any states to hold delegate selection contests outside the DNC's window. Tired of being at the end of the process and knowing that candidates were just as happy not to have to compete in a state that was a bottomless pit for campaign money, some Democrats were pushing a bill in the state legislature that would move the California primary up to the first day of the window in March. Lamenting the situation, California assemblywoman Maxine Waters said: "By the time they [presidential candidates] get to California, they are either disgusted, broke or just don't care anymore."[19]

Added to these complaints was a new one. Iowa and New Hampshire's preeminence was seen by some as having contributed to the generally poor quality of the post-reform era Democratic nominees. While partisans of the two early contests argued that if their states' roles were diminished it would be hard for candidates to "break through the barrier of obscurity and begin to gain national reputations," other Democrats, on and off the commission, were wondering if having an obscure candidate become the nominee of the Democratic Party was such a good idea after all.[20] As William Mayer, then at Harvard University, testified before the Hunt Commission, "Why in the world would we want to give an unknown, inexperienced person a good chance to become President in the first place? Given that the Presidency is one of the most difficult and important jobs in the world it seems absurd to me to argue that we would want to confer it on a person who had temporarily caught the fancy of a few New Hampshire voters."[21]

Members of the Hunt Commission were presented with several options for shortening the nomination season and reducing the impact of the first contests. The toughest option was to rigorously enforce the existing window period and allow no exemptions to the rule, not even for Iowa and New Hampshire. This position had the strong support of the AFL-CIO, whose members held 20 percent of the votes on the commission. The hard-line, no-exemptions position was also favored by some of Senator Kennedy's partisans on the commission and by members from some of the large, late-primary states, such as California.

However, the no-exemptions position was eventually defeated. Both Iowa and New Hampshire put together formidable lobbying efforts in order to retain their early positions. At a hearing before the commission in September 1981, nearly all of the forty witnesses testified to the terrific value of the early contests to the Democratic Party. Only one witness, an official of the Iowa State AFL-CIO, argued against the righteousness of the early caucuses. The Democratic governor of New Hampshire, Hugh Gallen, not only testified before the full commission but also hired some well-known Washington political consultants to work on strategy for the state of New Hampshire. But perhaps the most important part of the Gallen strategy, one that would continue to be effective even as the antipathy of other states to New Hampshire increased, was to let it be known that he (Gallen) would be watching the proceedings of the Hunt Commission, especially the actions of the presidential candidates who would soon be coming to New Hampshire.[22] This was the first time—but it would not be the last time—that New Hampshire officials blackmailed prospective candidates into supporting their first-in-the-nation primary.

A second reason the no-exemptions position ultimately failed was the realization by many of the commissioners that the hard line would be, for all practical purposes, unenforceable. Although the U.S. Supreme Court had on more than one occasion given the political parties broad latitude to decide the rules by which they governed themselves, their only sanctions lay in the ability to seat or not seat delegates at a nominating convention.[23] New Hampshire officials conveyed (to those who had not already figured it out on their own) that if the state party were forced to choose between holding the first-in-the-nation primary or having its twenty-two votes (out of 3,933) cast at the convention, it would choose the former.

A similar warning came from Iowa. Commissioner John Law, a former executive director of the Iowa Democratic Party, told commission members early on in their deliberations:

> The problem is . . . we don't have a way to make the Republicans move. We would be put at a tremendous competitive disadvantage. . . . If the only solution is to go into the window and thus give the court to the Iowa Republican Party, it is a price that will simply be too great for us to pay. They [the Iowa Democratic Party] would do the honest thing in my view of simply obeying the state statutes, forgetting about the national party mandate, and taking [their] chances on whether [the] delegates would be seated."[24]

To these early states the attention and money that came with an early presidential nomination contest paid enormous dividends in building organizational strength for all the other state and local races that state parties cared most about. To give up a first-in-the-nation contest was, for them, the equivalent of unilateral disarmament.

Third, the hard-line position failed because fears were raised that by enforcing the window the party would create, in effect, a national primary: many states would hold primaries simultaneously, making the first day of the nomination season even more determinative of the eventual outcome than it already was. Several members of the commission's Technical Advisory Committee, which was composed of political consultants, raised this issue.[25] As the commission was meeting, California and New York politicians were considering moving the dates of their presidential primaries earlier in the season than they had been in 1980, thus increasing worries that eliminating the pre-window contests could create a national primary. Pat Caddell, who had been President Carter's pollster, was among those who voiced this concern.[26]

In an attempt to keep some state primaries later in the season, the commission briefly explored incentive systems that would prevent the process from becoming even more front-loaded. Allowing states to adopt delegate allocation schemes that made participation more appealing to candidates and giving later states better convention facilities were two of the incentive schemes considered. (Allocation schemes are discussed in chapter 4.) But incentive plans were ultimately rejected by the commission, only to return twenty-five years later in a major assault on Iowa and New Hampshire in 2008.

Last but by no means least, the hard-line position failed because the Mondale campaign's representatives on the commission worked against it. Having concluded that there would be a first-in-the-nation New Hampshire primary and early Iowa caucuses regardless of the actions of the Hunt Commission, Mondale's operatives decided to score points with Democratic politicians in both states—particularly New Hampshire—by supporting their requests for specific exemptions.[27]

Kennedy representatives on the commission, however, sided with organized labor in trying to enforce the window rule without exceptions. When that effort failed, they did not support the exemption language preferred by both Iowa and New Hampshire. For Kennedy, as for later Massachusetts presidential candidates (Senators Paul Tsongas and John Kerry), the New Hampshire primary was a lose-lose proposition. Because the Boston media market so dominates New Hampshire news, Massachusetts politicians are well known in New Hampshire. But for that reason (as Massachusetts senator Paul Tsongas discovered in 1992), a victory by a Massachusetts presidential aspirant in New Hampshire is frequently devalued because the Massachusetts politician is thought to have a "home-state" advantage. On the other hand, losing New Hampshire can be devastating for a Massachusetts politician and thus high-risk.

In January 1982, the Hunt Commission decided to allow exemptions to the window rule. It also voted 47 to 16 to limit the pre-window period in which exempted states could hold primaries or caucuses in order to shorten the nomination process. The final language adopted by the commission on January 15, 1982, added the following sentence to the existing text: "A rule 20 exemption shall not be granted from Rule 10A in excess of 7 days prior to the second Tuesday in March for primary states and 15 days prior to the second Tuesday in March for caucus states."[28] More important, however, the new rule gave Iowa and New Hampshire specific, upfront exemptions from the window: "provided, however, the New Hampshire primary may be held no earlier than seven days before the second Tuesday in March and the Iowa precinct caucuses may be held no earlier than fifteen days before the second Tuesday in March."[29]

Iowa and New Hampshire were now not only officially exempt from the provisions of the window rule; they were also protected from other states with aspirations to be "first in the nation." Opponents of this rule tried to limit the Iowa exemption to eight instead of 15 days, but this formulation was adamantly protested by both states and ultimately failed, since it would place the Iowa caucuses on a Monday night one day before the New Hampshire balloting.[30]

The final rule was hailed by Governor Hunt as a significant step because it shortened the primary season by five full weeks.[31] The Mondale campaign was pleased because the new rule greatly reduced the amount of time during which a second- or third-tier candidate could use a surprise showing in Iowa or New Hampshire to turn his new national prominence into financial and organizational strength, as Carter had done in 1976 when six full weeks separated the Iowa caucuses and the New Hampshire primary. Mondale also won a friend in Governor Gallen by supporting the grandfathering of his state's early primary. In contrast, the position of the Kennedy campaign angered the governor and resulted in negative press coverage in New Hampshire.

The Mondale campaign's victory turned out to be ephemeral. Kennedy ended up dropping out of the 1984 nomination race, and Mondale lost the New Hampshire primary in a surprise upset to Senator Gary Hart of Colorado, a candidate who had had no role in the machinations over the New Hampshire primary date. Nonetheless in future years, politicians in the early states would understand and use the power they had over presidential candidates.

The "Trigger"

Once the rules for the 1984 season were adopted, states began to submit delegate selection plans to the DNC for approval. As that progressed it became evident that the carefully negotiated window rule, Rule 10A, was fatally flawed. Under the existing rule, New Hampshire was allowed to hold its primary one week before the second Tuesday in March, or March 6, 1984.

Iowa would be allowed to hold its precinct caucuses 15 days before the beginning of the window, or February 27, 1984. The Compliance Review Commission (CRC) could grant an exemption to a state that had been outside the window in 1980, but it could not allow a primary state to go earlier than March 6, 1984, or a caucus state to go earlier than February 27, 1984.

Enter the Vermont primary. For some years Vermont had held a nonbinding presidential preference primary to coincide with the state's early-March town meetings. Because the primary was a beauty contest and did not have anything to do with the selection of delegates in either party, it received much less attention than the New Hampshire primary. That fact helped explain why the Hunt Commission's drafters forgot about Vermont as they considered how to rewrite the window rule. Nevertheless, the Vermont primary posed a problem because of New Hampshire's "trigger" law. Adopted in 1975 to protect New Hampshire's first-in-the-nation status, chapter 653:9 of the New Hampshire State Statutes, "Election of Officers and Delegates," requires that the state's primary be held: "on the second Tuesday in March or on a date selected by the secretary of state which is 7 days or more immediately preceding the date on which any other state shall hold a similar election, whichever is earlier."[32] In a provision that has turned out to be very important, the law gives the secretary of state the sole discretion to determine what constitutes a "similar election."

New Hampshire's secretary of state, William Gardner, took the position, along with most other state officials, that the Vermont primary was a "similar" enough election to force the New Hampshire primary to be held one week earlier, on February 28, 1984, regardless of the fact that the new delegate selection rules did not permit any primary before March 6, 1984. The possibility that New Hampshire's primary would move to February 28, 1984—one day after the Iowa precinct caucuses—caused considerable consternation in Iowa. Iowa Democrats foresaw that the impact of their precinct caucuses would be seriously diminished as news from Iowa was reported and then swamped by the results of the New Hampshire primary just 24 hours later. Consequently, party leaders began to think about scheduling the caucuses as early as February 20, 1984.

Thus began a test of wills between state parties and the DNC, the first of many similar fights waged with some regularity ever since. New Hampshire officials were determined to prevail in this contest. The state's voters enjoyed the attention they received from potential leaders of the free world every bit as much as their politicians and elected officials. The story of the woman who responded, "I don't know; I haven't met him yet," when asked how she felt about presidential candidate Birch Bayh, may be apocryphal, but it illustrates how close the average voter in New Hampshire gets to the potential candidates. News coverage of the primary controversy almost never failed to make the front page in the New Hampshire papers, and every Democratic politician in the state was careful to be on the right side of the controversy.

At first the issue did not have the same degree of intensity in Iowa as it did in New Hampshire. Iowa's first-in-the-nation tradition was not as old as New Hampshire's, and since Iowa was a caucus state, not a primary state, a smaller proportion of the electorate was directly involved. In addition, Iowa Democrats held different positions on the issue, depending on the preferences of their favored presidential candidates. Nonetheless, former state party chair Ed Campbell told reporters that when he agreed to the February 27 date for Iowa's precinct caucuses, it was with the understanding that they would he held eight days ahead of New Hampshire's primary.[33] The Republican governor of Iowa also threatened to use his veto power to make sure that the Iowa Democrats held their caucuses ahead of New Hampshire's primary and did not capitulate to DNC demands.[34]

On the DNC side, Chairman Chuck Mannatt and CRC chair Nancy Pelosi were equally determined not to give way. They maintained that since the Vermont primary was a beauty contest only, it was not subject to DNC rules and should not cause New Hampshire to change the date of its primary. In public and in private, Mannatt repeated that a deal had been made with regard to the dates of the two first contests and that short of reconvening the entire DNC to reconsider the rules, nothing could be done.[35]

Mannatt and Pelosi felt strongly enough about not granting any further exemptions to Iowa and New Hampshire that Mannatt began to threaten that the DNC would exercise a never-before-used rule to turn the New Hampshire primary into a beauty contest and force the state to elect delegates via a separate process inside the window.[36] Theoretically, the DNC has the power to go into a state that does not comply with party rules and form a committee that sets up a delegate selection process that does conform to national party rules.[37] No national party leadership had ever seriously contemplated doing this for the obvious reason that it would cause resentment and hard feelings—especially if there was unanimity of opinion in the state in favor of its own laws and traditions. Yet throughout 1983, Mannatt, Pelosi, and members of the DNC staff spoke of this option both publicly and privately in hopes of forcing Iowa, at least, to comply with national party rules.

Reactions from Democratic and Republican leaders in New Hampshire were predictably vehement. Chris Spirou, Democratic minority leader in the New Hampshire House, accused the national Democratic Party of having "chained New Hampshire to a position of political oblivion. It was a clear and strategized attempt to discredit New Hampshire's first-in-the-nation primary. The fault is with the Democratic National Committee."[38]

As it became clear that DNC officials were not about to budge, New Hampshire politicians pressured the presidential candidates to declare that they were solidly on the side of New Hampshire. In March 1983, State Senator Richard Boyer wrote to all the candidates urging them to support a change in the rules that would allow New Hampshire to move up its primary. In another letter, U.S. Representative Norman D'Amours asked them to pledge to seat the delegates that would be elected in New Hampshire's primary.

The Mondale campaign calculated that it had the most to lose from an earlier start to the primary season. Campaign advisers reasoned that the more time that elapsed between the first two contests and "Super Tuesday" (the first day of the window period, when eleven primaries and caucuses would be held), the greater would be the possibility that an unknown candidate could emerge as a threat. For a time, Mondale avoided choosing between the DNC and the New Hampshire position by stating that he would not run in any primary before the New Hampshire primary. In urging the other presidential candidates to do the same, the Mondale campaign hoped to diminish the threat posed by the Vermont primary to New Hampshire's preeminence as the first test and thereby lead New Hampshire officials to rule that their primary could be held on March 6, as party rules required. In contrast, Senator Alan Cranston sought to win friends in New Hampshire by becoming an early and vocal proponent of New Hampshire's right to hold its primary on February 28. In response to Representative D'Amours's letter, he pledged that he would support seating New Hampshire delegates if they were challenged for having been elected in an early primary. Senator John Glenn also pledged his support for seating New Hampshire delegates.[39]

On June 16, 1983, the Compliance Review Commission met to review the first delegate selection plans. Iowa and New Hampshire submitted plans that included both the date set in the Hunt Commission rules and the fact that state statutes in both states would most likely require earlier dates. By then, the Iowa legislature had united in favor of its first-in-the-nation status and had adopted its own trigger rule, which read: "Delegates to county conventions of political parties and party committee members shall be elected at precinct caucuses held not later than the fourth Monday in February of each even numbered year. The date shall be at least eight days earlier than the scheduled date for any meeting, caucus or primary which constitutes the first determining stage of the presidential nominating process in any other state."[40] The CRC ruled both states to be in noncompliance with the rules and instructed them to resubmit their plans to the CRC with the correct dates.

The impasse continued into the fall of 1983. In early October the New Hampshire secretary of state issued his political calendar calling for the presidential primary to be held on February 28. Although the attorney for the New Hampshire Democratic Party, in an attempt to keep peace with the national party, appealed quite eloquently to Attorney General Greg Smith that the statute did not require a February 28 date, the attorney general upheld the earlier date as expected.

This move forced Iowa Democrats to confront the issue in their state. Dave Nagle, the state party chair, was a forceful proponent for Iowa's moving the caucuses to February 20, eight days ahead of the New Hampshire primary. Aligned with Nagle were sixty-four of Iowa's ninety-nine county chairmen and John Law, the former executive director of the Iowa party and director of the Cranston campaign. Most of the politicians opposed to moving the date were Mondale supporters such as Iowa's labor leaders, the Senate majority leader, Lowell Junkins, and U.S. Representative Tom Harkin.

On October 14, 1983, the CRC met once again to consider the Iowa and New Hampshire delegate selection plans. The night before, a group of presidential campaign representatives met with the state chairs of Iowa, New Hampshire, and Maine (which was seeking an exemption to hold early caucuses). They sent a message to Mannatt to the effect that the presidential campaigns were opposed to having the DNC punish the states by running alternate delegate selection systems and that they preferred the earlier set of dates for Iowa and New Hampshire, as well as a March 4 date for Maine and a March 10 date for Wyoming.

The meeting had little impact on Mannatt and Pelosi, who by then were committed to a no-compromise position. When the full CRC met, the delegate selection plans from Iowa and New Hampshire were, once again, voted in noncompliance with national party rules. In addition, the CRC sent out its strongest warning yet: if New Hampshire law dictated an earlier date for the primary, then the state party would have to submit an alternate delegate selection system, which complied with the 1984 Delegate Selection Rules, to the Compliance Review Commission.[41]

With the DNC decision holding firm in the face of opposition from all of the presidential campaigns, except that of former Florida governor Reubin Askew (who understandably would have liked the season to officially begin with the Florida primary and who ended up finishing last in the New Hampshire primary), New Hampshire state chair George Bruno and his Iowa counterpart Dave Nagle decided to use the occasion of the upcoming New Hampshire State Convention to ask all the presidential candidates personally to support their position on the date controversy. The two state chairs issued a letter from the presidential candidates to Chairman Mannatt in which the candidates pledged to support the early dates for Iowa, New Hampshire, and Maine and to boycott any alternate delegate selection process that might be set up by the DNC. No candidate had any option other than to sign the public letter; in the words of the Mondale campaign's state coordinator in New Hampshire: "We were held up at the convention."[42]

With that, the controversy died down in New Hampshire but raged all the more intensely in Iowa. On November 19, 1983, the Iowa State Central Committee voted 20 to 10 to set the date of the Iowa caucuses for February 20, 1984. The decision followed a heated internal party battle that pitted the state chair and many of the county chairs against much of the state's elected leadership. The fact that the opposition to the February 20 date came from the top Mondale supporters in the state led many observers to wonder about Mondale's position on the date controversy. On November 23, Senator Cranston wrote to Mondale to ask, "Which side are you on?"[43] The letter was also released to the press. Mondale responded immediately that he supported the earlier date for Iowa. This was the public position of the Mondale campaign. Yet top Mondale aides had been quietly urging their friends in

Iowa to try to win acceptance of the later date. The play did not go unnoticed by the political reporters in Iowa, one of whom noted, "Mondale forces are trying to have it both ways."[44]

The thinking behind the Mondale strategy in Iowa was simple and prophetic. Peter Hart's polling for Mondale showed him to be weaker in New Hampshire than in any other early state.[45] By keeping the Iowa and New Hampshire contests close together, Mondale's top aides hoped to magnify the impact of a hoped-for strong showing in Iowa on the New Hampshire results and leave as little time as possible for a strong challenger to emerge in New Hampshire.

The final chapter was written in U.S. District Court in Iowa. Three Mondale supporters—former state chair Ed Campbell, DNC member Jean Haugland, and Charles Gifford, the top UAW politico in Iowa—sued the Iowa Democratic Central Committee, alleging that by violating DNC rules the state party had harmed the plaintiffs by jeopardizing their chances of being seated at the nominating convention.[46] The Cranston campaign and the Glenn campaign intervened on the side of the Iowa state party. On January 17, 1984, the court ruled against the plaintiffs and in favor of the Iowa state party on the grounds that "the interests of the candidate interveners in this action and the other candidates outweigh those of the plaintiffs and prevent this Court from granting the equitable relief plaintiffs are entitled to. Changing the date of the Iowa caucuses would result in severe inequities to the presidential campaigns."[47]

The Emperor Has No Clothes

Faced with the intransigence of the New Hampshire and Iowa state parties, the DNC's Executive Committee voted to establish a 19C Committee, a party-run committee that would be vested with the power to run alternative delegate selection systems in Iowa and New Hampshire. Yet it was clear to all sides that this committee would not attempt to act. Doing so would have been sheer folly given that the candidates and the press had already invested enormous resources in the first two contests. At this point, any action by the national party would only prove that when it came to enforcement, the emperor had no clothes. Iowa, New Hampshire, Maine, and Wyoming (the latter two having received formal exemptions at the last minute) ran delegate selection systems outside the window. The result was the outcome most feared by the Mondale campaign: an interval of time that was sufficient enough to allow for a long-shot candidate—Senator Gary Hart of Colorado—to emerge and threaten the front-runner.

Seven years after the Democratic Party's first attempts to decrease the importance of the early caucuses and primaries, it was clear that the window rule was a failure. In 1984, Gary Hart's New Hampshire win, reinforced by subsequent wins in the early states of Maine and Wyoming, catapulted him into competition with the vaunted Mondale juggernaut, a competition he was able to keep alive until the very end of the 1984 nomination season. The effects of the early contests on the subsequent contests were enormous. With no resources to speak of—no organization, no endorsements, no money (in the pre-Internet world it took weeks to get money in the bank), Hart competed against Mondale on Super Tuesday on momentum and free media alone. In contrast, despite substantial financial resources, celebrity status, high name identification, and a position on the ideological spectrum closest to southern voters, John Glenn's capacity to compete on Super Tuesday was destroyed by his inability to place in the early contests.

The window rule's failure to have its desired effect was due in part to the calculations of Democratic presidential candidates who heavily influenced both its drafting and its enforcement. The window rule could have been much tougher or enforced more strictly had the candidates not sought to curry favor with New Hampshire politicians and voters. But this outcome was inevitable once momentum became a major factor in primary politics. Even a candidate as well funded as Mondale could not afford to compete everywhere on the new frontloaded Super Tuesday that he had helped create. Thus even Mondale needed to create momentum in an early, small, and therefore inexpensive state.

The power of the early contests is an unavoidable by-product of the modern nomination system. Once candidates were forced to compete in a sequence of public events in all 50 states, even well-funded front-runners had to rely on the free media that came with the establishment of momentum to win later, more costly primaries. To skip an early contest meant taking the risk that someone else would capture the imagination of the press and the public—in short, the momentum. As candidates invested time and money in the early states, so did the press, on the lookout for the earliest possible clues as to who among the contestants would do best with the voters. In response, more and more states moved their votes earlier in order to get in on the action.

The window rule was a weak and fruitless effort in the face of these underlying dynamics. Not only was it nearly impossible to enforce; it was counterproductive. As more states moved toward the front of the window, Iowa and New Hampshire became even more important as launchpads for a successful campaign. And as they became more important, more and more states moved up, nearly creating what the Winograd Commission had sought to avoid—a national primary.

Iowa and New Hampshire: Inching Forward

Since 1984 the Iowa caucuses and the New Hampshire primary have reigned supreme. Other states have attempted to go early, but the automatic triggers in both states' laws meant that Iowa and New Hampshire simply moved their contests earlier—even when it was determined that the offending state would be a beauty contest only. As a result, both contests have been inching forward in time. As table 3-1 indicates, New Hampshire's primary used to be in March; then it moved into February and, most recently, into early January!

To further defend their first-in-the-nation status, the parties in both states threatened the presidential campaigns that if the candidates attempted to campaign in any other early states they would turn this into an issue with their voters who, more than voters in any other state, cared about their first-in-the-nation status. In 1996, for example, pressure from Iowa and New Hampshire Republicans forced the party's candidates to boycott two early voting states, Louisiana and Delaware. Thus states that held votes early in the calendar found that no one came to campaign.

Following the 1996 election, the Republican Party attempted to do something about the early states and what they considered to be a dangerously frontloaded nomination system. Senator Bob Dole, the favorite of the Republican establishment, had had a rocky start to the nomination. The conservative Pat Buchanan managed to come in a close second to Dole in the Iowa caucuses, buoyed by the strength of Christian evangelical voters. He then upset Dole in New Hampshire. His New Hampshire victory, fueled again by hard-core conservatives, posed a stark challenge to the Republican

Table 3-1. *The Ever Earlier New Hampshire Primary, 1952–2008*

Year	Date of primary
1952	March 11
1956	March 13
1960	March 8
1964	March 10
1968	March 12
1972	March 7
1976	February 24
1980	February 26
1984	February 28
1988	February 16
1992	February 18
1996	February 20
2000	February 1
2004	January 27
2008	January 8

Source: Congressional Quarterly, *Presidential Elections since 1789* (Washington: Congressional Quarterly, 1987); and Office of the Secretary of the Democratic National Committee, Washington.

establishment—that coalition of Wall Street and Main Street that composed the nonreligious portion of the Republican Party. But the South Carolina "firewall" that Lee Atwater had constructed to stop John Connally and then Bob Dole himself in 1988 saved Dole from Buchanan in 1996 and saved the Republican Party from a man that some saw as too extreme to win a general election, the Republicans' version of Jesse Jackson on the Democratic side.

After South Carolina, Dole went on to win every primary in the month of March and win the nomination and then lose the general election to President Clinton. But the Buchanan experience worried more mainstream Republicans. The conservative (and some thought too-radical) base of the Republican Party had shown itself to be pretty powerful in the two early states. But by 1996 it was clear that taking a direct run at the early states was very difficult. So instead of taking them on directly the Republicans tried to decompress the calendar by passing a resolution that required all primaries and caucuses to be held between the first Monday in February and the third Tuesday in June. The idea was to entice states to go later in the season, thus allowing the momentum from early-state victories to wear off in time for other candidates to get momentum. And so they offered "bonus delegates" to those states that held primaries later in the system—an idea adopted by the Democrats in 2008.[48]

With this move, the Republicans finally had their own window rule—and a window that opened before the Democrats'. This increased the pressure on the DNC to allow more states to go early. In 2000, backed by the White House and Vice President Gore's supporters, the Democratic National Committee was able to hold the line. As table 1-4 shows, only 2 percent of the Democratic delegates that year were elected before March. But holding the line came at a price. Democrats in South Carolina and in Michigan had kept their contests within the window, only to watch with envy as the Republican Party held high-profile early contests between George W. Bush and John McCain in 2000, attracting enormous amounts of attention and new voters. These two states complained bitterly that the national party had put them at a competitive disadvantage with the Republicans in their states.

Prodded by concerns from these two states in particular, in the runup to the two major party nominating conventions in the summer of 2000 members of the Democratic Party's Rules and By-Laws Committee met quietly with their counterparts at the Republican National Committee. The object was simple: to have both parties' nominating systems start on the same date, so that neither party would be disadvantaged. Progress was made and then, at the last moment, Joe Allbaugh, one of Bush's top political operatives, acting on behalf of Karl Rove, George W. Bush's campaign manager, vetoed the resolution coming out of the Republican National Committee's Rules Committee at the Philadelphia convention. Like many nominees before and since, George W. Bush felt that there was nothing wrong with the system that had gotten him this far.

The decision was a real disappointment to the Democrats and Republicans who had worked in good faith to get a common starting date as a means of stemming the increasing tendency toward frontloading. In the absence of agreement on a common starting date, the Democrats had no alternative but to move up their window in order to be in sync with the Republicans. More states went earlier, with the result that 25 percent of the convention delegates were selected in January and February 2004, compared to 2 percent in

January and February 2000. Iowa and New Hampshire grew ever more important, and their citizens more protective of the unique position they held in the nomination process.

This lesson was brought home to Howard Dean in 2004. He had had one of the more brilliant preelection seasons ever in 2003, raising unprecedented sums of money over the Internet, mobilizing thousands of young people to join the party, and generally upsetting the applecart of more seasoned politicians such as Massachusetts senator John Kerry. Then came Iowa. Dean's defeat in Iowa was as dramatic as his earlier rise to the front of the pack. Dean's downfall resulted from the lack of Iowans in his state organization and his engagement in an intense negative campaign with U.S. Representative Dick Gephardt that allowed John Kerry to emerge unscathed as the winner. But Dean was also hurt by remarks about the Iowa caucus system that he had made years ago on Canadian television. These comments came back to haunt him at a critical point in the Iowa campaign. "If you look at the caucus system," said Dean, "they are dominated by the special interests in both sides, in both parties. The special interests don't represent the centrist tendencies of the American people, they represent the extremes. Say I'm a guy who's got to work, and I've got kids. On a Saturday, is it easy for me to go cast a ballot and spend 15 minutes doing it or do I have to sit in a caucus for eight hours? And listen to everyone else's opinion for eight hours about how to fix the world."[49] Resurrected 10 days before the caucuses, Dean's remarks contributed to the deflation of his presidential bubble. At the time, polls had Dean and Gephardt tied for first place, with Kerry in a close third. The several days Dean had to spend explaining his comments took their toll.[50] Not even his subsequent endorsement by Senator Tom Harkin, the state's most popular Democrat, could reverse the downward slide. Dean finished third in Iowa, with a humiliating 18 percent of the vote.

Yet Another Democratic Party Commission

Despite their seemingly unassailable position, after 2000, Iowa and New Hampshire continued to face challengers for primary preeminence. Chief among these was Michigan. Between presidential elections, politicians who were not former or future presidential candidates tended to forget about whatever inequities they perceived to have resulted from the impact of these two early states. But not Senator Carl Levin of Michigan. Starting in 2003 he has waged a sometimes lonely crusade to end the "stranglehold" that Iowa and New Hampshire, in his view, held over the system.[51] To Levin, Iowa's dominance in the process gave an unfair advantage to agricultural issues and interests, and New Hampshire's dominance gave an unfair advantage to the Northeast. Missing was any representative of the manufacturing base of the country, such as Michigan.

In 2004, just when the Democrats thought they had outgrown rules commissions, Levin forced DNC Party Chairman Terry McAuliffe to create a new commission to study the "timing" problem. In return, Levin agreed not to push for an early Michigan primary, which would force New Hampshire to move even earlier in the process. And so, the Commission on Presidential Nomination Timing and Scheduling was born, chaired by Representative David Price and former labor secretary Alexis Herman.

I delivered the opening testimony at the first meeting of the commission. My remarks focused on the lessons of history recounted in this chapter. I warned that the DNC really had no sanctions available to enforce its will, since Iowa and New Hampshire would rather be early than have their delegates seated at the convention; that presidential candidates would bow to blackmail from politicians in the two states; and that voters in those two states actually cared about the issue of timing, whereas there was no evidence that voters in any other state (including Michigan) even knew there was an issue.

The other testimony that day was from Professor Ron Walters, a veteran of Jesse Jackson's two presidential campaigns and a leading voice in the African American community. After recounting how difficult it was for African American candidates, such as Jesse Jackson, Carol Moseley Braun, and Al Sharpton, to do well in the all-white states of Iowa and New Hampshire, he made a fascinating civil rights case. "A legal case could be made," he said, "with respect to the Voting Rights Act. If Section 2 suggests that we shouldn't dilute the vote of minorities, and if it is the case that having these, this system of Iowa and New Hampshire the way they are and the way they have been, dilutes the vote, then I think, at some point, maybe in 2007 when people are thinking about renewing the Voting Rights Act, people will begin to think about the way in which this impacts on political party structures, as well as having the effect of diluting the black vote."[52]

Walters's argument was to have a powerful effect on the course of the commission's proceedings. Along the way the mandate of the commission morphed into something a bit easier to handle than doing away with the Iowa and New Hampshire primaries: the issue of demographic representation. At the very first meeting the die was cast. As commissioners emerged from small group meetings, co-chair David Price reported, "There was considerable sentiment for diversifying the early states, diversifying demographically and ethnically and so forth."[53] The evolution of the commission's mandate was articulated by Alexis Herman, the other co-chair, in the *Washington Post*. According to political writer E. J. Dionne, "Herman says that what began as a 'big state/small state' discussion is morphing into 'a larger conversation about the party's values.' She notes that the way the primary calendar is structured also affects which voices within the party are the loudest, which issues are given the most prominence. Where, she asks, is the voice of the manufacturing worker? How can the seemingly intractable divisions between 'red' and 'blue' states be eased?"[54]

Subsequent hearings and meetings bore out Herman's characterization of the commission's debates. Under a barrage of lobbying from Iowa and New Hampshire, and reluctant to admit to the weakness of the DNC's enforcement capacity, the commission quickly shed its focus on the perennially difficult issue of who was first. By October a consensus was forming that rather than take on Iowa and New Hampshire head on, the commission would recommend adding one or two states to the pre-window period so that the early contests would reflect the racial and geographic diversity of the party.

Both Senator Carl Levin and Democratic National Committeewoman Debbie Dingell (wife of longtime Michigan representative John Dingell) felt betrayed. On November 6, 2005, the Michigan state party met and issued a strongly worded resolution urging the commission "to end the monopoly of Iowa and New Hampshire."[55] In the resolution the Michigan party recounted that it had been prepared to challenge the system in 2004 by moving its own primary up to early January. But it had been dissuaded from this action by then DNC chairman Terry McAuliffe, who had promised to create the commission. The clear implication was that Michigan had been betrayed by the DNC and its commission.

After nearly a year of deliberations, the Price-Herman Commission issued its final report to the DNC on December 10, 2005. Once again, the party allowed Iowa and New Hampshire to retain their privileged positions, but the DNC was instructed to add two states to the early lineup and to take racial and geographic diversity into account in selecting the states.[56] At least on paper, this gave Michigan one more chance. On July 22, 2006, the DNC's Rules and By-Laws Committee concluded a two-day meeting in Washington at which states that wanted to be considered for one of the two early slots in the calendar presented their case. Most of the states that applied were small states, and most of them had some claim to expanding the diversity of the early contests. The emerging consensus was that one of these states should be in the South and one in the West and that they should represent African Americans, Hispanics, and labor unions. Michigan also applied, arguing that it had greater ethnic, racial, and economic diversity than any of the other contenders. But Michigan never really had a chance. For one thing, Iowa, a midwestern state, was still first. Second, the consensus was that the early contests should be in small states where retail campaigning was possible. In the end, the committee chose South Carolina, a southern state with a large black population, and Nevada, a western state with a large Hispanic population and a large number of labor union members, to round out the early calendar.

Florida and Michigan Attempt to End the Monopoly

Senator Levin was not pleased. The commission he had brought into being did not, in the end, do anything about the problem of Iowa and New Hampshire. And so, in the summer of 2007, the Michigan Democratic Party, acting under instructions from Senator Levin and Debbie Dingell, withdrew its initial plan and resubmitted a proposal for a January 15 primary. The clear intent was to challenge the primacy of the New Hampshire primary.

At about the same time, the Florida Republican Party decided to hold its primary on January 29, 2008. Included on the January 29 ballot was an item that would limit property tax assessments and thereby constrain public spending. Public sector unions and the Democrats in general feared that this proposal would pass only if the Republican presidential nomination race were on the ballot, skewing turnout against the Democrats. (The proposition did end up passing, to the delight of conservatives in the state.) Thus, largely inspired not by animus against Iowa and New Hampshire but by local concerns, Florida Democrats joined their Republican counterparts in pushing for an early primary.

The DNC's Rules and By-Laws Committee turned down both plans but kept negotiations open with each state throughout the year, hopeful that something could be worked out. Instead, as 2007 wore on, uncertainty and anxiety about the calendar increased. Presidential campaigns were acutely sensitive to both the starting date and the sequence that would follow. News organizations needed to plan their coverage. And party insiders worried about the possibility that Iowa and New Hampshire's "triggers" would push those contests into December, in defiance of a Democratic Party rule requiring that all steps in the delegate selection process be held in the year of the convention.

On August 25, 2007, the DNC's Rules and By-Laws Committee met in Washington, D.C., to settle, once and for all, the issue of timing. Using their authority to punish states that violated the window rule, the committee members stripped Florida and Michigan of 100 percent of their delegates to the 2008 nominating convention. (Seeking to void this decision, Florida filed a lawsuit against the DNC in October 2007, only to have it thrown out on grounds that the national party had the clear authority to set its own rules for its own nominating system.) The Republican Party had already enacted an automatic 50 percent cut in the delegates of all the early states—including Iowa, New Hampshire, Nevada, South Carolina, Florida, and Michigan. Interestingly, the Republican penalty was enacted without a whiff of protest.

Less than a week later, the four early states—Iowa and New Hampshire, now joined by South Carolina and Nevada—sought to rally the presidential candidates behind the DNC's decision on Florida and Michigan. South Carolina Democratic Party chair Carol Fowler circulated a letter to all the Democratic presidential candidates asking them to pledge not to campaign in any state holding a caucus or primary before February 5, 2008, other than the four that had been chosen in the DNC process. First to sign were New Mexico governor Bill Richardson, Connecticut senator Christopher Dodd, and Delaware senator Joseph Biden—candidates for the presidency who had raised little money in 2007 and who could barely afford to compete in the small states making the request, let alone in big states like Florida and Michigan. A few days later, Senator Barack Obama, former senator John Edwards, and last but not least, Senator Hillary Clinton came on board. In

October of 2007 five Democrats—Obama, Biden, Edwards, Richardson, and Dennis Kucinich—took their names off the Michigan ballot, leaving only Clinton and Dodd on the ballot. There was no such option in the Florida primary, so everyone's name remained on that ballot.

Throughout this process, as was his habit, New Hampshire's long-serving secretary of state, William Gardner, kept his cards close to the vest as to what date he would choose for the New Hampshire primary, even hinting at one point that he would call the primary for 2007.[57] Finally, on November 21, 2007, Gardner set the date of the New Hampshire primary for January 8, 2008—one week before the Michigan primary. It was the shortest period of time in history between the setting of the date and the actual date of the primary. For his toughness Gardner was named Citizen of the Year by the state's largest newspaper.

The political class breathed a sigh of relief; the calendar fell into place, with the earliest starting date in the modern history of the nominating process. Reporters shook off their New Year's Eve hangovers and headed out to Iowa for the January 3 caucuses. The Republicans held six heated nomination contests in January, one of which—Florida's—ended the presidential bid of Rudy Giuliani. True to their pledges, the Democratic candidates did not campaign in Michigan or Florida, but they waged intense campaigns in the four early states sanctioned by the DNC. Like others before him, Senator Levin had come up against the immovable object of the New Hampshire primary and failed to budge it. Iowa and New Hampshire reigned supreme once again.

Conclusion

Neither Iowa nor New Hampshire set out to dominate American presidential nominating politics. But once the dynamics of the modern nomination system thrust them into the spotlight they grew fond of their place and held on to their positions fiercely. Although many presidential hopefuls have no doubt cursed these two states' early contests in the privacy of their homes, no one has dared cross them and so the system survives with the help, every four years, of yet another batch of presidential candidates.

The politics of these two early states in the nomination system are a perfect example of the problem of intensity in a modern democracy. As the revered political scientist Robert Dahl noted in his thinking about James Madison:

> What if the minority prefers its alternative much more passionately than the majority prefers a contrary alternative? Does the majority principle still make sense? . . . Madison might argue that government should be designed to inhibit a relatively apathetic majority from cramming its policy down the throats of a relatively intense minority."[58]

Neither Dahl nor Madison could have predicted how, in the evolution of the modern American presidential nomination system, an intense minority of voters would prevail. Voters in Iowa and New Hampshire have become accustomed to their privileged position; most voters in other states can only imagine what it is like to be courted by someone who actually becomes president. And therefore, delegates or no delegates, Iowa and New Hampshire remain in first place.

4

PROPORTIONAL REPRESENTATION

Why Democrats Use It and Republicans Don't

In the modern nominating system, sequence is strategy, with Iowa and New Hampshire dictating who moves on and who doesn't. For the vast majority of presidential candidates in the post-reform era, one or both of these two states have spelled the end of the road. But the tendency to frontload the modern nominating system means that for those few candidates who make it past the first hurdle, the measure of success changes quickly. Instead of concentrating on who is winning states, candidates (and the press) soon shift their focus to who is winning delegates.

This business of counting delegates often comes as a surprise to presidential candidates and the public alike, and for good reason. In the 20 nomination contests between 1972 and 2008, only five nominees—George McGovern in 1972, Gerald Ford in 1976, Jimmy Carter in 1980, Walter Mondale in 1984, and Barack Obama in 2008—have had to fight for the nomination from the very first to the very last primary. In the other 15 contests, either an incumbent ran unchallenged or one presidential candidate dominated the first few contests to such an extent that everyone else was forced out of the race long before the last primary.

Sequence works the same way for both political parties—Iowa and New Hampshire and the states that serve as "firewalls" are as important to Republicans as to Democrats. But the method of allocating delegates to presidential candidates differs significantly between the parties. Democrats use a proportional representation system that tends to reward candidates who lose narrowly and awards relatively few delegates to those who win narrowly. Republicans tend to use winner-take-all systems that reward candidates who win by even the slimmest margins.[1] This difference means that Democratic contests that make it past the early states can go on much longer than Republican contests. It also helps explain why four out of the five contested nomination contests listed above were in the Democratic Party. The same pattern held in 2008, when John McCain was able to wrap up his nomination several weeks before Barack Obama, in part because his primary wins were yielding greater results in the delegate count.

Tables 4-1 and 4-2 show how different the two parties' rules are. On the Democratic side, national party rules called for winner-take-all primaries at the state level to be eliminated by 1976. Other systems with winner-take-all effects survived, at least for a while. For instance, in states that elect delegates directly, the presidential candidate's name appears after the name of local candidates for delegate. In these systems, slates of well-known local candidates tend to be elected as a block, yielding winner-take-all results by district. In other states (mostly in the Republican Party) all the delegates in a congressional district are awarded to the presidential candidate who wins that district. In two years, 1984 and 1988, the Democrats used a bonus system that awarded an extra delegate to the winner of the congressional district. But by 1992, even systems with the potential to result in winner-take-all outcomes at the congressional district level had disappeared completely on the Democratic side.

In contrast, the Republican Party employs a wide variety of rules for allocating delegates to presidential candidates, including proportional rules and variations on winner-take-all systems. In addition to direct election of delegate states, winner-take-all by congressional district states, and winner-take-all-by-state states, some states on the Republican side have employed hybrid systems that award a presidential candidate all the delegates if he or she exceeds a certain percentage of the vote.

Why such a difference between the parties? First, while the Republican Party got swept up in the trend to move from party caucuses to primaries for both competitive and legal reasons, the decision on how to allocate delegates following a primary has been left up to state parties. The Republican Party has never had a national fight over allocation rules. As Representative David Price says in his 1984 book, *Bringing Back the Parties,* "In its national

Table 4-1. *How Democrats Allocate Convention Delegates to Primary and Caucus State Winners*

Item	Proportional representation	Direct election of delegates	Winner-take-all by congressional district[a]	Winner-take-all by state	Other[b]
1972[a]					
Primary states only	13 states (16%)[c]	9 states (33%)	6 states (14%)	5 states (12%)	
1976					
Primary and caucus states	41 states (58%)	14 states (41%)	1 state (1%)	0	
1980					
Primary and caucus states	54 states (94%)	2 states (6%)	0	0	
1984					
Primary and caucus states	38 states (47%)	8 states (29%)	0	0	10 states (24%)
1988					
Primary and caucus states	39 states (54%)	7 states (15%)	0	0	10 states (24%)
1992	56 states (100%)				
1996	56 states (100%)				
2000	56 states (100%)				
2004	56 states (100%)				
2008	56 states (100%)				

Sources: Office of the Secretary, Democratic National Committee. Data for 1972 come from newspaper accounts of the delegate race.

a. Since 1972 was a transitional year, data on caucus states are difficult to come by, so only primary states are included here.

b. National party rules allowed for the existence of a "bonus rule" in 1984 and 1988 only, whereby the winner of a congressional district was able to win the first delegate before the proportional formula was applied.

c. The first number in each column is the number of states using a given system; the second number is the percentage of total convention delegate votes elected in those states. There are usually more delegates than delegate votes because of fractional votes. States total more than 50 because Puerto Rico and territories are included.

Table 4-2. *How Republicans Allocate Convention Delegates to Winners, Presidential Primary States Only, 1972–2008*

Year	Proportional represen- tation	Direct election of delegates	Winner- take-all by congressional district[a]	Winner- take-all by state	Other[b]
1972	3 (7%)[c]	11 (29%)	6 (14%)	3 (9%)	
1976	11 (17%)	10 (32%)	5 (11%)	2 (8%)	
1980	15 (26%)	11 (28%)	8 (14%)	2 (9%)	
1984	12 (23%)	10 (26%)	6 (12%)	1 (8%)	
1988	15 (20%)	6 (19%)	6 (16%)	5 (14%)	1 (5%)
1992	13 (20%)	12 (25%)	7 (18%)	5 (14%)	2 (7%)
1996	7 (11%)	4 (10%)	8 (23%)	12 (23%)	6 (12%)
2000	10 (16%)	6 (17%)	7 (19%)	13 (24%)	3 (8%)
2004	10 (15%)	3 (8%)	7 (23%)	10 (17%)	2 (8%)
2008	10 (14%)	3 (7%)	7 (20%)	12 (23%)	6 (12%)

Sources: Data compiled from *Congressional Quarterly Weekly Reports*; and "Delegate Selection Overview" available from the Republican National Committee. (Data for 1996 are from newspaper accounts.)

a. In some winner-take-all-by-congressional-district states a bonus is given to the statewide winner as well.

b. States in this category are hybrids. They use proportional rules to allocate delegates at the congressional district and at-large levels, *unless* a presidential candidate wins more than a given percentage (usually 50 percent) of the vote in a congressional district or statewide. For instance, in 2008 in Alabama, Arkansas, Mississippi, and Texas, if a candidate won more than 50 percent of the votes in a district he or she won all the delegates; otherwise delegates were awarded according to proportional representation rules. In Tennessee, delegates are awarded using proportional representation rules unless a candidate wins 66 percent of the vote, and then the candidate can win all the delegates in a congressional district or the state. In Louisiana a candidate can win all the delegates in the state if the candidate wins 50 percent of the votes; if not, all the delegates are "uncommitted."

c. The first number in each column is the number of states using a given allocation system; the second number is the percentage of total convention delegates elected in those states. Because caucus/convention states are not included, the totals do not equal 100 percent.

rules . . . the Republican Party has not gone down the 'fair reflection' path of the Democrats."[2] The Republicans had a brief flirtation with party reform, Democratic style, when, at their 1972 convention the party created a committee to look at the relationship between the Republican National Committee and the state committees. Chaired by Representative William A. Steiger of Wisconsin, the committee set out to test some of the ideas being explored by Democrats. Among the issues considered was proportional representation. But Republicans specifically rejected mandating proportional representation, arguing that they wanted the nominating system to mirror the winner-take-all aspects of the general election and the Electoral College system. Ultimately most of the reform ideas raised in the Steiger Committee were rejected in favor of a states'-rights approach to delegate selection.

Republican opposition to proportional representation has lasted for many decades. When I asked Frank Fahrenkopf, former chairman of the Republican National Committee, why they never mandated proportional representation, he replied: "We Republicans would never do that. Since the Electoral College is winner-take-all, why would you adopt a primary system that's different? When we go into a state all the candidates build statewide organizations, and then they are prepared to run in the Electoral College."[3] Thus the story of why Democrats use proportional rules and Republicans do not is a story that takes place largely within the Democratic Party.

While proportional representation is widely used in democracies around the world, especially parliamentary democracies, it is almost never used in the United States.[4] The system was a favorite of the early-twentieth-century progressive reformers who saw proportional representation as a way to break the power of big-city political machines. After a brief spell of popularity, however, proportional representation was abandoned for a variety of reasons, including the fact that in some places it resulted in Communists' getting elected to city councils. So what explains the Democrats' decision to mandate proportional representation when translating primary votes into delegate votes? To answer this question, we have to look back to 1968 and one of the 1968 convention's most hated rules—the unit rule. This rule allowed all the votes of a state's delegation to be cast according to the preferences of the majority of the delegation. Thus, to the extent that a small number of antiwar delegates had managed to get themselves into state delegations, application of the unit rule meant that their voices would never be heard. Arguing that "unrestrained application of majority rule in primary, convention and committee systems produced much of the bitterness and divisiveness characteristic of 1968," reformers set out to abolish the unit rule and to ensure "fair representation" at earlier stages in the delegate selection process.[5] Although the reformers were immediately successful in abolishing the unit rule, it took them two decades to mandate proportional representation throughout the Democratic nomination process.

Fair Representation and McGovern's California Challenge

Initially, most politicians were unfamiliar with proportional representation. Thus the McGovern-Fraser Commission (officially, the Commission on Party Structure and Delegate Selection), which was set up in 1969, did not use the term, instead choosing the more ambiguous "fair reflection." Moreover, commission members could not agree on whether the 1968 mandate to ban the unit rule included proportional representation. (Commissioner Fred Dutton of California, who sought to maintain his state's winner-take-all primary, led the fight to avoid use of the term "proportional representation.") Consequently, the final version of McGovern-Fraser guideline B-6 used the term "fair representation" instead. The final guideline simply "urged" state parties to "adopt procedures which will provide fair representation of minority views on presidential candidates," meaning that the rule would be nonbinding for the 1972 convention.[6] Following this ruling, a few states did adopt proportional allocation systems for 1972, but the unresolved issue of proportional representation was left for the 1972 nominating convention where, to the dismay of reformers, it became the test vote of the convention.

It all began with the 1972 winner-take-all California primary, where George McGovern's narrow win over Hubert Humphrey netted him all 271 California delegates.[7] In the weeks before the convention, while McGovern's managers were preoccupied with control of the Platform Committee, the ABM (Anybody but McGovern) forces concentrated on controlling the Credentials Committee. Thus when the Credentials Committee met to consider its record number of 82 challenges, a challenge to the seating of California's delegates was among them. ABM forces controlled a majority on the committee, thanks to the fact that the ten McGovern members from California could not vote. (Credentials Committee members are not allowed to vote on challenges involving their own state.)

Debate in the Credentials Committee centered on some of the same issues that had arisen in the McGovern-Fraser Commission, such as whether the unit rule prohibition enacted at the 1968 Convention had been intended as a ban on winner-take-all primaries. In addition, committee members raised the question of whether the state of California had even tried to comply with the McGovern-Fraser guidelines, as well as the fact that several other states with statewide or district winner-take-all schemes were not facing credentials challenges. Ultimately, however, this challenge, like convention challenges before and after, was not about abstract rules but about political power. Voting 73 to 65, the Credentials Committee decided to deprive McGovern of 151 of his California delegates and distribute them to the other contenders on the grounds that "the California winner-take-all primary functionally disenfranchised 56 percent of the California Democratic electorate who did not vote for George McGovern."[8]

While the Credentials Committee was meeting, the Rules Committee convened in a somewhat less politicized environment. There the unfinished work of the McGovern-Fraser reformers was being done. Advocates of mandatory proportional representation understood that one of the stumbling blocks to achieving proportional representation for 1972 was the confusion surrounding the 1968 convention language on the unit rule. It was thus important that the 1972 convention go on record in favor of proportional representation in the delegate selection process. Testifying before the Rules Committee, Ken Bode, research director of the McGovern-Fraser Commission, urged the 1972 convention to require all states to adopt proportional systems for the future. In a carefully documented presentation, he outlined the inequities of winner-take-all by district systems in addition to the inequities of the more highly publicized winner-take-all by state primary. "It is not an effective remedy to eliminate California's primary [where George McGovern won 45 percent of the popular vote and 100 percent of the delegate vote], but leave standing the Florida primary [where George Wallace captured 43 percent of the popular vote and 93 percent of the delegate vote]," Bode argued.[9]

Liberals like Bode, who made up the majority of the Rules Committee, were strongly affected by segregationist George Wallace's strong showing in the 1972 primaries. Of the 21 primaries that year, he placed first in five (Florida, Tennessee, North Carolina, Maryland, and Michigan) and a close second in six (Wisconsin, Pennsylvania, Indiana, West Virginia, Oregon, and New Mexico). In particular, they were concerned that winner-take-all rules could help future candidates like Wallace reap large delegate gains by winning conservative districts or by winning a plurality of votes in a state in multicandidate contests. Thus the Rules Committee passed and the 1972 convention adopted strengthened provisions mandating "fair reflection" for the 1976 Democratic convention. Section 4 of the Rules Committee report read as follows: "Resolved, further, that the Call for the 1976 Democratic National Convention shall include provisions that assure that delegates to the 1976 Democratic National Convention shall be chosen in a manner which fairly reflects the division of preferences expressed by those who participate in the presidential nominating process in each state, territory and the District of Columbia."[10] At the same time, the 1972 convention voted to seat the delegates elected in California's winner-take-all primary—reversing the ruling of the Credentials Committee—even though many of those voting for the measure had to hold their noses through the vote. After all, the California delegates were essential to McGovern's nomination; the reformers could wait another four years.

Fair Reflection versus Proportional Representation

Thus the 1972 California credentials challenge set the stage politically and the 1972 Rules Committee resolution set the stage legally for requiring proportional representation in all of the 1976 delegate selection systems. Nevertheless, in 1976 advocates of proportional representation were to find their goals thwarted once again. In the year following the 1972 debacle, two more commissions were formed to codify Democratic Party rules. One, the Charter Commission, was created by the 1972 convention to write a charter that would govern the Democratic Party. The other, called the Commission on Delegate Selection (more commonly referred to as the Mikulski Commission after its chair, then–Baltimore city councilwoman Barbara Mikulski), was given the task of writing delegate selection rules for the 1976 nomination season.

The Mikulski Commission began its work under an extensive mandate to make appropriate revisions in the McGovern-Fraser rules, adopt guidelines for the Call to the 1976 Convention (the Call to the Convention establishes the rules under which the convention will operate and the nominee will be chosen), and establish a monitoring and compliance mechanism to make sure that affirmative action was taking place in each state. The commission was divided between party regulars and reformers eager to continue and solidify the changes adopted to govern the 1972 process. The regulars included a large number of state party chairmen and AFL-CIO members who wanted to avoid the large number of credentials challenges brought in

1972 and, more important, were determined to avoid the exclusion of party regulars from the nomination process, which they blamed in large part for the party's loss in 1972.

The primary focus of concern for the Mikulski Commission and later the Charter Commission was the controversial quota system that had been in place for the 1972 convention. States at that convention had been challenged if the number of women or the number of minorities in their delegations did not match the presence of these groups in the electorate of the state. A numerical quota system had been specifically prohibited by the McGovern-Fraser rules but was nonetheless enforced by the Democratic National Committee and the 1972 convention. This was of great concern to party regulars, who were finally waking up to the full implications of the reform rules. The effect of the quota rule had been felt most intensely in Illinois, where, after a challenge at the 1972 convention, the powerful Mayor Daley and his delegation of party regulars were unseated in favor of a delegation of liberal insurgents led by reform activist William Singer and civil rights leader Jesse Jackson. As in Illinois, the rule meant that the traditional leaders of the Democratic Party in many states, white men who held elective or party office or who made large contributions to the party, were being pushed aside in favor of women and minorities, many of whom were, at the time, new to the process and more liberal than the established party leaders. One regular party delegate to the 1972 convention summed up the problem with the new rules as follows: "There is too much hair and not enough cigars at this convention."[11]

Fights about affirmative action took up an enormous amount of time and attention in the early days of the reformed nominating system. But as intense as fights over affirmative action and quotas were for symbolic reasons, they had little to do with winning or losing, and thus they were not of as much interest to presidential candidates, who in the end did not care about the sex or race of their delegates, just that they had delegates. In contrast, a less visible but still controversial agenda item than the issue of quotas was the ongoing question of proportional representation, which did, after all, affect winning and losing. Section 4 of the 1972 Rules Committee report required the commission to make sure that delegates to the 1976 Convention were chosen in a manner that "fairly reflected" the preferences of those participating in the nominating process. In the minds of many reformers, "fair reflection" meant proportional representation and had been settled by the 1972 convention before the commission ever met. But in her opening remarks to the commission, Chairwoman Mikulski reopened the question by stating, in reference to Section 4 of the Rules Committee Report, "This is going to be a problem."[12]

Adopting proportional representation across the board would affect not only the California winner-take-all system but also the direct election of delegates system that was used by several large and powerful northern states, including Illinois, New York, Pennsylvania, and Ohio. Under this system, delegates were usually elected by slate in a district, producing winner-take-all outcomes by district. That result usually did not parallel the division of voter preferences as expressed in the nonbinding beauty contest portion of the ballot and was therefore seen as a "loophole" to the proportional representation that many believed was required by the fair reflection rule. Consequently, states using direct election of delegates came to be known as "loophole primary" states.

With minimal visibility, representatives of the Mikulski Commission and the Charter Commission got together and agreed on language that would ban winner-take-all by state systems such as California's but continue to allow for direct election of delegates. Party reformers Ken Bode and Alan Baron and party regulars Don Fowler and Bob Vance negotiated the compromise so quietly that one member of the Mikulski Commission did not realize what had been done until the 1976 primary season was in full gear.

According to Don Fowler, then state chair of South Carolina and a member of the Charter Commission, "The simple truth of the matter is that neither commission wanted to get pinned down to specific, mathematical proportional representation."[13] Moreover, liberal commission members, who were the strongest proponents of proportional representation, were for the moment reluctant to press hard. A primary concern for liberals was the expected repeat candidacy of George Wallace, who had proven to be a very powerful candidate in 1972, winning four primaries after the assassination attempt on him in May 1972 in Laurel, Maryland. Although Wallace ultimately was too debilitated by the attempt to run much of a race in 1976, that was not evident in 1973, when he looked like a potentially serious candidate. Therefore, liberals saw a strategic advantage in preserving the existing loophole primaries, rather than insisting on strict proportional representation. According to Ken Bode, "Loopholes tended to be in northern party states. . . .

The feeling among liberals was that Wallace would not do well in those sorts of primaries."[14]

In addition, party reformers, sensitive to the criticisms of the McGovern-Fraser rules that had gathered force in the wake of the 1972 defeat, were focused on preserving the progress they had already made. By 1973 a coalition of party regulars had formed, uniting traditional labor and more conservative Democrats. The Coalition for a Democratic Majority created a counterpressure to the reformers,[15] and the more conservative faction of the labor movement attempted at one point to contest the Democratic Party's authority to set delegate selection rules, a decision that could have undone all of the reforms.[16] Requiring all states to adopt proportional systems would require major party and legislative changes in most of the large industrial states. As Bode explained, "The feeling was that if you took on all these big states at once the whole effort at having national party rules would collapse."[17] This feeling was shared by new DNC chair Robert Strauss, a very practical politician who was attempting to right the balance between reformers and regulars by, among other things, substantially increasing the power of the party regulars on reform commissions.

Thus mathematical proportional representation in the nominating process, a goal of many of the original party reformers, was delayed once again—sacrificed to the greater goal of preserving the reform movement and to the political calculation of defeating George Wallace. The rule on delegate allocation reported out of the Mikulski Commission in December 1973 included the following critical language: "For the purpose of fairly reflecting the division of preferences, the non-binding advisory presidential preference portion of primaries shall not be considered a step in the delegate selection process. In such primaries where votes are also cast for individual delegate candidates, the votes for such individual delegate candidates shall constitute a fair reflection of the division of preferences provided that such delegates shall be elected from districts no larger than a congressional district."[18] This language was adopted by the full DNC and incorporated into the Call to the 1976 Convention.

The following year it was the Charter Commission's turn to rule on proportional representation. In the winter of 1974 the commission released a draft charter that met with strong opposition from party regulars. Labor leaders, the Democratic governors, and more than 150 of the 248 Democratic

House members voiced strong objections to the draft charter. Among the subjects of complaint were the requirement that the party hold a midterm convention, the proposal to set up a Judicial Council, (a body that would act as a sort of final court of appeals for party disputes), and of course, affirmative action and proportional representation. This set the stage for an open confrontation at the commission's last meeting.

Amidst complaints that Strauss's assistant Mark Siegel had called only the party regulars on the commission to urge them to attend, the Charter Commission met in August 1974 in Kansas City. According to political reporter Michael Malbin: "When most 'reform' members of the commission reached Kansas City, they fully expected to lose votes on the mandatory party conference and judicial council issues. But they were not prepared for a move by the 'regulars' to try to change the affirmative action and proportional representation proposals."[19]

The most heated controversy revolved around affirmative action and quotas. The Mikulski Commission's approach to these issues had been to the liking of reformers, who now tried to get the same language inserted into the charter. Led by Willie Brown of California (later to become speaker of the California Assembly and mayor of San Francisco), a group of African American members threatened to walk out if the commission changed anything in the draft Article 10 (the charter provision requiring affirmative action). After hours of debate and caucusing, a walkout was averted with an agreement to send four different versions of Article 10 to the Conference on Party Organization and Policy, a special midterm conference that would convene in Kansas City in December 1974 to approve the new party charter.

Having avoided near disaster over the questions of affirmative action and quotas, the commission proceeded to the ticklish question of proportional representation. The chief opponents of including proportional representation in the charter were members of the Coalition for a Democratic Majority and John Perkins, an AFL-CIO official. Commission member Tom Carroll of Kentucky argued that proportional representation would give "extreme candidates a voice they otherwise would not have."[20] Perkins feared that proportional representation would lead to many presidential candidates' having small numbers of delegates, thereby requiring a brokered convention. Therefore they argued in favor of striking the "fair reflection" language from the charter and leaving it simply in the Mikulski Commission rules, which as party by-laws would be easier to amend. However, the amendment they supported had the unintended effect of removing not only the fair reflection language but also the language that would require delegate selection to take place in the calendar year of the convention *and* the language prohibiting the unit rule!

Reaction was immediate and dramatic. Reformers, already feeling defensive over the losses they had sustained on party organization questions and the proposed weakening of the all-important language on affirmative action, were so taken aback by the attack on the unit rule prohibition that they abandoned the proceedings. Willie Brown announced that he was walking out, with the warning that "the November elections would be spread with black blood and women's blood."[21] Several white reformers followed the commission's African American members out the door, and shortly thereafter Chairman Terry Sanford adjourned the meeting for lack of a quorum.

Over the next few months, Chairman Strauss worked hard to iron out differences between the various factions in order to prevent a repeat of the August walkout when the party met in December. Ultimately, the language proposed by Strauss and adopted by the midterm conference was, in the words of Mark Siegel, "abstract enough to mean anything."[22] The new party charter required that delegates to the national convention "be chosen through processes which (ii) assure that delegations fairly reflect the division of preferences expressed by those who participate in the presidential nominating process."[23] Strauss and his people argued that the DNC would be able to decide for itself before each presidential election year exactly what "fairly reflect" meant. This solution briefly papered over the deep differences within the party. Nevertheless, organized labor was never happy with the charter language, maintaining that "Strauss had sold them out to the liberals," and labor officials remained wary that fair reflection would come to mean proportional representation.[24] Meanwhile, as the 1976 convention drew near, it became increasingly clear that reformers were still adamant about making fair reflection synonymous with proportional representation.

Jimmy Carter Wins

The 1976 Democratic Convention convened amidst remarkable unity, and for good reason. In the fall of 1976 the Republicans' prospects were not looking good. Democrats would be running against President Gerald Ford, who had become vice president after Spiro Agnew resigned due to scandal, and then became president when Richard Nixon resigned following the Watergate scandal. Ford had narrowly survived a powerful challenge for the nomination from the right wing of his party by California governor Ronald Reagan. For Democrats, victory was in the air, and this confident mood no doubt was reflected in the dramatic decrease in the number of challenges filed to delegates' credentials. The decrease in credentials challenges also indicated that by 1976 the reform rules had become accepted and implemented by most state parties and presidential candidates and that moreover, by the time of the convention, Jimmy Carter faced no serious challengers for the nomination.

Carter came into the convention with a substantial delegate lead. According to the June 16, 1976, Associated Press delegate count, Carter had 1,345.5 delegates to 598.5 for "uncommitted," the next highest preference. (Votes cast by delegates from small entities like Democrats Abroad and from territories such as Guam and the Virgin Islands counted as half votes.) This lead was due in large part to his wins in some of the 14 "loophole" primaries held in 1976. For instance, in the important Texas primary, Carter won 92 of the 98 delegates on the primary ballot, compared to 6 for Senator Lloyd Bentsen, the favorite son. Carter won 94 percent of the delegates with 47.6 percent of the popular vote (thereby making the Texas Democratic Party forever opposed to future loophole primaries).

But as in so many rules sagas, the next steps were shaped by the previous presidential nomination contest—in this instance by supporters of defeated U.S. Representative Mo Udall, a favorite of the liberal reformers. The 1976 Convention Rules Committee was composed, in part, of reformers led by U.S. Representative Don Fraser of Minnesota, who regarded abolition of the loophole primary as an important piece of unfinished business. Their first step was to enlarge the mandate of the Commission on the Role and Future of Presidential Primaries (called the Winograd Commission after its chairman, Michigan Democratic Party chair Morley Winograd), which had been created by Chairman Strauss in January 1976, to draft changes in delegate selection rules for 1980. Fulfilling the worst fears of organized labor, they also proposed that the commission be required to implement a rule that had the effect of banning loophole primaries and thereby requiring across-the-board proportional representation for the 1980 primary season. The loophole ban was supported by a coalition of Udall delegates, reformers such as Don Fraser who were still dedicated to completing the McGovern-Fraser reforms, and members from more liberal labor organizations, notably the National Education Association (NEA) and the United Auto Workers (UAW). Most of the Carter delegates and delegates from loophole primary states opposed the measure.

No one rose up to defend the loophole primary per se. Instead they argued that the issue was of sufficient complexity and ambiguity that it should be resolved by the full commission after appropriate study and debate. Eventually the loophole primary ban passed the convention's Rules Committee, but narrowly, with 58.5 in favor and 58.25 opposed. Section 9 of the majority report of the Rules Committee was then reported to the full 1976 convention as follows: "Resolved further that in reviewing and modifying the Delegate Selection Rules, the Commission on Presidential Primaries shall construe Article II, section 4, clause (ii) of the Charter to bar the use of delegate selection systems in primary states which permit a plurality of votes at any level to elect all the delegates from that level. This amendment shall not be amendable as a By-Law."[25]

On the Sunday before the opening of the 1976 convention, Chairman Strauss, the presumptive nominee Jimmy Carter, and several state chairs, including Morley Winograd, met to discuss the issues that had been generated by the Rules Committee report.[26] The most controversial issue, a minority report that would have required equal numbers of men and women delegates at future nominating conventions, was opposed by Carter, who was adamant in asserting that the country did not like quotas. Of less importance, but still on the agenda, was Section 9 of the majority report to the Rules Committee, which would abolish the loophole primary. The Carter campaign, which had accumulated a large share of its delegate lead through such primaries, supported a minority report that left them in place. Abolishing the loophole primary would affect many of the largest states, requiring not just changes in party rules but also changes in state statutes. Strauss assured Carter that it would be easy to pass the minority report to Section 9, and that all that was required would be to take it up on Thursday afternoon of the convention, when very few delegates would be on the floor.

But Strauss's prediction was wrong. Unfortunately for the Carter campaign, delegates *did* show up for the Thursday afternoon session; moreover, the delegates who showed up were liberals, not party regulars. Furthermore, as the Carter campaign found out, their own delegates were not of one mind on this question. The NEA and the UAW were strongly aligned with the reformers, and the Carter campaign found they had to "release" their delegates to vote as they pleased on this issue. After a relatively short debate punctuated by pleas to "close the electoral loophole which gives power to the few over the many" and by exhortations to "close the loophole which allows 13 states to stack the deck while the other 37 states play fair," the minority report failed on a voice vote.[27]

The White House Tries to Rewrite the Rules

In the context of what was widely considered a very successful convention, the controversy over loophole primaries was not even noticed. It was the typical low-priority rules issue that candidates at their convention tend to try to ignore. However, it was to come back and haunt the Carter White House as the president's advisers tackled the first political chore of their reelection effort—the writing of the 1980 delegate selection rules. No one knew better than Carter's delegate hunter Rick Hutcheson and his pollster Pat Caddell how important loophole primaries had been to Carter's nomination. Together with Mark Siegel, formerly Strauss's aide at the DNC, they made up the team that was to decide White House policy on the new rules commission, the Commission on the Role and Future of Presidential Primaries, otherwise known as the Winograd Commission. (Anne Wexler was the fourth White House official on the Winograd Commission, but her long history of involvement as a party reformer put her in an awkward position vis-à-vis the president's strategists, and therefore she took part only occasionally in commission business.)

Early on in the new administration, the White House operatives on the commission opened a discussion of the convention mandate on loophole primaries with Chairman Winograd and his staff. In short order, they concluded that for legal as well as political reasons, the 1980 rules could not include loophole primaries. Legally, it was clear that convention mandates (defined as formal resolutions passed by the full convention) were binding on other, lesser, party bodies. Politically, while the White House had increased the size of the Winograd Commission with loyal Carter supporters and White House staffers, their margin of control over the commission was fairly small, and the reformers were a cohesive group.

Thus the Winograd Commission began deliberations under instructions to write rules that would guarantee the use of proportional representation systems for all states in 1980. In the nine years since the party had begun the process of delegate selection reform it had always avoided this step. This had been possible because of the ambiguity in the term "fair reflection." The 1976 convention mandate had removed that ambiguity. Now an incumbent president faced the job of running his reelection campaign under a purely proportional system. Party operatives and White House officials feared that moving to proportional representation would create a plethora of factions in the nominating process, as minor candidates attempted to gain delegates to use as bargaining chips against the incumbent. Therefore commission members began to look for ways to dull the impact of proportional representation. Reporting on the discussion in his subcommittee, Don Fowler of South Carolina put it this way: "Given the elimination of the winner-take-all primary . . . some mechanism needed to be in our delegate selection process that was consensus building in its intent and effect."[28]

The main options centered on the question of the "threshold," or the percentage needed by a presidential candidate in order to be eligible to receive a proportion of the delegates. The 1976 rules had set 15 percent as the maximum threshold for states using proportional representation, but allowed states to use a lower one. Don Fowler's subcommittee presented several options to the commission. The first was to make the threshold mandatory instead of optional. Second was to raise the threshold, lower it, or keep it at 15 percent. The third option was a thinly disguised White House proposal that came to be known as the "sliding window."[29] Under this option, the threshold would be 15 percent for the states holding the determining step of their delegate selection process (first-tier caucuses in caucus states and the primary itself in primary states) in the first four weeks of the primary season, 20 percent for states whose determining steps fell in the next four weeks, and 25 percent for states falling in the final four weeks. Thus as the nomination process advanced, it would become increasingly difficult for minority candidates to accumulate delegates.

The "sliding window" became the centerpiece of the White House's position on delegate allocation. In its defense, the White House and its allies on the commission argued the dangers of a purely proportional delegate selection system. To do this, the issue had to be taken out of the context of the next election (an almost impossible task in the history of party reform, especially given that an incumbent president was involved). Nevertheless Pat Caddell, the president's pollster, tried: "I, for all the undercurrents, don't think this is really relevant to 1980. . . . I think for all the talk we have about the success of '72 and '76 in terms of the process, I think it's fair to say that we're really playing a game of Russian roulette. Sooner or later if we change the process more and more to a proportional system, we are going to end up with a situation where a candidate . . . is going to win a slew of primaries and go to a convention and be denied the nomination because of inability at that stage to coalesce into a majority."[30]

Reformers, however, remained suspicious of the White House proposal. They saw it as a way to protect President Carter's nomination by keeping potential challengers from winning any delegates. Speaking in opposition to the sliding window, Commissioner Scott Lang of Massachusetts maintained that the proposal would "make sure that minority candidates are unable to run."[31] He calculated the effect that the sliding window would have on the 1980 calendar (assuming primary and caucus dates remained the same) and found that only 14 percent of the 1980 delegates would be elected under a 15 percent threshold (because of the number of states having early contests), while a full 57 percent of the delegates would be elected under a 25 percent threshold.[32] Thus the sliding window would *increase* the threshold for most contests or cause states to move early, both of which were opposed by reformers on the commission.

The sliding window proposal and a proposal making the proposed thresholds mandatory were adopted in two identical 30–25 votes. These measures, along with the creation of a "window" for delegate selection and some minor changes to the rules on filing deadlines, became known as the White House package. Not surprisingly, the report of the Winograd Commission was promptly and widely criticized in the press for its perceived positive impact on President Carter's renomination. The *New York Times* wrote that it was "intended to hinder any Democratic challenge to Mr. Carter's nomination in 1980."[33] The *Washington Post* ran an editorial claiming: "All in all, it seems pretty plain that the changes are in the direction of closing up the race again, and protecting the President from a primary challenge."[34] Even the *Economist* devoted a story to the rules fight, observing: "In defending the proposals, the White House pleads innocent to trying to fix the rules, which is perhaps over modest, since one thing nobody has ever seriously criticized Mr. Carter's staff for was not knowing how to win primary elections."[35] The reputation of the Carter operatives for understanding the modern nominating system had caught up with them.

Almost immediately reformers began to organize against the commission's majority report in preparation for the meeting of the Democratic National Committee that would pass final judgment on the 1980 rules. First to act was ADA (Americans for Democratic Action), which met one week after the final meeting of the Winograd Commission and passed a resolution condemning both the final report and the White House's influence.[36] The Democratic Conference, an ADA offshoot dedicated to monitoring party processes, sent out a package urging its members to lobby the DNC against the sliding window and several other provisions in the package. Carrin Patman, a DNC member from Texas who had served on the commission, began her own lobbying effort against the report, soon supplemented by a letter from Nancy Abrams, a DNC member from Florida, and 123 other DNC members and Democratic elected officials. The Democratic Task Force of the National Women's Political Caucus came out in opposition to the sliding window as well. George McGovern, grandfather of the reform movement, got into the act with a letter to "Fellow Democrats" opposing the commission's final report and advocating that the threshold be lowered to 10 percent. "We should not be in the position of disenfranchising Democratic voters in states whose delegate selection processes begin later," he argued.[37]

Opposition to the Winograd Commission report coincided with a larger problem, the growing perception that President Carter was not in control of his own political party. Problems between Carter and the Democratic Party had festered since his nomination. He had run not only as an outsider to the Washington establishment but as an outsider to the Democratic Party establishment. The elevation of early Carter supporters (ECSs, as they were known) over other longer-term party activists was one of many bones of contention between DNC Chair Ken Curtis and the White House. In December 1977, Chairman Curtis resigned after several run-ins with the White

House over management of DNC politics. Several months later, Mark Siegel, the former Strauss aide who had been responsible for White House–DNC liaison activities and instrumental in the ouster of Ken Curtis, resigned his White House post amidst disagreements with the White House on Middle East policy. This left the White House without a firm link to party regulars on the DNC. Thus the pending fight over the Winograd Commission report began to be perceived by some as a test of "outsider" Carter's ability to control his own party.[38]

By the spring of 1978, concern over Carter's relationship with the party, not to mention concern about his renomination prospects, helped place the report of the Winograd Commission on the top of the White House political agenda. In a memorandum to the president, Hamilton Jordan and newly appointed DNC Chair John White put the case bluntly: "Because of the President's standing in the polls, disappointments over patronage, the Mark Siegel resignation, the lack of a long historical relationship between early Carter supporters and Party regulars, DNC approval of what we recommend is not automatic."[39]

The issues at stake thus took on an added dimension: they became a test of Carter's ability to control his own party. The White House and DNC staff planned a three-part strategy. Some issues, such as the early filing deadlines desired by the White House, were compromised away. Opposition to other issues, such as the new window rule (see chapter 3) and the proposal that party and elected officials make up 10 percent of the convention delegates, was defused by making minor adjustments to the draft rules. Finally, the controversial "sliding window" proposal was dropped altogether and replaced with what became known as the "floating threshold."

The new threshold rule had the same effect as the old one but avoided using a particular number or series of numbers that could easily be attacked in debate. The new formulation rested on the premise that the threshold should be that percentage of the vote required to win one whole delegate in a district. Calculated by dividing the number of delegates in a district into 100 percent, the threshold would vary from district to district. More important from the perspective of the president's strategists, this new formulation would, in effect, raise the threshold around the country since most districts contained either four or five delegates, yielding either 20 percent or 25 percent thresholds.

In May 1978, the DNC Executive Committee met to consider the proposed changes to the Winograd Commission report. The maligned "sliding window" had been replaced with the following language:

> At all stages of the delegate selection process, delegates shall be allocated in a fashion that fairly reflects the expressed presidential preference or uncommitted status of the primary voters or if there is no binding primary, the convention and caucus participants, except that preferences securing less than the applicable percentage of votes cast for the delegates to the National Convention shall not be awarded any delegates. The applicable percentage in presidential primary states shall be calculated by dividing the number of National Convention delegates to be elected in that congressional district or other smaller delegate selection unit into 100, provided, however, that the applicable percentage shall be no higher than 25 percent.[40]

The impact of this new formulation was not lost on experienced participants in reform politics. Writing in the *New Republic,* Ken Bode had this to say: "Clear away the mumbo jumbo about consensus building and what you have in the new White House floating threshold scheme is the same thing as the discarded sliding window: a system that tips to the advantage of the frontrunners. This is what the system's authors assume the President will be in 1980. If past experience is any guide, only about three districts in ten will elect 6 or more delegates in 1980, meaning that the threshold in 70 percent of the districts will be well above the 15 percent level of 1976."[41]

On June 9, 1978, the full Democratic National Committee met to consider the final Winograd Commission report. In an effort to defeat the White House package, reformers on the commission offered Minority Report C, which would set the threshold at a maximum of 15 percent and make its application optional by state. In essence, the minority report language was the same as the 1976 threshold rule. Following a close voice vote, Chairman John White ruled that the Minority Report failed. Someone called for division (a show of hands instead of a voice vote), and the chair ruled that the Minority Report failed. Someone else called for a roll call vote, and the chair ruled against the request. Thus the 1980 delegate selection rules, as designed by the Carter White House, were adopted amidst complaints about the chair's "strong-arm tactics."[42]

Now all that remained was the implementation of the Winograd Commission rules. This proved considerably easier than their passage, given that the Compliance Review Commission was composed almost entirely of people loyal to the White House. Nevertheless, two decisions were made that were to alter the operation of the allocation rules for 1980 and once again delay across-the-board application of proportional representation. The first decision was to permit some loophole primaries; the second was to permit some winner-take-all outcomes.

Under instructions from the DNC, most former loophole primary states proceeded to write delegate selection plans that would transform their systems into proportional systems. Proportional representation had failed in both the Mikulski and the McGovern-Fraser Commissions in part because those drafting the rules could not figure out how to meet the fair reflection requirements and at the same time guarantee minority representation. By the time the CRC implemented the Winograd Commission rules, its task was even more complex: proportional representation was required everywhere, racial quotas (now called goals and timetables) were firmly in place, and at the midterm conference the DNC had just mandated that state delegations to the 1980 convention be composed of equal numbers of men and women.

In order to comply with this bewildering set of potentially conflicting rules, half of the 1976 loophole primary states simply dropped delegate names from the ballot and elected delegates in caucuses held before or after the primary. (Caucuses held before the primary rank-ordered candidates for delegate. Then, depending on the outcome of the primary, if a presidential candidate was entitled, for example, to two delegates, the delegate candidates ranked number one and number two on that candidate's list were sent to the convention.) Although the election process was still fairly complicated, the "right" outcome, meaning the proper mix of men and women, minorities, and candidate preferences, was easier to achieve in a meeting of party activists than on a primary election ballot.

But for loophole states that chose *not* to adopt a pre- or post-primary caucus, the beauty contest portion of the primary election became binding on the allocation of delegates. The votes for individual delegates now established a rank order among them. But receiving the most votes did not guarantee that a candidate would end up going to the convention. The presidential candidate he or she supported would have to win a sufficient percentage of the vote to be entitled to one or more delegates, and even then the poor delegate candidate might not be elected. For example, suppose John Doe was the second highest vote-getter for Carter in a congressional district with five delegates. Suppose Carter was entitled to two delegates and the first seat went to the highest vote-getter—Harry Smith. The next delegate then went to the highest vote-getting woman—Mary Jones. Thus John Doe could not go to the convention as a delegate even though he had received more votes than Mary Jones. Such was the plan submitted by the Pennsylvania Democratic Party. The Pennsylvania plan came under some criticism, but when the CRC suggested that maybe the equal division requirements could be relaxed to avoid this unfairness, the outcry from organized women's groups was sufficient to bury the suggestion, and the Pennsylvania plan was approved in spite of its enormous complexity.[43]

While most of the loophole states were changing their systems, one state, Illinois, refused to change. In Illinois the process of electing delegates on the ballot was dear to the hearts of both reformers, who felt it gave them a chance, albeit a small one, of keeping the election out of the back rooms of the Cook County machine, and party regulars, who knew how to get their delegates elected and who preferred not to have to deal with the complications of presidential politics. Aware of this local sentiment, the new DNC chairman, John C. White, promised Jack Touhy, the state chair of Illinois, that if he delivered the votes of the Illinois delegation in favor of the Winograd Commission report, White would make sure that the CRC looked favorably on Illinois's request for an exemption from the ban on loophole primaries.

The decision to allow Illinois to keep its loophole primary was dictated by the White House political team, which assumed that Illinois would be a good state for President Carter. He had won the primary there in 1976 with strong support downstate. As an incumbent he expected to be favored by the pragmatic politicians in Chicago interested in federal grants. The loophole primary was therefore expected to give him a large delegate boost.

Thus the CRC staff began guiding the state party of Illinois through the various "provable positive steps" that it would need to take in order to qualify for an exemption to the rule banning loophole primaries. Legislation was introduced to change the primary to a proportional primary, testimony was taken, the party went on record supporting the change, and finally, as expected, the Republicans defeated the bill. On May 25, 1979, Illinois Senate president Phil Rock sent a letter to state party chair Jack Touhy informing him that Senate bills 604 and 607 had been defeated with almost unanimous Republican opposition.

But as the date for the CRC to take final action neared, a series of events clouded the political calculus, showing yet again just how difficult it is to anticipate the outcome of primary politics. On October 9, 1979, the *Washington Post* reported that Chicago's mayor, Jane Byrne, was supporting President Carter for reelection. The next day, Mayor Byrne sought to "clarify" her comments. By October 16, the mayor was hedging her support, and on October 28, barely three weeks after allegedly endorsing Carter, Mayor Byrne said she would support Ted Kennedy for president.[44]

At the time, I was the CRC's executive director. In mid-October, Carter's new delegate hunter, Tom Donilon, asked me if the CRC could deny Illinois's request for an exemption. After discussions with John White and others, we concluded that the earlier decision, which was now looking like a bad one to the White House, had to stand. The exemption was granted despite a mid-October poll that showed Kennedy beating Carter in Chicago, 44 percent to 40 percent.[45] By January 2, 1980, however, the same polling company found Carter beating Kennedy in Chicago, 73 percent to 15 percent. And when the Illinois primary finally took place, the White House decision was validated: Carter won 91 percent of the delegates with 65 percent of the primary vote.

Other than Illinois, only one other state, West Virginia, was allowed to conduct a loophole primary in 1980. But in this case the exemption was more by accident than by design. As is true in some small states, the West Virginia legislature meets only briefly and at the beginning of each year. By the time the CRC notified the state party that it needed to secure changes in the law governing West Virginia's primaries, the legislature had gone out of session until 1980. By then it would have been too late to amend the primary law and write a new delegate selection plan for the 1980 election. Therefore West Virginia was granted an exemption to the prohibition on loophole primaries.[46]

But the debate over proportional representation and winner-take-all systems did not end there. One last battle was fought around the CRC's efforts to carry out its mandate to "adopt regulations to prevent winner-take-all outcomes at the Congressional District or other smaller delegate selection unit."[47] At its February 1979 meeting, the CRC adopted Regulation 6.15, which read as follows: "If only one candidate reaches the applicable threshold a delegate shall be awarded to the next highest vote getter."[48] The goal of this measure was to ensure that no candidate could win 100 percent of the delegates without winning 100 percent of the vote.

As states began to write delegate selection plans, they realized the potential absurdity of this rule. Every state had fringe candidates. In southern states, for example, candidates belonging to segregationist sects frequently filed and gained access to the Democratic primary ballot. Regulation 6.15 gave them a chance to win delegates even if they won only a very small percentage of the vote and another candidate—presumably President Carter—won the rest. Not surprisingly, the Georgia state party was among the first to protest the regulation, arguing in July: "Fringe presidential candidates with possibly only a very slight percentage of the popular vote will be able to have a separate caucus and forum in many Congressional Districts in the nation. . . . The rule as it now stands will be an inducement to fringe candidates to enter the presidential primary."[49]

Similar letters were received from state party chairs and executive directors all over the country. The state chair of Florida called the regulation "unacceptable in the spirit of fairness and common sense," and the vice chair of the Louisiana state party protested the "absurd interpretation of the ban on winner-take-all primaries."[50] In response to this wave of sentiment, the CRC adopted a new Regulation 6.15, which read:

> At the CD or other smaller National delegate selection unit, if only one candidate reaches the threshold the next highest voter getter shall be awarded one delegate, except in the following situations: a) If one preference receives 85 percent or more of the vote, or b) If the frontrunner is 50 or more percentage points ahead of the second place preference and the second place preference has 15 percent or less of the vote. In either situation a or b the frontrunners shall be awarded all the delegates.[51]

This fourth version of the regulation was finally adopted. But even its language did not meet the test of the true believers in proportional representation. For some people, any winner-take-all outcome needed to be prohibited in order to fulfill the mandate of the 1976 convention. On October 4, 1979, five Democratic activists who had been active in party reform politics brought a complaint before the Judicial Council of the Democratic Party, in which they argued that since Regulation 6.15 did not prevent winner-take-all outcomes it violated the convention mandate and Rule 12B (the rule on fair reflection) of the delegate selection rules.[52] The complaint stated: "In absolute terms no winner-take-all means that under no circumstances shall a candidate receive all the delegates unless he or she receives all the votes."[53]

In a rare example of common sense triumphing over the extreme antipathy of reformers to winner-take-all outcomes, the Judicial Council ruled in favor of the CRC. The complaint, absurd as it was on the face, was a fitting conclusion to years of efforts to enforce mathematical proportional representation on a party that was deeply ambivalent about the wisdom and consequences of its use. In 1980 the party came closer than ever before to a thoroughly proportional system. Yet the system was to operate in a way that few could have foreseen. As we will see in chapter 5, the new proportional rules worked in Jimmy Carter's favor not by keeping a minority candidate from winning delegates, but by keeping the winning candidate in some states from winning delegates. Similarly, years later, another presidential candidate, Barack Obama, would benefit greatly from the party's proportional representation system.

The Democrats Decide to Pick a Winner

The drubbing Democrats took in the 1980 election, losing not only the presidency but the Senate as well, brought the party's love affair with outsider candidates to an abrupt end, and the debate over delegate allocation took a new turn. Until Carter's defeat in 1980, the debate on fair reflection had been characterized by a preoccupation with the rights of "minority candidates" and the rights of the voters who voted for these candidates. In this context, "minority" referred to numerical, not racial, minorities, but so many people confused the two that proportional representation often took on the emotional importance associated with affirmative action issues. It sometimes seemed as if the party had spent 12 years writing rules that had been designed just in case a black or Hispanic were to run for president and receive only black or Hispanic votes.

Following the 1980 election, party leaders had a new preoccupation: rewarding winning candidates, not losing ones. The failure of the Carter presidency had resulted in a shift even among some former reformers, who now argued that the party needed to nominate well-known Democrats like Kennedy or Mondale and stay away from unknown quantities like Jimmy Carter. In practical terms, this meant rewriting the rules to favor candidates who won at the state level, especially in big industrial states, where traditional Democratic Party constituencies, including labor, remained strong. In 1980, Senator Ted Kennedy's challenge to President Carter had been seriously hampered by the fact that his late wins in these states yielded him few delegates because of the workings of proportional representation. By the same token, the large industrial states—many of them strongholds of the traditional Democratic Party—had suffered a sharp decline in their influence over the party's choice of a nominee. Thus the nomination race between Carter and Kennedy that had just ended and the race between Kennedy and Mondale that lay ahead defined the context within which the party's next rules commission, the Hunt Commission (the Commission on Presidential Nominations), began its work in 1981.

By then, the party reform movement was nearly a decade old. Many of the original advocates of party reform in general and proportional representation in particular were no longer involved in party politics. Ken Bode had become a television journalist with NBC; Eli Segal, his colleague on the McGovern-Fraser Commission staff, was running the family business in Massachusetts. Other veterans of the early party reform battles had been involved in Kennedy's 1980 campaign and thus brought candidate concerns, not party reform concerns, to the Hunt Commission. Carol Casey, a party reformer and staunch defender of proportional representation on the Mikulski Commission, had been one of Kennedy's delegate hunters in 1980, along with Scott Lang, a Massachusetts lawyer and former head of the CRC, and Harold Ickes Jr., a veteran of New York City reform politics. They found themselves advocating rules that they had spent years opposing in order to create a system that would be more likely to produce a Kennedy nomination in 1984. As we shall see, this effort left Minneapolis mayor Don Fraser and Texas party reform advocate Carrin Patman virtually alone in trying to preserve the original reform objective of across-the-board proportional representation.

The bulk of the discussion on proportional representation at the Hunt Commission's first several meetings came from the delegate selection experts, who were all critical of proportional representation. As a member of the Technical Advisory Committee (TAC), I was one of those experts. At the commission's first meeting, on August 13, 1981, I presented a paper that argued that the problem with the current allocation rules is that they did not reward candidates for winning. A later options paper was prepared by the TAC made a point of showing how the rules had worked against winners in the large industrial states. Similarly, Pat Caddell's presentations on timing suggested that if the commission wanted states to keep their contests later in the process they should offer states the option of winner-take-all systems.

Discussion by commission members themselves was repeatedly delayed. At the commission's second meeting, Carrin Patman tried to engage in a discussion of proportional representation and was cut off by the chairman.[54] By what was supposed to be the final meeting of the commission, there still had not been a full-fledged debate on this topic. However, as debate on other rules unfolded, it became clear that an agreement had already been reached on what was to happen to the fair reflection rule.

The future of mandatory proportional representation and important proposals, such as reinstating loophole primaries, *had* been fully aired in meetings of the Technical Advisory Committee and in meetings within the Mondale and Kennedy camps. The other presidential candidates were largely left out of the discussions, even when they were present at the table. For instance, in one meeting of the TAC it became clear that one of the candidate's representatives did not know what a loophole primary was; nor did he know that Ohio had held one in 1976—an astounding knowledge gap in the minds of the assembled "rules freaks." Much later in the process, the supporters of Senators John Glenn and Gary Hart would complain that the new allocation rules were designed to help the front-runners—and they were. But these concerns were expressed too tentatively and too late.

Moreover, even had the objections been raised on time, they would have been unlikely to prevail. Like the Kennedy and Mondale campaigns, the other two power blocs on the Hunt Commission, the AFL-CIO and the state party chairs, were also in favor of changing the allocation rules. The AFL-CIO's John Perkins had opposed strict proportional representation since his days on the Charter Commission. Once assured by both the Mondale and

Kennedy camps that labor delegates would be slated (placed on the ballot) in loophole states if the AFL-CIO endorsed a presidential candidate, labor got behind reinstatement of the loophole primary. The state chairs were, very simply, in favor of any rule that gave states options and did not require them to change their state statutes or go through the contortions that Pennsylvania had undergone in 1980 in order to comply with national party rules.

Thus they offered little opposition to yet another measure that significantly undercut proportional representation, the proposal to allow elected officials to attend the 1984 convention as unpledged delegates. The proposal was created in the House Democratic Caucus by Representative Gillis Long and his aide Al From. It was presented to the Hunt Commission by the House Caucus secretary, Representative Geraldine Ferraro. Immediately it faced opposition from feminist groups who objected to the creation of a group of "superdelegates" that would be mostly white and mostly male. (More on this in chapter 6.) In reality the Ferraro proposal did very little to weaken the charter provision on equal division between the sexes and a great deal to weaken the charter provision on fair reflection as it had been interpreted in 1980. The proposal created a significant portion of the 1984 convention delegates, 14 percent, who would not be allocated to presidential candidates on the basis of any public demonstration of presidential preferences, such as a primary or a first-tier caucus vote.

And yet the opposition, such as it was, came over the question of who the delegates would be (mostly men), not how the proposal would affect the process of choosing a nominee—a pattern familiar to those who had sat through prior party debates on these issues. Hours of debate and hundreds of pages of transcript show only minor interest in the effect of the Ferraro proposal on the fair reflection rule. Robert Friebert, attorney general of Wisconsin, was one of the few who seized on this point, arguing that the Ferraro proposal "does serious damage to proportional representation. I do not believe the title. . . . I believe that those delegates will be elected solely because of who[m] they support for President of the United States. . . . They will be committed in everything but title. . . . I think what we are doing is in many ways fooling ourselves with the phrase 'uncommitted delegate.'"[55]

The ease with which this aspect of the controversial rule on automatic delegates was passed by the commission was to foreshadow the ease with which the commission would make major changes in the fair reflection rule.

The Ferraro proposal creating superdelegates passed on a vote of 47 to 6. The next day, the commission proceeded to take up the rule on allocating delegates to presidential candidates (Rule 12). The new version of Rule 12 changed the 1980 language on fair reflection in two important ways. First, it raised the threshold in caucus states and in at-large delegations from an optional 15 percent or 20 percent to 20 percent.[56] Second, it deleted the provision that called for the CRC to adopt regulations preventing winner-take-all outcomes, eliminating the need for the ridiculously convoluted Regulation 6.15. In an indication of how far the party had come, these two changes stimulated absolutely no debate, a far cry from the Winograd Commission, where small changes in the threshold were denounced in the strongest terms.

Debate did occur, however, on the proposal to allow states to choose between two delegate allocation systems: proportional representation and direct election of delegates. (Members of the TAC had decided that step one in resurrecting the loophole primary would be to rehabilitate its image, and it was subsequently referred to in all commission working papers and draft rules as the "direct election of delegates primary.") The opposition was led by Don Fraser and Carrin Patman, the only remaining party reformers who wished to argue the virtues of strict proportional representation. Patman presented voluminous data to show how unfair the results of loophole primaries could be, especially when someone with 35 percent or 45 percent of the vote won all the delegates. Her opposition to loophole primaries echoed the concerns of past reformers who had argued that presenting the views of all candidates, especially losing candidates, was paramount: "Proportional representation is our promise to every person who comes in at the grass roots level . . . that if you come in and vote with the Democratic Party . . . we are going to guarantee that your voice will be heard in fair share."[57]

Mayor Fraser attempted to move the debate from the Hunt Commission to the party charter, thereby moving it to consideration before the full Democratic National Committee, in hopes that reformers could win the two-thirds vote needed to enshrine their definition of "fair reflection" in the charter. But the ploy received little support. After nearly a decade of debate, party activists were still reluctant to equate fair reflection with proportional representation. Bob Torricelli of New Jersey, one of Mondale's two representatives on the commission, argued: "What has been previously proposed [proportional representation] does not constitute fair reflection. There is nothing that anymore fairly reflects the voter sentiments than to allow the candidate who has the most votes to win."[58] Similarly Don Fowler commented, "I think it is very very important for everybody to understand that in doing away with winner-take-all and putting the fair reflection language in the Charter, this Party did not adopt proportional representation."[59]

Proposed new Rule 12 governing the allocation of delegates to presidential candidates passed the Hunt Commission easily—48 in favor and 10 against. The rule allowed states to choose one of three options for awarding delegates: proportional representation, direct election of delegates, or the "bonus plan." The bonus plan was the brainchild of John Reilly, Mondale's senior representative on the Hunt Commission. It awarded a bonus delegate to the winner of a congressional district in order to avoid the situation where the winner (in districts with an even number of delegates) simply split the delegate votes with the losers. As we will see in chapter 5, when there are only two candidates competing in a congressional district with an even number of delegates, the rules call for the winner to get half and the loser to get half, an outcome that Kennedy had faced repeatedly in 1980. The trend since the McGovern-Fraser Commission had been toward more and more proportional representation. Yet with amazingly little opposition, the Hunt Commission turned back the tide by allowing states to choose delegate allocation systems that would permit a candidate to win all the delegates in a district (in loophole states) or a large proportion of them (in bonus states).

The new Hunt Commission rules were adopted by the DNC on March 26, 1982. Carrin Patman led the token opposition to the new version of Rule 12. Even the other presidential candidates at the time did not organize to oppose a rule that had been initiated and strongly backed by Mondale and Kennedy operatives. With both Mondale and Kennedy in the race, each second-tier candidate's goal was to become a major contender by knocking one of the front-runners out of the race early. None of the candidates were interested in staying in the race if all they could win was a fraction of the vote. Thus the number of delegates to be won with 10, 15, or 20 percent of the vote was not a question of sufficient importance to cause more than grumbles from the other presidential candidates.

Jesse Jackson Contests the Rules

Jesse Jackson was not a candidate for the Democratic nomination when the 1984 rules were passed. But one year later, the entrance of the party's first black presidential candidate into the race reopened the debate over proportional representation of minority candidates, and this time "minority candidate" had a double meaning—racial as well as numerical. Jackson's candidacy was born in 1983 when, to the anger of many black leaders, Walter Mondale endorsed Richard Daley and Ted Kennedy endorsed Jane Byrne in the Democratic primary for mayor of Chicago. The third candidate in the race, Harold Washington, a black U.S. representative, was outraged that two major leaders in the Democratic Party would get involved in a Democratic primary in the first place and against a black candidate. The fact that both Mondale and Kennedy issued their endorsements before Washington became a candidate did little to decrease the resentment.

Although there was no love lost between Jesse Jackson and Harold Washington, Jackson took the opportunity to reinforce what had become a frequent complaint among black Democrats—that they were taken for granted by the Democratic Party because of their loyalty at election time. "What we have," he said in an interview from Mississippi, where he was working to register black voters, "is the combination of the Democratic Party breaking the law and the Republican administration not enforcing the law. Our leadership focuses on the Republicans, but the Democrats are failing two major tests as well: they are not making room for blacks [as candidates, as slate-makers and, in some cases, as voters] who want to be Democrats, and they are failing the test of character, expecting blacks to vote for white candidates, but not the other way around."[60] The complaint was not unique to Jackson. Other black leaders such as Georgia state senator Julian Bond said, "The Democrats take us for granted. . . . The reason I think somebody black must run is to renegotiate the contract between the blacks and the Democratic Party."[61]

The Harold Washington incident gave Jackson the argument he needed to justify his entrance into the presidential race. Mondale endorsed Daley on February 15, 1983; by March 11 Jesse Jackson was in Des Moines, Iowa, testing the waters for a presidential bid. This development caused deep concern within the Mondale campaign. With the emergence of John Glenn as a strong contender among white southern voters, Mondale needed to win black votes. Thus in the spring of 1983 the Mondale campaign began a dialogue with the Jackson campaign that continued through the primary season. Initially, the Mondale campaign hoped to dissuade Jackson from running. To the representatives of the Mondale campaign, all veterans of mainstream party politics, the task was straightforward: find out what Jesse wanted and then bargain with him. But as the "unusual dialogue" (in the words of *Washington Post* reporter Dan Balz) progressed, it became clear that Jesse Jackson was no ordinary politician.[62] He was not interested in a Cabinet post or in the control of "street money"—he wanted to win delegates to the Democratic convention.

During the spring and summer of 1983, one of the Mondale campaign's chief strategists, Tom Donilon, was assigned the task of explaining the complexities of a presidential campaign to Jackson. Donilon first addressed the complexity of the Federal Election Law with regard to presidential nominating campaigns—the contribution limits, spending limits, eligibility for matching funds, and so on. He then proceeded to explain the new rules governing the allocation of delegates to presidential candidates, the higher thresholds in most states, the even higher thresholds in bonus states, and the winner-take-all properties of loophole primaries. The new rules meant that a candidate who won a small share of the total vote would not amass many convention delegates. Mondale's advisers hoped that once Jackson realized how hard it would be to win delegates to the convention he would rethink his candidacy.

Predictably, in retrospect, these considerations did little to deter Jackson. As Donilon tells the story, after he had gone through the details of a presidential campaign and emphasized the need for an early organization and an early start, Jackson looked at him and said: "That's what you need. I just need me, Lamond [Lamond Godwin, a Jackson aide], and a lawyer to do this shit."[63]

On November 3, 1983, Jackson announced that he was a candidate for the Democratic nomination for president. However, the discussions with the Mondale campaign had not been totally unproductive. By the time he announced, Jackson was well aware of the challenges he faced, and within a week of his announcement he attacked the party's delegate allocation rules, charging that they discriminated against the poor and against racial and ethnic minorities.[64] Jackson kept up the attack on the party's rules through November and December. In a December 20 letter to party chair Charles Mannatt, he outlined the changes he wanted the DNC to make in the 1984 delegate selection rules. He opposed the 20 percent thresholds, loophole primaries, and superdelegates, and he requested that the DNC adjust its delegate allocations to states to take into account an alleged census undercount of the black population.[65] Mannatt finally agreed to allow Jackson to present his complaints about the rules to the January 1984 meeting of the DNC's Executive Committee. The meeting was preceded by a long night of negotiations involving Mannatt, Jackson, Mondale campaign manager Bob Beckel, and Tom Donilon. When the Executive Committee was to begin meeting, the negotiations were still going on.

In the meantime, Kathy Vick of Louisiana, president of the Association of Democratic State Chairs, and individual state chairs, such as Robert Slagle of Texas, had gotten wind of the fact that Mondale's representatives and Mannatt were about to compromise with Jackson by allowing states to set their own thresholds for the awarding of delegates to presidential candidates. They were vehemently opposed to this solution, not wanting to repeat in their states the debate that had been taking place nationally for so long and that had just been given new life by Jesse Jackson. In the face of their opposition, the negotiations broke down. Jackson refused to come downstairs from his hotel room to address the Executive Committee. Instead they heard a rather heated harangue from his campaign manager, Gary, Indiana, mayor Richard Hatcher, who was also a vice chair of the DNC. The Executive Committee adjourned without making any changes in the 1984 delegate selection rules. But Jackson continued to voice complaints throughout the 1984 delegate selection season, as his delegate count fell below his proportion of the vote in many of the states in which he competed.

Until the Hunt Commission rewrote the rules, the party had emphasized the importance of guaranteeing minority candidates representation at its convention. Jesse Jackson's continuing outrage arose in large part from the fact that in 1984 the party had consciously adopted a set of rules designed to favor winners, not losers. The representation of minority candidates had taken a back seat to the desire to nominate a winner. It had also fallen prey to the political manipulations of the then leading presidential candidates.

Yet despite the new fair reflection rules, the 1984 race did not come to an early end. Nearly half the delegates that year were still elected in proportional representation systems. Neither higher thresholds, bonus plans, nor direct election primaries were sufficient to provide Mondale with the knockout punch that he needed to get Jackson and Gary Hart out of the race. Nor were the new rules sufficient to allow Hart to make a serious challenge to Mondale's delegate lead. Despite the candidates' efforts to write rules that would allow winners to win, the 1984 delegate allocation system was still influenced by proportional systems, which guaranteed the Democrats nothing more than a candidate who went, limping and wounded, into the general election.

Jackson versus Dukakis and the Final Triumph of Proportional Representation

Jesse Jackson was not the major story in the 1984 nomination race, which turned into a dramatic contest between the front-runner, Walter Mondale, and that year's surprise insurgent, Senator Gary Hart of Colorado. By the end of the primaries Jesse Jackson was an afterthought and an aggrieved candidate. He kept up a steady drumbeat of criticism of Mondale, but he also focused a great deal of criticism on the party rules that Mondale had helped engineer. He was especially irritated that he had so few delegates at the San Francisco convention; even among black delegates, Mondale had a clear lead.[66] The Mondale campaign worried that Jackson's continued unhappiness would decrease black turnout, which would have to be very high in the upcoming difficult race against the popular incumbent, Ronald Reagan. So in the tradition of giving losing candidates a chance at righting the wrongs they had allegedly suffered, the 1984 convention created yet another rules commission, called the Fairness Commission and chaired by South Carolina party chair Don Fowler.

At the commission's hearings in August 1985, Representative John Conyers Jr. of Michigan laid out Jesse Jackson's objections to the presidential nomination system. "After the defeat of President Carter," said Conyers, "there appeared to have been a concerted effort by the Democratic Party to have a controlled selection process which resulted in a system where some candidates for the presidential nomination felt that process disenfranchised them and their supporters. Secondly, there is a feeling that as the party considers new directions for the presidential race in 1988, the important role of minorities, who are overwhelmingly Democratic, may be diminished as the Democratic Party attempts to recapture those who have, hopefully only temporarily, left the party."[67] Conyers proceeded to lay out a series of criticisms of the system, including complaints about caucuses and frontloading—not things the Fairness Commission could do much about. However, Conyers also brought up high thresholds, the direct election of delegate primaries, and the bonus delegate plan, cloaking his critique of these rules in the powerful civil rights language of "disenfranchisement." He made the same critique of the new category of superdelegates.

Conyers was followed by Jesse Jackson himself, who argued that the combination of the 20 percent threshold and the superdelegates meant that while he got 21 percent of the vote in the 1984 primaries, he ended up with only 11 percent of the delegates to the 1984 convention. In typical Jackson style, he said that the Hunt Commission rules "favored the big-shots over the long-shots and the sling shots."[68]

But the members of the Fairness Commission were in no mood to reverse what the Hunt Commission had done. On October 18, 1985, they decided to lower the threshold for getting a delegate from 20 percent to 15 percent. But they allowed states to continue to use the direct election of delegates system or the bonus system, and they increased the number of superdelegates to the 1988 convention by adding Democratic governors and all members of the Democratic National Committee—despite what appeared to be a 1984 convention directive in the opposite direction.[69]

Jackson was not pleased and wrote a strongly worded letter of protest to DNC chairman Paul Kirk several days later. In the letter he accused the party of "creating a national gerrymandering process . . . stacked against independents and minorities."[70] But Jackson's concerns did not carry the day. In the end, the 1988 delegate selection rules had a slightly lower threshold but more superdelegates and only slightly fewer delegates elected in winner-take-all systems than in 1984.

In 1988, Jesse Jackson ran for president again: he was older, wiser, and more determined than ever to win delegates and thus be a force at the 1988 convention. This time he made sure that his campaign at least tried to file full slates of delegates and that he broadened his message to create a coalition of blacks and liberal whites.[71] (Nonetheless, he missed the deadline to file delegates in the all-important states of Pennsylvania and Ohio.)[72] Although the rules were basically the same as they had been in 1984, the dynamics of the 1988 race were different. Jackson managed to stay above the fray as Missouri representative Dick Gephardt, Tennessee senator Al Gore, and Massachusetts governor Michael Dukakis battled it out. Once Dukakis emerged as the winner of the southern Super Tuesday and Al Gore failed to win any states outside the South, it was clear that none of the other candidates had much of a chance. One by one they dropped out of the race, leaving Jackson as Dukakis's major opponent throughout the remainder of the primaries.

The political establishment never saw Jackson as anything more than a protest candidate, but he did extremely well in 1988, winning Alabama, Georgia, Louisiana, Mississippi, and Virginia on Super Tuesday and the Michigan primary. He also increased his overall vote and delegate count from their 1984 levels. Appealing to a coalition of blacks and very liberal voters, he nearly doubled his 1984 vote in Florida and Indiana and nearly quadrupled his 1984 vote in Massachusetts.

Success made Jackson even unhappier with the process. As Dukakis began his inexorable climb to the nomination, Jackson began to complain to the press once again that the system was unfair. By May 1988, after Dukakis had won the Ohio and Indiana primaries, Jackson reopened his complaints about the nomination process, telling reporters that his popular vote totals (28 percent for Jackson to 37 percent for Dukakis) were not reflected in his delegate totals and that he would challenge the seating of delegates to the 1988 convention.[73] He appointed Washington lawyer Ron Brown; Eleanor Holmes Norton, chair of the Equal Employment Opportunity Commission in the Carter administration; and veteran party infighter Harold Ickes to handle convention negotiations with the Dukakis campaign on two fronts: the contents of the Democratic Party's platform and the rules. This experienced team was backed up by over 1,000 delegates to the 1988 convention. If Dukakis wanted peace at his convention, he needed to pacify Jackson. Dukakis chose to compromise on the rules, agreeing to get rid of superdelegates (a deal he could not keep since he didn't win the election and control the party subsequently) and systems, such as the direct election of delegates and the bonus system, that rewarded winners in the presidential nomination process. The deal prompted the *Washington Post* to editorialize: "One difference between the political parties is that the Republicans let their winning candidates set the rules for the next election and the Democrats let their losing candidates rewrite the rules."[74]

And so the 1988 Democratic Convention passed a resolution stating: "Resolved that paragraph (ii) of Section 4 of Article Two of the Charter shall be construed to prohibit the direct election of delegates, the use of so-called 'bonus delegates' or any other method whereby delegates are allocated in a fashion other than by which they proportionally represent the expressed presidential preference (including uncommitted status) of the primary voters, convention or caucus participants as the case may be."[75] In supporting the resolution, D.C. mayor Marion Barry told the convention delegates, "I stand here on behalf of more than 1,300 delegates and 7 million Americans who supported the candidacy of Reverend Jesse Jackson. . . . I also represent those Americans who because of our rules felt left out, locked out and kept out of the voting process."[76]

When the Democratic National Committee's Rules and By-Laws Committee met in 1990 to pass the rules for the 1992 nomination season, the prohibition on direct election and loophole primaries passed without opposition. It had taken 20 years, but proportional representation was now mandated in the Democratic Party rules and has been ever since.

Conclusion

The trajectory of the fight over proportional representation reflected assumptions about primary politics over two decades. The idea was born in the fury of the antiwar protesters at the Democratic National Convention in 1968. Its attractiveness to liberal reformers waned in the face of segregationist George Wallace's strong showing in 1972 and collapsed briefly in the aftermath of Jimmy Carter's failed presidency. It was brought back by Jesse Jackson and became cloaked in the aura of the civil rights movement. It shapes the progression of the delegate count for Democrats, just as the Republicans' more varied allocation system shapes the delegate count on their side. It is to the delegate count and how it shapes momentum that we now turn.

5

DEVIL IN THE DETAILS

*How the Delegate Count Shapes
Modern Nominating Campaigns*

On the morning of March 5, 2008, newspapers all over the United States ran some version of the following headline: "John McCain Clinches GOP Nomination." The night before, he had won four critical contests and four critical sets of delegates. In Ohio he won 100 percent of the delegates by winning 60 percent of the primary vote to 30 percent for Mike Huckabee, the former Arkansas governor who was his closest remaining rival. In Vermont he won 100 percent of the 17 delegates, in Texas he won 99 out of 137 delegates, and in Rhode Island he won 13 out of 17 delegates. Once all the votes were counted, McCain could claim a majority of the 2,380 delegates who would attend the convention. The Republican race was over.

On that same morning in March 2008, the Democratic race was still on. Senator Hillary Clinton had won a solid victory in Ohio, a key general election state, but her 10-point victory there netted her only 75 delegates while her rival, Senator Barack Obama, won 66 delegates. Her Texas win didn't even result in a delegate win; there she won the primary and lost the delegates to Obama, 94 to 99 (due to a combination of proportional rules and a bizarre caucus system tacked on to the primary), and in Rhode Island her primary win gave her five more delegates than Obama received there.

The contrast between the outcomes of the Democratic and Republican primaries on March 4, 2008, dramatically illustrates how allocation rules shape the path to a major party nomination. As we saw in chapter 2, presidential candidates work hard to establish a favorable sequence of primary wins in order to create momentum. But after the initial primaries, the contests tend to come in multiples, and the delegate count replaces the number of wins as the key measure that can accelerate or decelerate a candidate's momentum. The Republican rules reward winners by boosting their share of the delegate count, relative to their share of the vote; the Democratic rules reward losers in the same way. Consequently, Republican candidates can secure their party's nomination with a relatively small number of narrow wins, while Democratic candidates need to rack up a large number of early big wins or commit themselves to the arduous task of consistently winning by smaller margins in state after state after state.

No one can describe John McCain's path to the Republican nomination as easy: at one point he had run out of money, fired his staff, and been left for dead. But once he rebounded and began to win primaries, his wins with the voters translated into even larger delegate gains. He won 12 out of the 14 winner-take-all Republican primaries, thereby building up a substantial lead in delegates. In contrast, when Hillary Clinton began to win late important primaries, the proportional rules of the Democratic Party prevented her from catching up with Barack Obama in the delegate count.

The Democrats' proportional rules do more than simply make Democratic nominating contests lengthier and costlier than Republican ones (sometimes lasting well into the summer), while the presumptive Republican nominee gets an early start on the general election campaign. They have also fundamentally altered the balance of power within the Democratic Party. It is typically much harder for a candidate to win by large margins in the larger, more diverse states that dominate the later reaches of the calendar. Therefore these states cannot be counted on to significantly boost a candidate's delegate count. This makes smaller, homogeneous early states loom even larger in a campaign's calculations.

In addition, both parties' delegate allocation rules shape campaigns in less public ways. Getting the right rules in place has been an important part of many candidates' pre-primary strategy, particularly on the Republican side, where they have choices. And once the rules are in place, campaigns have risen and fallen by their ability to understand and respond to the requirements the rules impose. Successful candidates have understood the importance of looking beyond vote tallies to the mechanics of the delegate count, which often operate behind the scenes; unsuccessful candidates have often learned this lesson too late.

Trying to Set the Rules

The first strategic imperative facing presidential candidates is to try for winner-take-all rules (or rules that reward winning) in states that they feel they can win and for proportional rules in states that they feel they may lose. This strategic option has not been available to Democrats since 1992, when party rules mandated the universal use of proportional representation, but it was frequently practiced before then. In the Republican Party, where the choice of allocation rule is up to each state party, jockeying for favorable allocation rules has been a strategic tactic as common as jockeying for a favorable sequence of contests.

In 1976, for example, supporters of Gerald Ford in Massachusetts sought an opinion from the state Supreme Court on the meaning of the state statute that said that delegates to nominating conventions must "reflect the preferences expressed by the voters in the presidential preference portion of the ballot."[1] (The language in the statute was the result of Democratic Party reforms.) The Republican state party argued that the law required proportional representation. Ford supporters, knowing that Massachusetts would be a good state for Ford against Reagan, wanted the system to be winner-take-all by congressional district. The court deferred to the state party and Ford lost. This was an unfortunate setback for Ford. When Massachusetts held its Republican primary, Ford beat Reagan 62 percent to 35 percent, but because the rules were proportional, he gained 27 delegates and Reagan gained 15. Given that Ford's margin of victory at the convention later that summer was a mere 117 votes, the closest contest in modern history, Ford's supporters could have used all of the 15 delegates they would have won under winner-take-all rules.

Following President Ford's defeat in the 1976 general election, Ronald Reagan emerged as the clear front-runner for the 1980 Republican nomination. In 1979 the other Republican hopefuls teamed up to try to change the California Republican winner-take-all primary to a primary in which the state's 168 delegates would be awarded on a proportional basis. (By switching to proportional rules, they hoped to deprive Reagan of at least 80 delegates.)[2] Not surprisingly, they faced an uphill battle in the state that Reagan had governed for two terms. In September 1979, the Reagan-controlled Republican State Convention rejected a proposal to award delegates by proportional rules. In response, supporters of Reagan's challengers formed the Fair Presidential Primary Committee, with the purpose of collecting enough signatures to place a proposition ending the winner-take-all primary on the June ballot.

The Fair Presidential Primary Committee was headed by State Senator John Schmitz of Orange County, a supporter of John Connally, and by Representative Peter McCloskey, a supporter of George Bush. It was financed largely by Leonard K. Firestone, who had been President Ford's ambassador to Belgium and who was Ford's next-door neighbor in California. Other money came from a combination of moderate Republican Bush backers and Texas oil interests who favored Connally.[3] Despite their support, the initiative failed to get enough signatures to get on the ballot, an outcome widely seen as a boost for Reagan. Opponents of the winner-take-all system then went to court, where their efforts also failed. On April 18, 1980, the California Supreme Court upheld the ruling of a lower court that declared the winner-take-all primary to be constitutional.[4]

Three years later it was the Democrats' turn to fight over allocation rules at the state level. During the summer of 1983, former vice president Mondale's campaign was predicting a tough fight for the Democratic nomination with Ohio senator John Glenn. In an effort to help Glenn, the Ohio Democratic Party adopted a "loophole" primary, which, as discussed in chapter 4, usually resulted in winner-take-all outcomes by congressional district. But in their haste to secure all of Ohio's delegates for their favorite son, the drafters of the delegate selection plan included a provision that allowed voters to cast one vote for John Glenn and thereby vote for all the delegates in that district who were Glenn supporters. This variation on the loophole primary violated Rule 12 of the 1984 Delegate Selection Rules, which required that votes be cast for each individual delegate.[5] So the Compliance Review Commission handed the plan back to the Ohio state party with directions to amend it.

Seizing the opportunity presented by the CRC's move, Tim Hagan, the flamboyant Cuyahoga county commissioner and Mondale state chairman, challenged the delegate selection plan and took his attack on the "unfair" state party to the press.[6] After several months of criticism directed at the state party for its refusal to adopt a proportional system, Hagan was able to convince party leaders to adopt the bonus delegate plan. This plan was not nearly as advantageous to Glenn as direct election of delegates because it allowed a second-place finisher (presumably Mondale) to win some delegates.[7] Of course by the time of the Ohio primary John Glenn was no longer in the race, and it was Senator Gary Hart who went on to win a narrow victory over Mondale. Given the narrowness of Hart's victory (42 percent to 40 percent), the existence of the bonus plan helped him add 12 sorely needed delegates to his totals.[8]

Understanding allocation rules and engineering them to increase a candidate's expected delegate count can be important elements of a winning campaign. But at the same time, it is important to keep the rules' significance in perspective. Allocation rules are not the only aspect of the nominating process that shapes both momentum and the delegate count. Sequence is at least as important. Ignoring the interaction between sequence and allocation rules can lead to disaster. As Rudy Giuliani's failed candidacy shows, candidates can be so blinded by the big delegate prizes available in winner-take-all states that they miss the fact that sequence still matters.

As we saw in chapter 2, Giuliani's strategy was to use a strong showing in the Florida primary as a springboard to victory in the delegate-rich contests that followed Florida. Part of this strategy involved upping the stakes in the post-Florida contests where Giuliani looked strong. Of the 21 states planning to hold contests on Super Tuesday 2008 (February 5), Connecticut and New York, obviously good states for Giuliani, had used winner-take-all rules (on the Republican side) in 2004 and were planning to use them again. Oklahoma and Missouri had also used winner-take-all rules in 2004 and would be using them again. California, a very good state for Giuliani, used winner-take-all-by-district rules in 2004 and would use them again in 2008. And Illinois elected delegates directly on the ballot in 2004 and would use that system again in 2008. That left New Jersey, which had moved its primary up from June to February 5 for 2008 and needed to establish an allocation rule.

In 2007, Giuliani's Republican neighbors in New Jersey saw that he was doing well in the national polls and calculated that if they all got behind Giuliani, his strength on the presidential ticket and his attractiveness to New

Jersey voters might bring enough money in and enough voters to the polls to help get other New Jersey Republicans elected. That was why a hardcore conservative right-to-life activist like David Von Savage, Cape May county chair and a former Pat Buchanan supporter, decided to back Giuliani in the New Jersey primary, despite Giuliani's pro-choice record. In the spring of 2007, Savage, along with a few other county chairs, got himself placed on the state committee that had to make decisions about the following year's Republican primary.

In the past, New Jersey Republicans had elected delegates directly on the ballot without regard for the outcome of the presidential preference primary, which was merely a "beauty contest." But in an effort to help Giuliani, Savage and other supporters proposed that the 2008 New Jersey primary award all the delegates to the candidate who won the most votes statewide. In Savage's words, "It was tantamount to going to Atlantic City and putting all your chips on red. . . . If you win you win big; if you lose you lose big."[9] The change was made at a June 2007 meeting of the New Jersey Republican Party's Rules Committee amid some controversy.

The addition of New Jersey to the February 5 lineup allowed Mike Duhaime, Giuliani's campaign manager, to argue in favor of the Florida-plus strategy as follows: "I think one of the things to also look at is which of those states are winner-take-all and which . . . award their delegates in a different way. I think looking at this mathematically, obviously, when you have states like New York, New Jersey, Connecticut and Delaware that are all winner-take-all—New York with over 100 delegates, New Jersey with 52, Delaware with 18 and Connecticut with 30—you have over 200 delegates right there."[10]

The Giuliani strategy would have made sense in a system of simultaneous primaries, as illustrated in table 5-1, but in a sequential system it failed to take into account just how powerful the early contests are in defining and creating momentum. By the time of the Florida primary, Giuliani had been out of the news for nearly a month. In the meantime Republican voters had been gripped by the comeback story of Senator John McCain and the come-from-behind story of former Arkansas governor Mike Huckabee. Giuliani's third-place showing in Florida was so weak that he never made it to the other winner-take-all states where he might have been expected to pull in substantial numbers of delegates. He dropped out of the race shortly after Florida and endorsed John McCain.

Table 5-1. *What Might Have Been: Giuliani's Winner-Take-All Strategy, 2008*

Date	Contest	Number of delegates[a]	Delegate allocation rule[b]	Average Giuliani advantage, fall 2007[c]	Potential delegate harvest[d]
Feb. 5	California	173	WTA-CD	+ 14	Est. 130
Feb. 5	Illinois	70	DE	+ 02	Est. 53
Feb. 5	Missouri	58	WTA-S	+ 07	58
Feb. 5	New York	101	WTA-S	+ 33	101
Feb. 5	New Jersey	52	WTA-S	+ 33	52
Feb. 5	Connecticut	30	WTA-S	+ 25	30
Feb. 12	Virginia	63	WTA-S	+ 14	63
Mar. 4	Ohio	88	WTA-CD	+ 13	Est. 53
Apr. 22	Pennsylvania	74	DE	+ 20	Est. 53

Sources: Polling data are from Real Clear Politics website in the fall of 2007 (www.realclearpolitics.com (archives). Delegate data are from: Republican National Committee 2007–2008 Rule No. 15(e), Delegate Selection Overview Summaries for Presidential Primaries, Caucuses, and Conventions. Rhodes Cook, *Race for the Presidency: Winning the 2008 Nomination* (Washington: CQ Press, 2008). "New York Times Election Guide 2008" at http://politics.nytimes.com/election-guide/2008/results/votes/index.html [April 1, 2009].

a. Delegate numbers count automatic RNC members.

b. Abbreviations for Delegate Allocation Rules: WTA-CD means winner-take-all by congressional district; WTA-S means winner-take-all by state; DE means direct election of delegates.

c. The average Giuliani advantage is the Giuliani advantage (positive spread) or disadvantage (negative spread) over his closest rival in the polling. If there was more than one statewide poll in 2007 the polls are averaged.

d. Delegate counts from states that award delegates to the winner of a congressional district cannot be estimated from statewide polls. However, when a candidate has a healthy lead in statewide polls he or she can be counted on to win a plurality of congressional districts. Here I estimate that Giuliani could have won 75 percent of delegates in winner-take-all-by-congressional-district states if his numbers had held up.

In the end it was John McCain, not Rudy Giuliani, who benefited from the existence of so many winner-take-all states. By the time the 2008 nomination season was in full swing, the conservative base of the Republican Party had spent a year mourning the fact that they didn't really have a candidate they could be enthusiastic about. Several Republican candidates tried out for the conservative mantle, figuring that coming out of Iowa there would be "one front-runner and a conservative."[11] When Mike Huckabee, a Southern Baptist minister and former Arkansas governor, emerged into the national spotlight from the Iowa caucuses, social conservatives had finally found their

Table 5-2. *Mike Huckabee's Second-Place Finishes*

State	Total delegates	Delegates awarded to Huckabee
Alaska	29	6
Washington[a]	40	8
South Carolina	24	5
Missouri	58	0
Oklahoma[c]	41	6
Virginia[b]	63	0
Maryland[c]	37	0
Wisconsin[c]	40	3
Texas	140	16
Rhode Island	20	4
Ohio[c]	88	0
Mississippi	39	0
North Carolina	69	8
Indiana[c]	57	0
West Virginia[a]	30	18
Kentucky	45	0
Total	790	74

a. In Washington and West Virginia some delegates are awarded at the primary and some at a party caucus.

b. The state is winner-take-all statewide.

c. The state is winner-take-all by congressional district.

candidate. By the end of January, as he campaigned in Alabama, the press was reporting: "A crowd estimated at 2,200 heard Huckabee pound away in support of values long espoused by social conservatives for whom such values drive voting decisions. Pro-life, pro-traditional marriage between a man and a woman, a strong military, a society that values a divine creator—all areas Huckabee devoted attention to Saturday, all areas that have made him the favorite among evangelicals."[12] As other, better-known Republicans dropped out of the race, Huckabee continued, buoyed by the enthusiasm of the religious portion of the Republican Party base.

While Huckabee won a few contests outright, mostly he came in second place. However, as table 5-2 shows, his second-place finishes added little to his delegate count, thus denying him not just a shot at the nomination but the ability to be a strong advocate for social conservatism at the convention.

The winner-take-all rules of so many Republican states meant that even substantial showings, such as Huckabee's 41 percent of the vote in Virginia, left him without any delegates. Under the Democratic Party's proportional rules, Huckabee would have won a much greater number of delegates. For instance, Virginia had 60 pledged delegates to the Republican convention and three automatic delegates who were members of the Republican National Committee. Under the Democrats' proportional rules, Huckabee's 41 percent of the vote (to 50 percent for McCain) could have netted him as many as 25 delegates, rather than zero. Similarly in Oklahoma, under proportional representation, Huckabee's 33 percent of the vote (just 4 percentage points behind McCain) could have yielded as many as 17 of the state's 38 pledged delegates.

Sustaining Momentum: It's the Delegates, Stupid

In order to create momentum in the first stage of the primary process, candidates have to win votes; in order to sustain it in the second stage, they have to win delegates. These processes are not always the same, as some candidates have learned the hard way.

Bush versus Reagan, 1980

By anyone's account, March 1980 was a great month for Ronald Reagan. He was winning primaries by large margins and delegates by even larger margins thanks to the winner-take-all rules in effect in many southern Republican state parties. His main opponent, George H. W. Bush, was obviously in trouble. In a *Washington Post* story entitled "The Eagle's Nose Dive," Bill Peterson and Robert Kaiser wrote: "Now the eagle is in a tailspin, his wings bruised and battered. The fresh face of January is etched with the lines of disappointment and defeat of March."[13]

Nevertheless, Bush's prospects for a comeback should have been good. The same news story pointed out that Bush was due $2.6 million in matching funds from the federal government. At the same time, the Reagan campaign was cutting back on staff spending and travel because it had already spent more than two-thirds of the money permitted by the FEC for the primary season. Moreover, the primaries were moving north to territory less favorable to Reagan. Gerald Ford had beaten Reagan in most northeastern states in 1976, and given his Connecticut background, Bush was thought to have a good shot at doing so as well.

But by that point in the race, attention had moved to the delegate count. Momentum was no longer defined by the outcomes of individual primaries or caucuses, but by the cumulative effect of each contest on the delegate count. On March 25, Bush won the Connecticut primary, but his victory was swamped by Reagan's win in New York the same day. Not only did New York have more delegates than Connecticut, but it used a direct-election-of-delegates system, which translated into lopsided gains for the victor. Reagan captured 73 delegates in New York to six for Bush, while under proportional rules Connecticut allocated almost equal numbers of delegates to the winner (15 for Bush) and the loser (14 for Reagan).[14] The absence of a presidential preference vote on New York's Republican ballot meant that it received little news attention, compared to the Connecticut primary. Nonetheless the *Washington Post* was quick to point out: "Reagan remains far out front in the most vital measure—the delegate count."[15] The following day political columnist David Broder observed: "The mathematics of the presidential balloting in the Democratic and Republican parties require Kennedy and Bush to win about five of every eight delegates remaining to be chosen if they are to overhaul frontrunners Jimmy Carter and Ronald Reagan.[16]

What happened to Bush in New York? In states that elect delegates directly, victory is determined by the slating process, and Reagan had a stronger organization in the state. Thirty-four Reagan delegates ran unopposed, while only one Bush delegate ran unopposed.[17] Thus Reagan had won the New York State primary in the winter of 1980 when slating had to be done.

The next major opportunity for a Bush comeback was the Pennsylvania primary. The Bush campaign proceeded to concentrate all its efforts in the state. Reagan, near the limit imposed by the FEC for spending in the primaries, could not match Bush's investment. Reagan spent a total of $250,128 in Pennsylvania whereas Bush spent $1,369,807 in the state.[18] When primary day came, Bush beat Reagan 54 percent to 45 percent in the beauty contest vote, scoring his most significant victory over Reagan since Iowa.

But Bush's Pennsylvania victory did almost nothing to restore the magic "Big Mo" to his campaign—for while Bush was winning the beauty contest, Reagan was winning the delegates. Of the 77 Pennsylvania delegates elected on primary day, Reagan won 50, and Bush won fewer than 20. The Reagan campaign understood what it took to get delegates elected in this key state; the Bush campaign did not. Knowing that they would be outspent in the beauty contest, Drew Lewis and Rick Robb, Reagan's campaign managers in Pennsylvania, had "focused first on the delegate contest, seeking to obtain endorsement for Reagan from locally popular delegate candidates."[19] As a result, the pro-Reagan candidates for delegates were familiar to voters, while those who supported Bush were "fewer and generally less well known."[20] Adding to Bush's problems, a mailing identifying the Bush supporters on the ballot was filled with errors and reached homes too late to be of much good to the voters.[21]

As in New York, what the Reagan strategists had understood was that the first important step in winning the Pennsylvania primary had come on February 13, 1980, the date when delegate petitions had to be filed. The *Washington Post* summarized the campaign's strategy as follows: "Because ballot position has been important historically in the election of delegates, Reagan strategists filed as many delegate candidates as possible, hoping for top line positions. In the western Pennsylvania 21st district for example, Reagan supporters gained seven of the top eight ballot positions."[22]

The Bush team, in contrast, lacked a strong field organization. The few weeks between Iowa and the filing deadline in Pennsylvania left the understaffed Bush campaign too little time to do anything about its weak or nonexistent slates of delegates. Therefore campaign officials made a conscious decision to forgo a concerted effort in the delegate race and concentrate on the beauty contest.[23] In part this decision was dictated by tough choices about how to allocate campaign resources that were made back in January, when Bush chose to gamble on an early victory in Iowa or New Hampshire that would let him break away from the pack. But it also reflected the campaign's failure to understand how sustaining momentum would differ from obtaining it in the first place.

Bush's next major primary win was Michigan. But the other contests held that day gave Reagan enough delegates to claim the nomination, and shortly thereafter Bush left the race.

HART VERSUS MONDALE, 1984

Like George Bush, Gary Hart failed to understand or take advantage of the strategic imperatives of the delegate count. This made it impossible for his campaign to sustain its momentum, despite a stunning string of early and late primary and caucus wins.

In 1984, former vice president Walter Mondale was the heavily favored front-runner in the Democratic race for the nomination. The candidate who was expected to be his strongest opponent, Senator John Glenn of Ohio, saw his quest come to an early end when he made the rookie's mistake of thinking that the Iowa caucuses were like a primary. Glenn's stumble handed Mondale a stunning victory in Iowa, where he handily beat his next closest rival, Senator Gary Hart. But because Mondale was the front-runner and from a neighboring state to boot, his substantial victory was discounted by the national press corps, who focused on Hart's surprise second-place finish. Shortly thereafter and to the surprise of almost everyone in the political establishment, Mondale lost the New Hampshire primary to Gary Hart. Overnight, Hart became the beneficiary of the same momentum that Bush had experienced in 1980 after his Iowa upset over Reagan. With the loss in New Hampshire followed quickly by losses in the Maine and Wyoming caucuses, the Mondale campaign was clearly in trouble, and Mondale's top aides were giving serious thought to having Mondale drop out of the race. Mondale himself had begun to think of his southern swing as his valedictory.[24]

Against this backdrop, Super Tuesday, long hyped by the Mondale campaign and by others as the first really big test for the nomination, assumed even greater importance as everyone prepared to see whether Mondale would be forced from the race. Twelve delegate selection contests were held on Super Tuesday 1984 (March 13): primaries in Florida, Georgia, Alabama, Massachusetts, and Rhode Island, and caucuses in Oklahoma, Washington, Hawaii, Nevada, Wyoming, Democrats Abroad, and American Samoa.

By any objective criteria, Mondale did not do well on Super Tuesday. As table 5-3 shows, out of the five primaries, Hart won three and Mondale won two (Alabama by 14 percent and Georgia by only 3 percent). Hart also won three caucus states, including Oklahoma and Washington. Hart's six-point win in Florida and his 14 percent win in Massachusetts should have kept his momentum going—but to the surprise of many, Mondale was crowned the winner of Super Tuesday.

Jack Germond and Jules Witcover attribute Mondale's win on Super Tuesday to expert playing of the expectations game by the Mondale campaign. They quote Marty Kaplan, Mondale's chief speechwriter, on the press

Table 5-3. *Democratic Results for Super Tuesday, March 13, 1984*
Percent

State[a]	Mondale	Hart	Glenn	Jackson	Other and uncommitted
Alabama	34.60	20.66	20.85	19.56	4.33
Florida	33.36	39.29	10.85	12.20	4.30
Georgia	30.47	27.30	17.93	21.00	3.30
Hawaii	32.3	0	0	4.2	63.5
Massachusetts	25.50	38.98	7.20	5.04	23.26
Nevada	37.7	52.3	2.0	0.6	7.2
Oklahoma	39.7	41.4	5.0	3.8	10.1
Rhode Island	34.46	44.96	5.05	8.71	6.82
Washington	34	51	1	5	9
Wyoming	35.9	60.4	0.1	0.4	3.2

Source: Caucus data from *Congressional Quarterly Weekly Reports*, March 17, 1984, p. 626. Primary data from CQ Press, Voting & Elections Collection Search Form, retrieved November 2, 2008, from CQP Electronic Library website: http://library.cqpress.com.ezp-prod1.hul.harvard.edu/elections/searchform.php (access by subscription only).

a. States in italics are caucus states.

strategy for the evening: "As we watched the early network play, we believed that our game plan had the potential to succeed—namely that by claiming victory, by characterizing the race as 'now we're back in it' as opposed to 'now it's over' or that 'we're on our last leg', that we had a chance to get that across."[25]

And indeed, the networks tended to count Mondale "in" instead of "out" on the basis of the Super Tuesday results. Tom Brokaw of NBC led the pack with his comment that Mondale's friends in the South had "kept him in this race tonight."[26] The press surrounding Super Tuesday became more and more favorable as the week went on, and Super Tuesday became the beginning of the Mondale comeback.[27]

But there was more than just spin behind the media's take on Super Tuesday. There was also the delegate count, which the Mondale campaign had painstakingly played up since the New Hampshire primary. A four-page "talking points" memo distributed to campaign workers who dealt with the press highlighted the following message: "Our overall goals over the next three weeks are to . . . show a commanding delegate lead on Super-Tuesday with the backbone of our effort the winning of the massive Southern regional primary.... By March 20 we will have accumulated a commanding delegate lead over Hart."[28]

Two problems hampered Hart's ability to compete in the delegate race: his inability to compete in the race for superdelegates (in this case, unpledged delegates selected from Congress) and his failure to file complete slates of delegates in three critical loophole primary states.

The Mondale campaign had already begun its hunt for superdelegates in 1983. It put a top aide with extensive Capitol Hill contacts, Dick Moe, in charge of the delegate search on Capitol Hill and worked behind the scenes to urge Speaker of the House Tip O'Neill to set the date for the election of House delegates for January 1984, well in advance of both the Iowa caucuses and the New Hampshire primary. In essence, this turned the House delegate selection contest into the first primary, a move that paid off richly for Mondale. Not surprisingly, the combination of his early front-runner status and his years of personal relationships with many members resulted in a Mondale sweep of the House delegates. While formally unpledged, these delegates were routinely included in Mondale's column in all published delegate counts, giving Mondale a substantial lead over his opponents. With 164 members, the House delegation to the convention was larger than many big-state delegations.

The success of this strategy irritates former senator Hart to this day.[29] The *Washington Post's* delegate count of March 11, 1984, gave Mondale 124 delegates to 24 for Hart. At that time only 80 delegates, 58 from Iowa and 22 from New Hampshire, had been allocated in the traditional way. The bulk of the Mondale delegate count therefore consisted of delegates he had won in his large Iowa win, padded by congressional delegates who had made their preferences known to the media. While the number of congressional delegates included in the delegate counts varied according to the week and the source of the count, most boosted Mondale's numbers by 70 to 100 delegates. This was especially useful in helping the Mondale campaign mask its losses on Super Tuesday.

Hart's other problem with the delegate count occurred in the loophole primary states. Three states, Florida, Illinois, and Pennsylvania, had early deadlines for filing slates of delegates. Like the Bush campaign in 1980, Gary Hart's 1984 campaign was struggling to meet payroll from week to week and putting all its organizational efforts into Iowa and New Hampshire.

Meanwhile, filing deadlines passed in Florida (January 20, 1984), Illinois (January 11, 1984), and Pennsylvania (January 31, 1984). By the end of January it was clear that Hart was seriously behind. According to the Associated Press, "Hart has filed for only 34 of the 84 congressional level delegates at stake that day.... Making the overly optimistic assumption that all of Hart's delegates win, he still could not win the other 50 delegates. Since the remaining pledged Florida delegates are allocated based on the district delegates, Hart can end up with only 50 of the state's 123 pledged delegates, leaving 73 he cannot win in the primary."[30] The same problems occurred elsewhere, leading Evans Witt, an experienced AP reporter, to conclude that Hart had already forfeited 96 delegates in Illinois and 106 in Pennsylvania.[31] Similarly, in Alabama the Hart campaign had failed to file in one district and filed incomplete slates in the other six districts.

This failure was not entirely due to lack of money: other candidates with few resources did manage to file full slates. As noted in chapter 2, Jeff Berman, Barack Obama's 2008 delegate hunter, was working for John Glenn in 1983 and remains proud to this day of the fact that he managed to file complete slates in the same set of states. Other candidates in the back of the pack, such as California senator Alan Cranston and former Florida governor Reubin Askew, also managed to file full slates.

The cost of the Hart campaign's failure to file soon became clear. As the dust settled from Super Tuesday, it became apparent that while Hart had won Florida's primary, Mondale had won the most Florida delegates. In congressional district after congressional district, voters had picked Hart in the beauty contest and then, finding no delegates pledged to Hart on the second part of the ballot, had voted for delegates pledged to Mondale or Askew. These people tended to be well-known local politicians. Mondale consequently won 61 pledged delegates in Florida, followed by Hart with 35, former governor Askew with 24, Glenn with 2, and Jesse Jackson with 1, for a total of 123 pledged delegates.[32] (The remaining 20 Florida delegates were unpledged superdelegates.) Hart carried 15 out of 19 congressional districts in the beauty contest, but only four districts in the delegate race. If delegates pledged to Hart had been on the ballot and swept all the districts where he won in the beauty contest, Hart would have won an additional 42 delegates.

As the extent of their failure became apparent, Hart's advisers began to woo Askew's delegates. The campaign also challenged the Florida at-large selection process in an attempt get more delegates. While this challenge went nowhere, the Hart campaign was moderately successful in winning over former Askew delegates. Nonetheless, in terms of lost momentum, the damage had already been done. Hart's Super Tuesday victory had been lost in the delegate count. On March 11, 1984, as he was going into Super Tuesday, Mondale could claim a significant lead in delegates: 126 to only 24 for Hart.[33] Following Super Tuesday, the *Washington Post* showed that Mondale was still leading in the delegate count, although his proportions were not as high. The total delegate count was Mondale 373 and Hart 256. When the unpledged party leader delegates (mostly members of Congress) were subtracted from the vote, Mondale's delegate lead shrank to 259; Hart had 243.[34]

The delegate rout was repeated in Illinois, where Mondale's 5 percentage point victory in the beauty contest translated into the capture of the lion's share of the delegates: 96 for Mondale, 40 for Hart. (The Hart campaign filed no slates in 12 of the state's 22 congressional districts and incomplete slates in three.) By March 24, *Congressional Quarterly* gave Mondale 41 percent of the delegates being counted to 22 percent for Hart. Thus while Hart had won ten of the major delegate selection contests, Mondale had won nine, and four had remained uncommitted, Hart trailed in delegates by a margin of nearly two to one.[35]

Hart never was able to get near Mondale in the delegate count. Delegate under-filings in Pennsylvania produced a similarly lopsided delegate bonanza for Mondale, who won 45 percent of the beauty contest vote and 134 delegates to only 16 for Gary Hart. Altogether the Mondale campaign estimated that Hart's failure to file delegates in the three early loophole primary states probably cost him 293 opportunities to compete for delegates, the equivalent to losing the entire state of New York.[36]

The final loophole primaries of 1984 were held in New Jersey, California, and Maryland. By then, the Hart campaign had the organizational resources and the expertise needed to file complete slates. This allowed Hart to win a decisive delegate victory in California: 205 delegates to only 72 for Mondale. This unexpected victory prevented Mondale from claiming the nomination on the day after the primary. And so, as we will see in chapter 6, on the morning after the 1984 California primary, the modern nominating system turned into an old-fashioned search for delegates.

The Changing Democratic Calculus

As the failed campaigns of Gary Hart and George Bush show, the importance of understanding the difference between the primary count and the delegate count and the different organizational requirements they sometimes impose has affected Republican and Democratic candidates alike. But the allocation rules in force have had an even more profound impact on the Democratic side by changing how much different states count.

As we saw in chapter 4, with the exception of the 1984 and 1988 nomination seasons, all modern nomination contests on the Democratic side since 1992 have used proportional allocation rules. As Ted Kennedy and later Hillary Clinton discovered, these rules have increased the power of smaller, more politically homogeneous states and decreased the power of the larger industrial states, the traditional battlegrounds of the general election and the traditional home of postwar Democratic liberalism. This development was predicted by two political scientists, James Lengle and Byron Shafer, in 1976. Looking back at the 1972 primary season, they calculated that proportional representation would destroy the original delegate advantages enjoyed by the largest states, thereby shifting the balance of power among states.[37] Without proportional representation, they argued:

> A state's "political value"—the delegate margin obtained by the candidate who finished first in its primary—would have corresponded exactly with the size of delegation authorized by national party rules. The key battlefields would have been generally northeastern, urban, industrial, minority-oriented, populous, and two-party competitive in November, while the lesser ones would have been southern and western more rural, agricultural, homogeneous, sparsely populated, and politically one party.[38]

Proportional representation shifted the key battlegrounds to precisely those southern and western, smaller, homogeneous, early-moving states. While most of the party regulars saw affirmative action rules as the biggest challenge to their influence in the party, the real culprit was proportional representation, which turned the nominating contest (on the Democratic side only) into a contest where all 435 congressional districts were equal

(75 percent of delegates are apportioned by congressional district) and where the ability to win a plurality or majority in a big state (the key to electoral college victory) was simply not as important.

In addition, proportional representation had a big impact on candidate momentum. Late wins in a proportional system are simply not as valuable as early wins, and respectable but narrow wins in a few big industrial states are not as useful as lopsided wins in many small states. Even if buyers' remorse sets in as the primary season progresses, it becomes very difficult to change the course set early on.

To understand this better it will help to look at the mathematics of allocating delegates to presidential candidates. Delegates are awarded on a district-by-district basis, and the results are rounded to prevent fractional votes. Because there tend to be few delegates in most districts, the results sometimes veer far afield from mathematical proportionality. They are usually closest to proportionality in districts with an odd number of delegates. (Apportionment of delegates to congressional districts is based on a formula that takes account of population and Democratic performance in a congressional district. The vast majority of congressional districts have four, five, or six delegates.) In a five-delegate district with Candidate A receiving 55 percent of the vote and Candidate B receiving 45 percent, the formula is as follows:

.55 x 5 = 2.75 (Candidate A)
.45 x 5 = 2.25 (Candidate B)

Candidate A receives 2 delegates and Candidate B receives 2 delegates, and the fifth delegate is awarded to the candidate with the highest remainder—in this case Candidate A. Thus Candidate A has 55 percent of the vote and 60 percent of the delegates, while Candidate B has 45 percent of the votes and 40 percent of the delegates.

In districts with an even number of delegates, the mathematical correspondence between votes and delegates is much weaker. Using the same example as above:

.55 x 4 = 2.20 (Candidate A)
.45 x 4 = 1.80 (Candidate B)

Candidates A and B each receive two delegates, although Candidate A has a 10 point margin of victory. In a four-delegate district with only two candidates breaking the threshold, the winner must win with somewhere over 62.5 percent of the vote to win three delegates out of four; in a six-delegate district the winner must win somewhere over 58.5 percent of the vote to win four out of six delegates. These are very difficult margins to come by in large heterogeneous states. Since the number of even- and odd-delegate districts is, as one would assume, about even, the system as a whole is better to second-place winners than it is to first-place winners unless the first-place winner is able to win by enormous margins.

KENNEDY VERSUS CARTER, 1980

Ted Kennedy was an early victim of this system. In 1980, states representing 94 percent of the delegates to the Democratic convention had moved to proportional systems, and the incumbent Jimmy Carter had stacked Super Tuesday with the states that made up his southern base. Carter's wins in the South were so lopsided as to give him an enormous delegate advantage early in the season. In many congressional districts in the South, Ted Kennedy failed to reach the fairly modest thresholds needed to secure even one delegate.

Collectively, the South gave Carter a victory margin of 608 delegates (see table 5-4). He won the Alabama and Georgia primaries with 81.58 percent and 88.04 percent of the vote respectively, and won the Florida primary with 60.68 percent.[39] In the early South Carolina and Mississippi caucuses Kennedy was completely shut out of delegates, as he was in the Georgia primary. Many of these lopsided wins occurred before the presidential contests moved north, and they contributed to a delegate count of 409 for Carter and 148 for Kennedy three days before the New York primary.

In contrast, when Kennedy finally got to compete in the big northern industrial states, much more favorable territory for him, the primarily proportional allocation rules worked against him. Kennedy's substantial victory in New York State (58.9 percent to 41.1 percent for Carter) resulted in a proportional split of the delegates: 164 (58 percent) for Kennedy to 118 (42 percent) for Carter. The victory did not add much to Kennedy's delegate count. Nor did Kennedy's win in Connecticut. By April 5, 1980, the gap between the Carter and Kennedy delegate counts had narrowed, but not to the point where anyone could say that Kennedy stood the better chance of being nominated as illustrated in table 5-5. Carter's ability to win lopsided victories in

Table 5-4. *The 1980 Presidential Nomination Race in the South*

State	Carter (%)	Carter delegates	Kennedy (%)	Kennedy delegates
Alabama	81.58	43	13.22	2
Arkansas	60.09	25	17.52	6
Florida	60.68	75	23.20	25
Georgia	88.04	62	8.4	0
Kentucky	66.92	45	22.95	5
Louisiana	55.74	50	22.52	1
Mississippi	Caucus state	32		0
North Carolina	70.09	66	17.73	3
Oklahoma	Caucus state	36		3
South Carolina	Caucus state	37		0
Tennessee	75.22	51	18.07	4
Texas	55.93	108	22.81	38
Virginia	Caucus state	59		5
West Virginia	62.18	21	37.82	10

Source: CQ Press, Voting & Elections Collection Search Form, retrieved November 2, 2008, from CQP Electronic Library website: http://library.cqpress.com.ezp-prod1.hul.harvard.edu/elections/searchform.php (access by subscription only).

Notes: Percentages in the caucus states represent the percentages of delegates elected who will elect the national convention delegates. Initial vote percentages for caucus states are not shown here since they change from level to level before the final selection of national convention delegates.

small southern states was, in a proportional system, turning out to be more important than Kennedy's ability to win victories in larger states.

As tables 5-4 and 5-5 illustrate, the effect of having uniform proportional rules in every state is to reward candidates who can win lopsided victories and punish candidates who win only modest victories. If a candidate can win lopsided victories in certain states (as Carter and later Obama did in the South) they are advantaged in the delegate race even over candidates who can win victories in larger, more complex states (as did Kennedy and later Clinton). Hence proportional representation does not operate without a bias in the system, although, as with so many things, whether that bias is good or bad is in the eye of the beholder. As we will see, Carter's wins in the South were so big as to award him significant delegate wins; Kennedy's victories in the North were more modest, and thus while they allowed him to close the delegate gap with Carter, he was never able to overtake Carter or even to come close to him in the delegate count.

Table 5-5. *Effect of Kennedy Victories in Major Industrial States on the 1980 Delegate Count*

Primaries won by Kennedy	Carter delegates[a]	Kennedy delegates[a]	Other
March 22	409 (73%)	148 (27%)	1
March 25, New York primary			
April 5	623 (62%)	381 (38%)	2
April 22, Pennsylvania primary			
April 26	911 (64%)	506 (35%)	14
May 24	1,286 (63%)	711 (35%)	41 (2%)
June 3, California and New Jersey primaries			
June 7	1,764 (60%)	1,138 (38%)	60 (2%)

Sources: All delegate counts are taken from that week's *Congressional Quarterly Weekly Report,* 1980.

a. In each row, the first number is the *cumulative number* of delegates won; the second number is the *cumulative percentage* of delegates won.

On April 22, for example, Kennedy's very slight victory over Carter in Pennsylvania netted him only three more delegates than Carter, while Carter's ability to win big in Missouri (which had less than half the delegate strength of Pennsylvania) brought him 74 percent of the delegates. Thus following Kennedy's win in the major industrial state of Pennsylvania, Carter increased his share of the then committed delegates. Even Kennedy's seven-point win in California and his 18 point win in New Jersey served to decrease Carter's share of the delegates by only 3 percent—hardly enough to convince the party and the press corps that Carter's hold on the nomination was slipping.

Winner-take-all systems in the big states that Kennedy won would have made an enormous difference in the delegate count and therefore in the way that the Kennedy candidacy was perceived. As table 5-6 shows, Kennedy would have pulled ahead of Carter after the Pennsylvania primary if the four large industrial states he won (excepting Massachusetts, his home state, and Michigan, a caucus state) had used a winner-take-all allocation system. Kennedy would have gone into the convention with 1,531 delegates to Carter's 1,371—a far cry from the 626-delegate lead that Carter actually accumulated, mostly early in the season.

In fact, in the weeks before the 1980 Pennsylvania primary it became clear that the contest would be extremely close. Therefore, seeking to maximize their resources and looking toward the delegate count, both campaigns made

Table 5-6. *Effect of Kennedy Victories on the 1980 Delegate Count if States Had Had Winner-Take-All Systems*

Primaries won by Kennedy	Carter delegates	Kennedy delegates
March 25, New York primary		
April 5	505	499
April 22, Pennsylvania primary	702	715
June 3, California and New Jersey primaries		
June 7	1,371	1,531

Source: Author's calculations.

the same seemingly odd decision: spend no resources in congressional districts with an even number of delegates. They left behind some very bewildered locals as the campaigns closed up shop in some areas to concentrate on districts with odd numbers of delegates, where a given vote margin was likely to translate into a larger delegate gain.[40] For instance, they would close up shop in districts that had four delegates and move campaign organizers to districts with five delegates. Twenty-eight years later, Barack Obama's delegate counters took the same approach.

Clinton versus Obama, 2008

The candidate who fell victim to Barack Obama's delegate-hunting team was, of course, New York senator Hillary Clinton, who in 2007 had been the favorite to win the Democratic nomination. As a two-term senator from New York and the wife of the only Democratic president to win two terms since Franklin Roosevelt, she brought with her a huge amount of experience and an enormous and presumably expert political operation. Nonetheless, from February 5, 2008, onward, Hillary Clinton's campaign found itself behind in the delegate count. Like Ted Kennedy, George Bush, and Gary Hart before her, she recovered politically in the second half of the season, but she could never catch up in the all-important race for delegates and reverse Obama's early momentum.

It is tempting to blame the failure of the Clinton juggernaut on message, and clearly it did not help that, in a year when the public was clamoring for change, Hillary Clinton ran as the "inevitable" candidate with the most experience. Yet an equally important factor was her campaign's lack of a delegate strategy. Ironically, in this case, experience may have worked against her.

Clinton's presidential experience had been in her husband's 1992 and 1996 campaigns. In the first one, Bill Clinton's major opponents had evaporated early in the season. In the second one, Clinton was president and ran unopposed. Thus the former president had never experienced the problem winning delegates posed by the Democrats' system. At a meeting following the New Hampshire primary, some members of the staff talked about the delegate fight, and citing examples similar to those cited above, they talked about how candidates can lose even if they win. According to others who were there, Bill Clinton's reaction was, "God damn it, we didn't have these rules when I was running in 1992!"[41]

Somewhat later, Harold Ickes, Clinton's senior adviser, tried to explain the delegate dynamic to the campaign in a memo written on February 3, 2008, and later published in the *Atlantic Monthly*. "Finally, as we have discussed," he wrote, "proportional representation cushions on the down side and limits the upside and affects even numbered delegate districts differently than odd numbered delegate districts."[42] But by then it was too late. The Clinton campaign, which had raised nearly $100 million in 2007 and opted out of the federal financing system, had spent all its money on Iowa, New Hampshire, and the big Super Tuesday primaries, which loomed in two days. It lacked the resources to organize on the ground and continue the fight for delegates, state after state. Meanwhile, the Obama campaign had planned carefully, not only identifying key congressional districts to target in the high-profile Super Tuesday primaries, but also focusing on caucus states and on the critical contests that followed Super Tuesday.

The inability to match Obama's efforts on and after February 5, 2008, cost Clinton dearly. As a result of her campaign's failure to budget and plan for caucus states, she lost a series of states by such large margins that Obama created a delegate lead that proved to be insurmountable under the party's proportional allocation rules. Table 5-7 tells the story. In the two weeks after Super Tuesday, Obama picked up 244 delegates to 146 for Clinton.

Later in the season, Clinton scored wins in several big northern industrial states, but those victories did not result in enough delegates to reverse the tide. Beginning with her substantial victory in the Ohio primary (March 4), the Clinton campaign began to argue the importance of being able to win large industrial states. Yet absent winner-take-all rules, big states were no more important that a series of small states.

Table 5-7. *February 9–19, 2008, Establishes Obama's Delegate Lead*

Date	State[a]	Obama vote (%)	Obama delegates won	Clinton vote (%)	Clinton delegates won
Feb. 9, 2008	Louisiana	57	34	36	22
Feb. 9, 2008	*Nebraska*	68	16	32	8
Feb. 9, 2008	*Washington*	68	53	31	25
Feb. 10, 2008	*Maine*	59	15	40	9
Feb. 12, 2008	District of Columbia	76	11	24	4
Feb. 12, 2008	Maryland	61	42	36	28
Feb. 12, 2008	Virginia	64	54	35	29
Feb. 19, 2008	*Hawaii*	76	14	24	6
Feb. 19, 2008	Wisconsin	58	42	41	32
Total delegates			281		163

Source: Elections and Politics news from CNN.com at www.cnn.com/ELECTION/2008/primaries/results/state/#val=WI [April 1, 2009].

a. States in italics are caucus states.

As table 5-8 illustrates, the Clinton campaign would have had a very different nomination season under winner-take-all rules. The first column shows that Barack Obama came out of the February 5, 2008, primaries with a modest lead in delegates. But two weeks later he had nearly quadrupled his delegate lead. After that, the lead decreased somewhat, but it is clear that Obama had won the nomination by February 19, when he had established a firm delegate lead. The second column recalculates the 2008 delegate race, assuming that all the states are winner-take-all. Had that been the case, Hillary Clinton's victories in big states like California and New Jersey would have given her a 482-delegate lead over Obama on Super Tuesday.

Another, related way to look at the 2008 nomination race is to realize that Obama won every caucus state but one. Had Hillary Clinton mounted effective campaigns in caucus states she could have more or less split the delegates with Obama. However, by ignoring the early organizational and financial moves necessary to win a caucus state, the Clinton campaign lost them by margins large enough to result in large delegate wins for Obama. Obama's lopsided caucus wins, although in small states, did for him what Jimmy Carter's lopsided wins in southern states did for him in 1980: establish a delegate lead that could not be overcome, even by a candidate who went on to win later in larger industrial states. As table 5-9 illustrates, Obama's average

Table 5-8. *Obama-Clinton Pledged Delegate Race under Two Scenarios: Proportional Rule (as Calculated by the AP) and Winner-Take-All*

Actual delegate race, proportional rules			Delegate race assuming winner-take-all		
Date of contest (primary or caucus) awarding delegates	Obama	Clinton	Date of contest (primary or caucus) awarding delegates	Obama	Clinton
Jan. 3, 2008	28	14	Jan. 3	45	0
Jan. 8	41	23	Jan. 8	45	22
Jan. 15	71	58	Jan. 15	45	86
Jan. 19	85	69	Jan. 19	45	111
Jan. 26	118	81	Jan. 26	90	111
Jan. 29	156	133	Jan. 29	90	204
Feb. 5	1,009	967	Feb. 5	750	1,232
Feb. 9	1,113	1,024	Feb. 9	911	1,232
Feb. 10	1,128	1,033	Feb. 10	935	1,232
Feb. 12	1,237	1,092	Feb. 12	1,103	1,232
Feb. 19	1,293	1,130	Feb. 19	1,197	1,232
Mar. 4	1,476	1,317	Mar. 4	1,279	1,520
Mar. 8	1,483	1,322	Mar. 8	1,291	1,520
Mar. 11	1,503	1,335	Mar. 11	1,324	1,520
Apr. 22	1,576	1,420	Apr. 22	1,324	1,678
May 3	1,578	1,422	May 3	1,328	1,678
May 6	1,679	1,508	May 6	1,443	1,750
May 13	1,693	1,536	May 13	1,443	1,778
May 20	1,732	1,586	May 20	1,495	1,829
June 1	1,749	1,624	June 1	1,495	1,884
June 3	1,764	1,640	June 3	1,511	1,899

Sources: AP delegate tracker at: http://hosted.ap.org/specials/interactives/campaign_plus/delegate_tracker/delegate_tracker.swf [April 28, 2009]; *New York Times* delegate count at: http://politics.nytimes.com/election-guide/2008/results/delegates/index.html [April 28, 2009].

Notes: The DNC penalized Michigan for holding an early primary by awarding delegates half a vote each at the national convention. Delegate counts reflect the total number of votes at the convention; 128 pledged delegates and 29 unpledged delegates would attend the convention. Edwards and Obama withdrew their names from the Democratic ballot because Michigan broke party rules. On May 31, the DNC awarded Clinton 69 pledged delegates, or 34.5 pledged votes, and Obama 59 pledged delegates, or 29.5 pledged votes.

The DNC penalized Florida Democrats for holding an early primary by awarding delegates half a vote each at the national convention. Delegate counts reflect the total number of votes at the convention; 185 pledged delegates and 26 unpledged delegates would attend the convention. 52.5 pledged votes were allocated to Obama, 38.5 to Clinton, and 1.5 to Edwards.

Texas delegates include 126 delegates allocated by the primary and 67 delegates allocated by the caucus. Under the winner-take-all scenario, Clinton was allocated 126 delegates as the primary winner and Obama 67 delegates as the caucus winner.

Table 5-9. *Obama's Caucus Advantage, 2008*

Caucus state	Obama delegate advantage	Primary state	Obama delegate advantage
		Alabama	+2
Alaska	+7		
		Arizona	−6
		Arkansas	−15
		California	−38
Colorado	+17		
		Connecticut	+4
		Delaware	+3
		D.C.	+7
		Florida[a]	
		Georgia	+35
Hawaii	+8		
Idaho	+12		
		Illinois	+55
		Indiana	−4
Iowa	+13		
Kansas	+14		
		Kentucky	−23
		Louisiana	+12
Maine	+6		
		Maryland	+14
		Massachusetts	−17
		Michigan[a]	
Minnesota	+24		
		Mississippi	+7
Missouri	0		
		Montana	+2
Nebraska	+8		
Nevada	+3		
		New Hampshire	+3
		New Jersey	−11
		New Mexico	−2
		New York	−46
North Carolina	+19		
North Dakota	+3		
		Ohio	−9
		Oklahoma	−10
		Oregon	+10

Caucus state	Obama delegate advantage	Primary state	Obama delegate advantage
		Pennsylvania	−12
		Rhode Island	−5
		South Carolina	+21
		South Dakota	−3
		Tennessee	−12
		Texas	−4
		Utah	+5
		Vermont	+3
		Virginia	+25
Washington	+28		
		West Virginia	−12
		Wisconsin	+10
Wyoming	+2		
Average Obama delegate advantage in caucuses			+10.93
Average Obama delegate disadvantage in primaries			−0.32

Source: Elections and Politics news from CNN at www.cnn.com/ELECTION/2008/primaries/results/state/#val [April 28, 2009].

a. Since the status of delegates from Florida and Michigan was not determined until May 31, 2008, the delegate counts for most of the primary season did not include delegates won in either state.

delegate advantage over Clinton in caucus states was 10.93, while his average disadvantage in primary states was –0.32.

Like Mondale before her, Clinton made extensive use of superdelegates to compensate for her poor showing in actual pledged delegates. But unlike in 1984, when superdelegates were more or less folded into the overall delegate count without provoking much controversy, in 2008 the Obama campaign made the superdelegates an issue, arguing that they should reflect the will of the voters. The press kept a separate count of superdelegates, thereby exposing the true extent of Hillary's deficit in pledged delegates. And as the campaign went on and Clinton failed to reverse Obama's delegate lead, the superdelegates began to move to Obama. On May 11, 2008, Obama took the lead in the superdelegate count. Hillary Clinton continued to fight until the end of the primary season and conceded defeat in a speech in Washington, D.C., on June 7, 2008.

Conclusion

It would be foolish to build an explanation of any nomination contest on the structure of the underlying allocation system alone, just as it would be foolish to attribute the outcomes solely to television advertising or lack of it, the dominance of certain issues, or the looks of the candidate. Many factors converge to make a winner. Ted Kennedy, George H. W. Bush, Gary Hart, Rudy Giuliani, and Hillary Clinton all had other significant problems and strong opponents.

Nonetheless, it is clear that a candidate's ability to understand and use the delegate allocation rules to his or her advantage plays a crucial part in defining the nature of the nomination contest. Organizational prowess combined with a keen understanding of the system—especially the importance of superdelegates—helped Walter Mondale turn back a strong challenge from Gary Hart. The Obama campaign understood the importance of caucus states and calibrated their investments by the delegate opportunities offered in different congressional districts. Combined with the candidate's gifts as a communicator, this strategy helped Barack Obama take a commanding lead. Hillary Clinton fought back in a tough campaign, but the organizational weakness of her campaign in caucus states, and the Democratic Party's proportional allocation rules, combined with the closeness of the contest, made it impossible for her to close the delegate gap.

In the post-reform system, the delegate count has become an easy summary measure of a candidate's success or failure. It therefore plays a key role in creating and sustaining momentum in the nomination process. As the above examples show, allocation rules have profound effects on winning and losing in the delegate count, especially when combined with the sequential nature of the modern nomination process. It is more important to win in a state with winner-take-all or plurality rules than to win in a state with proportional rules. The delegate count and the rules that create it dominate the strategic rhythms of the modern nomination season. But that season still ends with a nominating convention—the topic of the next chapter.

6

DO CONVENTIONS
MATTER ANYMORE?

*Superdelegates, the Robot Rule, and
the Modern Nominating Convention*

It happens like clockwork. Every four years in the weeks before the Democratic and Republican conventions the press announces that it will cover an even smaller portion of the convention proceedings than it did four years earlier. The political parties complain. The press responds that the prime-time segment is just a show, that the convention is too choreographed, that there is no news. The pundits wonder if the nominating convention is dead. Increasingly the public wonders why we even have conventions in the first place.

This was not always the case. Conventions used to be where all the behind-the-scenes machinations of the previous year came together in a way the public could see. In the pre-reform era, each party actually chose its nominee at the convention. Costas Panagopoulos provides a glimpse of this bygone time:

> For over a century, nominating conventions were lively and animated events, settings for intense candidate and policy debates that frequently erupted in volatility and excitement. At the 1912 Democratic national convention in Baltimore, Maryland, for example, it took 46 ballots for Woodrow Wilson's supporters to break a deadlock and wrestle the nomination away from fellow contenders U.S. House Speaker Champ Clarke of Missouri, Representative Oscar Underwood of Alabama, and Governor Judson Harmon of Ohio. Twelve years later, after nine days

of stalemate, delegates at the Democratic convention in New York voted 103 times before Wall Street lawyer John W. Davis clinched the nomination as a compromise candidate between New York Governor Alfred E. Smith and Wilson's Treasury Secretary William G. McAdoo. That was the hey-day of nominating conventions, when fat cats in smoke-filled rooms did battle over contenders and the nomination was not a foregone conclusion before the convention even began.[1]

The demise of the convention as a decisionmaking body was the natural and inevitable outgrowth of a nomination system that had become, to use James Ceaser's term, a plebiscitary system.[2] Three developments in particular have played an important role in bringing about this transformation. First, convention delegates have become increasingly candidate-focused, rather than party-focused. Second, aside from superdelegates, uncommitted or unaffiliated delegates have virtually disappeared. And third, the plebiscitary nature of the modern nominating process has rendered the superdelegates themselves more or less irrelevant to the outcome.

Three conventions have bucked these trends and brought back some of the drama of the past: the 1972 Democratic convention, the 1976 Republican convention, and the 1980 Democratic convention. By and large, however, the outcome of the modern convention is known months ahead, and surprises are few and far between.

Candidate Right of Approval

Like many Democratic reforms, the fact that delegates owe their loyalty to candidates, not the party, can be attributed in part to the 1972 candidacy of segregationist George Wallace. That year, the former Alabama governor rode a tide of anti-busing sentiment to win the Michigan primary. Buoyed by an influx of Republican and independent voters who had nowhere else to express their anger (Richard Nixon was running unopposed for reelection), Wallace swept the Democratic primary, winning more than a million votes. But in some congressional districts, such as Michigan's 17th (then a liberal, Jewish enclave north of Detroit), there were no Wallace delegates on the ballot. When Wallace became entitled to delegates, McGovern supporters happily took their spots by packing the local caucuses. But the sweep of the state had also put some Wallace supporters in key positions in the party and when, at the state convention, it was discovered that McGovern supporters were masquerading as Wallace supporters, objections were raised.[3]

By that time, Wallace, who had been shot in an assassination attempt the day before the Maryland primary, had withdrawn from the Democratic race for the nomination. So the issue was dropped. But the ultimate result was a set of rules granting presidential candidates "candidate right of approval." Instituted in 1973 by the Mikulski Commission, these rules allowed each presidential candidate to approve every delegate seeking to run for election in his or her name. Initially presidential candidates were allowed to approve only one person for each delegate slot, leaving party loyalists with no role in the selection of convention delegates. In 1979 the Winograd Commission changed the rules by requiring presidential candidates to approve no fewer than three people for each slot. Nonetheless, the upshot was the same. As David Price explains in *Bringing Back the Parties,* these new rules "reflected a thoroughgoing shift away from any notion of the convention as a representative or deliberative body and toward a plebiscitary view: delegates were faithfully to reflect the array of preferences in the Democratic electorate as it existed as the moment of their selection."[4]

And Nelson Polsby observed: "What has changed is that candidates have gained and state party leaders have lost the right to designate who the delegates shall be."[5] This change, not surprisingly, altered the way delegates saw their role. Barbara Farah surveyed convention delegates from three post-reform-era conventions (1972, 1976, and 1980) and found that all delegates, with the exception of the 1972 Republican delegates, saw their role as representing candidate over party. Among delegates from primary states, this view was held by margins of better than two to one. The effects were not as strong for Republican delegates, who are not subject to candidate approval, but they were present there as well.[6]

Writing about their survey of delegates to the 1980 Democratic convention, Martin Plissner and Warren Mitofsky of CBS summarized the role of the post-reform delegate as follows:

As the role of binding primaries and, in the Democratic party, candidate control over the choice of delegates grew, the actual identity of the person who goes to the convention to cast a vote has become progressively less important. The bitterness of this year's Democratic Convention fight over the rule inescapably binding nearly all the delegates [to vote for the presidential candidate in whose name they were elected] may lead to some loosening of that particular rule. But the trend in Democratic Party practice toward making the delegate essentially a messenger from the primary and caucus participants is probably irreversible.[7]

This judgment has yet to be challenged, even though the party apparatus has succeeded over the years in reinserting itself into the delegate selection process. In large part this is due to the mechanics of the process. In contrast to the early post-reform period, the majority of states now choose their actual convention delegates in congressional district meetings *after* the presidential primary.[8] Thus by the time actual delegates are elected, the campaigns have usually moved on to the next state. As a result, candidates sometimes fail to exercise candidate right of approval altogether. If they do leave someone in the state with the authority to exercise approval rights, that person often has to negotiate with local party notables over who should have the delegate slots. The rule allowing presidential candidates to approve no fewer than three delegate candidates per slot sometimes allowed the locals to "game" the candidates. In one state in 2008, the local party people slated three names per slot for a candidate to approve and then had two of them conveniently "drop out" before the actual election—guaranteeing that the party's favorites would win the slots.[9]

Owing to such maneuvering, modern nominating conventions are still largely composed of local party notables and others who have held party office. John S. Jackson's studies of convention delegates show that, in 1968, 62 percent of the convention delegates had 10 or more years of party service behind them. That number drops to 54 percent in 1976, but a large portion of this drop can probably be accounted for by the fact that much of the party establishment that year guessed wrong when picking a presidential hopeful.

Table 6-1 shows the number of delegates who hold party office and the number of delegates who hold elected office in both the Democratic and Republican conventions wherever data are available. Party officials don't really disappear from the post-reform nominating convention, and over

Table 6-1. *Delegates Who Held Party Office or Elected Office,*
by Convention Year, 1968–2008
Percent

Year	Party office, Democrats	Party office, Republicans	Elected office, Democrats	Elected office, Republicans
1968				
1972	72			
1976	63			
1980		59		
1984	42	46	29	No data
1988	43	49	26	No data
1992	45	No data	24	No data
1996	58	61	No data	No data
2000	55	58	28	No data
2004	53	65	29	No data
2008	51	57	30	No data

Sources: John S. Jackson III, "A Decade of Reform: The Perspective of the Democratic Delegates," paper presented at the Annual Meeting of the American Political Science Association, August 31–September 3, 1979.

NYT/CBS Poll, "2008 Democratic National Convention Delegate Survey," for the August 25, 2008, issue, available at: http://graphics8.nytimes.com/packages/pdf/politics/demdel20080824.pdf [April 1, 2009].

NYT/CBS Poll, "2008 Republican Delegates: Who Are They?" for release August 31, 2008, at: www.cbsnews.com/htdocs/pdf/RNCDelegates_who_are_they.pdf [April 1, 2009].

time their numbers increase somewhat. However, they are no longer the free actors they were in the pre-reform era, and they no longer see their role in the same way.

Table 6-2 contains data on another measure of experience at the national conventions, and that is whether delegates are first-time convention delegates. As table 6-2 indicates, in 1968, the last year of the old-fashioned conventions, 67 percent of the delegates were attending their first convention. As the system became one where candidates instead of parties controlled delegates, we would expect that number to go up—and it does. In four out of the five presidential cycles in the 1970s and 1980s, more than three-quarters of the delegates to the Democratic Convention were attending their first convention. On the Republican side, this is true in three of the five conventions. By the 1990s, however, barely more than half of the delegates in both parties were first-timers! This shift coincides with the increasing use of post-primary

Table 6-2. *Percentage of Convention Delegates Attending Their First Convention, 1968–2008*

Year	Democrats	Republicans
1968	67	66
1972 (first post-reform convention)	83	78
1976	80	78
1980	87	84
1984	78	69
1988	65	68
1992	62	No data
1996	61	56
2000	51	54
2004	57	55
2008	57	58

Source: Harold W. Stanley and Richard G. Niemi, *Vital Statistics on American Politics 2007–2008,* (Washington: Congressional Quarterly Press, 2009) table 1-29: "Profile of National Convention Delegates, 1968–2000," p. 80. Data for 2008 come from the NYT/CBS Poll, "2008 Democratic National Convention Delegate Survey," for the August 25, 2008, issue, available at http://graphics8. nytimes.com/packages/pdf/politics/demdel20080824.pdf [April 1, 2009].

caucuses to select delegates and indicates that, far from being cut out of the new system, party regulars simply found a way back in.

Nonetheless, modern convention delegates by and large do not see their role as exercising their own independent judgment. State statutes and party rules both lend support to this attitude. Many state statutes explicitly require that delegates to both conventions vote to reflect the will of the primary voters on the first ballot at least. Similarly, on the Democratic side, Rule 11(H) of the Democratic Party's Delegate Selection Rules notes that delegates who are pledged to a presidential candidate "shall in all good conscience reflect the sentiments of those who elected them." In contrast to the earlier version of the "robot rule," which required that delegates who did not vote for the candidate to whom they were pledged be pulled off the convention floor and replaced by a loyal delegate, this language, which was adopted in 1982, returned some element of individual judgment to the delegates. Nonetheless, post-reform-era delegates have shown nearly 100 percent loyalty to presidential candidates, and the delegate count at the end of the primaries has accurately predicted the first ballot outcome at the convention in every single one of the post-reform-era nominating conventions.

Table 6-3. *Percentage of Uncommitted and Unaffiliated Delegates at Pre-Reform and Post-Reform Conventions at the End of the Primary Season, 1952–2008*

Year and party	Uncommitted	Favorite son	Total
1952 Democratic	33	18	51
1952 Republican	18	10	28
1956 Democratic	33	17	51
1960 Democratic	28	18	47
1964 Republican	24	11	35
1968 Democratic	n.a.	n.a.	n.a.
1968 Republican	n.a.	n.a.	n.a.
1972 Democratic	16	2	18
1976 Democratic	17	3	20
1976 Republican	8	0	8
1980 Democratic	3	0	3
1980 Republican	8	0	8
1984 Democratic	6	1	7
1988 Democratic	11	0	11
1988 Republican	11	0	11
1992 Democratic	12	0	12
1992 Republican	1	0	1
1996 Republican	7	0	7
2000 Democratic	3	0	3
2000 Republican	2	0	2
2004 Democratic	0	0	0
2008 Republican	0	0	0
2008 Democratic	0	0	0

Source: Data for 1952–2000 taken from William G. Mayer and Andrew E. Busch, *The Frontloading Problem in Presidential Nominations*, table 3.6: "Uncommitted and Favorite Son Delegates in Contested Nomination Races, 1952–2000." Data for 2004 and 2008 from http://use-lectionatlas.org/RESULTS/index.html [April 2, 2009].

The Disappearance of Uncommitted Delegates

To further understand why modern nominating conventions are so dull, we need to look beyond the candidate-focus of the delegates: namely, to the fact that convention delegates elected to represent "uncommitted" or a favorite-son candidate have all but disappeared. Table 6-3 shows the number of uncommitted and favorite-son delegates in the pre- and post-reform eras.

Beginning in the 1970s, favorite-son candidates, usually a governor or senator who runs only in one state for the sole purpose of controlling its convention delegation, virtually disappeared. There is nothing in the rules themselves that prohibits a statewide figure from putting his or her name on the ballot and seeking delegates. But politicians don't do it anymore, mostly because they risk embarrassment. George Wallace beat Senator Terry Sanford in Sanford's home state of North Carolina in 1976, and Carter beat Senator Lloyd Bentsen in Bentsen's home state of Texas that year as well. The risk for the local politician is great, and the gain is small, since most post-reform nominees are decided well before the convention, thus providing little opportunity for brokering.

The second reason for the disappearance of favorite-son candidates is structural. As states reformed their election laws to conduct presidential primaries, many of them gave the secretary of state authority to place all "nationally recognized" candidates for president on the ballot automatically. (This ballot provision explains why all the Democratic candidates for president were on the Florida ballot in 2008, even though Florida had been stripped of its delegates by the DNC.) Some state statutes specify that candidates must have qualified for federal matching funds in order to be placed on the ballot, and some do not. Most state statutes also allow a candidate to get on the ballot by circulating petitions and submitting them to the secretary of state, a task that made the somewhat quixotic business of running as a favorite son even more difficult.

Like favorite-son delegates, uncommitted delegates have tended to disappear in the post-reform era, largely because of changes in the rules that govern the nominating process. The disappearance of direct-election-of-delegate primaries and loophole primaries, which allowed local notables to be chosen as delegates regardless of the voters' presidential preferences, made it impossible, for Democrats at least, to go to the convention without pledging their support to a candidate. But most important, voters are simply not very attracted to "Mr. Uncommitted." With thresholds for winning delegates averaging 15 percent over the post-reform period, it is easy to see why uncommitted delegates cannot get elected in primary states: the uncommitted option rarely ever gets enough votes to be awarded even one delegate.

In the post-reform era, such uncommitted delegates as there are tend to come almost solely from caucus states. In 1976, for example, the uncommitted preference won 34 percent of the vote in caucus states but only 8 percent of the vote in primary states.[10] In caucus states where turnout is low and the presidential candidates are not mounting strong campaigns, a strong political figure or a strong interest group can organize uncommitted caucuses and win uncommitted delegates. Governor Martha Layne Collins of Kentucky, Governor George Ariyoshi of Hawaii, and Governor Richard Reilly of South Carolina all managed to elect fairly large numbers of uncommitted delegates to the Democratic Convention in 1984, principally because their states were not seriously contested by the major national candidates.

If we combine the number of uncommitted delegates and the number of favorite-son delegates, we can create a category of "unaffiliated delegates"—in other words, delegates who still had no known presidential preference at the end of the primary season. In the pre-reform conventions represented in table 6-3, 42 percent of the delegates, on average, fell into this category. In the post-reform years this number drops to 8 percent.

The existence of large numbers of unaffiliated delegates in the pre-reform era added a dimension of suspense to the convention. Candidates did their best to build the suspense, as the *New York Times* reported in 1952: "Each of the leading candidates has delegates in reserve who will not vote for him at the outset of the balloting. That is the set strategy at political conventions."[11] The idea was to create momentum or a bandwagon inside the convention hall. Today, with no one free to start the bandwagon moving in another direction, nominating conventions have little option but to reinforce the verdict delivered by the public portion of the process—even when the party could plausibly be better served by a candidate with few apparent followers inside the convention hall.

Superdelegates

The superdelegate category was created in part to counter the effect of binding public primaries, candidate right of approval, and the disappearance of unaffiliated delegates—a combination that has sapped the modern nominating convention of its ability to deliberate and perhaps save the party from a disastrous general election choice. The importance of deliberation was on the minds of many in the aftermath of the 1980 election, in which President Carter was beaten decisively by Ronald Reagan. The contested 1980 Democratic Convention had had a traumatic impact on the party, as had the fact that in the decade since the reform rules had taken effect the Democrats had nominated one sure-fire loser—McGovern—and one winner who was viewed at the time as a failed president—Jimmy Carter.

As the Hunt Commission met to reconsider the party's nominating rules, congressional Democrats, stung by their lack of impact on the 1980 process, banded together to ask that the House Democratic caucus be allowed to elect two-thirds of its members as uncommitted voting delegates to the 1984 Democratic National Convention. Led by Representative Gillis Long, chairman of the House Democratic Caucus, the representatives asserted that they had a special role to play in selecting the party's nominee and platform. In his testimony before the Hunt Commission, Long put the views of the Democratic Caucus as follows: "We in the House, as the last vestige of Democratic control at the national level, believe we have a special responsibility to develop new innovative approaches that respond to our party's constituencies."[12]

He found a receptive audience in commission chair Jim Hunt, who saw the inclusion of more elected officials in the nominating process as a top priority. Reflecting the sense of helplessness with which many elected officials had watched the events of the 1980 nomination season, Hunt said:

> We must also give our convention more flexibility to respond to changing circumstances and, in cases where the voters' mandate is less than clear, to make a reasoned choice. One step in this direction would be to loosen the much-disputed "binding" rule (11H) as it applies to all delegates [a step the commission did take]. An equally important step would be to permit a substantial number of party leader and elected official delegates to be selected without requiring a prior declaration of preference. We would then return a measure of decision-making power and discretion to the organized party and increase the incentive it has to offer elected officials for serious involvement.[13]

Hunt was joined by the AFL-CIO and the Democratic State Chairs Association in calling for 30 percent of the 1984 convention to be composed of uncommitted delegates drawn from the ranks of party leaders and elected officials. They argued that only a large number of unbound delegates—specifically, party leaders and elected officials—could return a modicum of flexibility or deliberativeness to the post-reform conventions. Ten years after the McGovern-Fraser reforms had dealt the regular party out of the nomination process, the regulars wanted back in.

Opposition to the proposal was voiced by supporters of Senator Ted Kennedy and by feminist groups. Kennedy's supporters feared, with good reason, that this large new bloc of delegates would favor his chief rival, former vice president Walter Mondale (whose campaign embraced the plan for the same reason). Feminists offered a more principled argument. Speaking on their behalf, Technical Advisory Committee member Susan Estrich of Massachusetts argued that the superdelegates would be drawn from Congress, the governors, and the state chairs, groups that were overwhelmingly white and male. Simply having equal numbers of women and men at the convention, argued Estrich, would not solve the problem of "equal power." The male superdelegates, because of their greater flexibility in the choice of a nominee, would have greater power than the female delegates who were committed to presidential candidates—hence the term "super" delegates.[14]

The issue put Representative Geraldine Ferraro in a tight spot, for she was both a loyal member of the House Democratic Caucus and a leading feminist. So Ferraro and DNC Chairman Charles Mannatt, also a supporter of the House proposal, began tense negotiations between Gillis Long and the feminist community. Opponents of the idea wanted elected officials elected by each state's Central Committee, where they would be subject to the results of the primary or caucus in the state. The compromise, "the Ferrarro plan," reduced the number of unpledged delegates to 566, or a total of 14.1 percent of the convention, but it left selection of the congressional delegates in the hands of the House and Senate as opposed to the State Central Committees.[15] The 14 percent number was far short of the original proposal that unpledged delegates make up 30 percent of the convention. However, if the number had been much larger, it would have been impossible in practice to meet the equal division requirements in the rules, and the politics of party reform still required preservation of the party's quota system for women. On the other hand, the compromise did preserve the freedom of members of Congress to endorse whomever they pleased—or not—without regard for the outcome of the primary or caucus results in their state, leaving them with some of the old-fashioned discretionary power that had been common in the pre-reform era.

Thus the Hunt Commission managed to do what prior commissions had felt was practically impossible: to include a large number of elected officials and preserve the party's requirement that delegations be equally divided between men and women. The cost was borne by white male party activists in the states, whose chances of being elected as at-large delegates virtually disappeared as the 1984 rules were implemented.[16] The at-large part of each delegation had to be disproportionately composed of women and minorities in order to achieve the party's affirmative action goals.

The category of superdelegates was expanded in subsequent years to nearly 800 elected officials including all members of the Democratic National Committee. Meanwhile, the Republican National Committee voted its members superdelegate status following the same logic as the Democrats: the people who oversee the delegate selection process, they argued, should be at the convention but should not be required to choose a candidate in advance. But for those who hoped that the superdelegates would return power to the convention and to the regular party, the history of superdelegates has been a disappointment. Superdelegates have played a role in only two of the nine post-reform conventions, and in neither one did they act contrary to the will of the voters as expressed in the primaries.

Superdelegates and the Mondale Campaign

In 1984, the Mondale campaign had worked hard to make the election of superdelegates "the first primary"—an achievement, as we have seen, that helped Mondale rebound from his unexpected loss to Gary Hart in New Hampshire. Nonetheless, at the end of the primary season, Hart's unexpectedly large victory in California left Mondale short of the number of delegates he needed to clinch the nomination. The campaign was in trouble. Earlier, James Johnson, Mondale's campaign manager had announced: "On the fourth of June, Mondale will have 1,750 delegates, and on the sixth of June he will have more than 1,967 [a majority] and we'll be the nominee."[17] Mondale himself had claimed that he would be the nominee by noon on June 5, the day after the California primary.

When it became clear that Mondale was losing to Hart in California by pretty substantial margins, the Mondale campaign had to find enough delegates to close the gap by the candidate's self-proclaimed deadline. The laborious work of doing the political research that would convince elected officials and party leaders to support Mondale fell to the delegate selection team in Washington, which I headed with the assistance of Tad Devine. On the morning after the California primary we passed the information we gathered on to a not-too-happy Walter Mondale, who sat in his hotel suite in California chomping on a cigar as he dialed. For several frantic hours, Mondale, his wife, Joan, and senior staff members worked the phones. The calls went out to uncommitted delegates, the congressional superdelegates, and delegates committed to candidates who had dropped out of the race months earlier. Throughout this process, Mondale never let it be known that he was in trouble. As recalled by Marty Kaplan, Mondale's chief speech-writer, and recounted by Jack Germond and Jules Witcover, "He never played that card directly, asking delegates to save his skin. Rather, he let them think he had the magic number and was appealing to them in the name of party unity."[18] Whenever a delegate committed, his or her name was passed back to our team in Washington, and we would immediately call David Lawsky, the delegate tracker for UPI, who would in turn call the delegate and confirm that the person was indeed publicly committed to Mondale.

The process was reminiscent of the delegate selection process in the pre-reform system, only carried out at warp speed. It was a process ideally suited to a candidate like Mondale, the quintessential insider. Gary Hart, the ideal post-reform candidate, made virtually no effort to court the superdelegates, leaving that task to his supporters in each state. This strategy was doomed to fail, both because it was decentralized and because Hart supporters tended to be new to state party politics.

Thus, for a brief moment in 1984, what had been stage two of the old-fashioned nomination process reappeared. On May 9, 1984, the internal Mondale campaign delegate count showed Mondale with 1,378.5 pledged delegates, or delegates won pursuant to the results in primaries and caucuses, and 171 superdelegates. By May 23, Mondale could claim 185 superdelegates; by June 4, he had 277 superdelegates in his camp; and by June 5, the day of the California primary, 323 superdelegates were for Mondale.[19] At noon on June 6, 1984, the day after the California primary, Mondale went downstairs to a hotel ballroom and in front of a sign that read 11:59, claimed the nomination. Almost immediately, the UPI delegate count, the count that had gained the most credibility during the nomination season, reported that Mondale indeed had the 1,967 delegates needed to nominate. Reporters and other insiders reveled in the details of the last-minute delegate operation. But as far as the rest of America was concerned, Mondale had won the nomination with the last primaries. By timing the conversion of the superdelegates to coincide with the end of the public portion of the process, the campaign managed to obscure the fact that Mondale had been put over the top by delegates who not been elected during the primary season.

In the end, Mondale won the allegiance of the majority of the superdelegates in every one of the states where he lost the primary or first-tier caucus (see table 6-4). These results were especially galling to workers in the Hart campaign, who saw the majority of elected officials in states where Hart had won a significant victory over Mondale go to Mondale. Although it was threatened that these discrepancies between the popular vote and the preferences of the superdelegates would become the basis for challenges at the convention, the challenges never appeared, probably because even had the superdelegates been subtracted from the final tally, Hart would have been unable to overcome Mondale's lead.

Hillary Clinton and the Superdelegates

In the years between 1984 and 2008, superdelegates were rarely mentioned. There were several reasons for this silence. By 1988, Gary Hart was the rising star of the Democratic Party and the front-runner for the 1988 nomination. Hart now stood to win a substantial number of superdelegates and had little incentive to alter the system. Furthermore, nomination contests from 1988 through 2004 on the Democratic side were wrapped up relatively early in the season, and in none of those years would the superdelegates' votes have been sufficient to change the outcome of the primaries and caucuses.

Only Jesse Jackson complained about the superdelegates, and he complained about them almost as much as he complained about the party's allocation rules. However, on this issue Jackson was ignored. Although the 1988 convention specifically moved that the number of superdelegates be decreased, the 1990 Rules Committee simply ignored this part of its mandate. In both 1988 and 1992, the Democrats elected 80 percent of the House and Senate Democratic caucuses as delegates to the convention, in addition to all the DNC members and other "distinguished leaders." By 2008 there

Table 6-4. *Presidential Preferences of Unpledged Superdelegates in Selected States Where Hart Won and Mondale Lost the Primary or First-Tier Caucus, 1984*

State	Hart	Mondale	Jackson	Uncommitted
Alaska	0	3	0	1
Arizona	2	4	0	1
California	13	19	1	6
Connecticut	3	5	0	0
Florida	0	14	0	6
Indiana	1	4	3	3
Louisiana[a]	2	4	0	6
Maine	1	2	0	2
Massachusetts	2	12	1	1
Nebraska	0	2	1	1
Nevada	2	3	0	0
New Hampshire	1	2	0	1
New Mexico	1	3	0	1
North Dakota	0	4	0	0

Sources: Richard M. Scammon and Alice V. McGillivray, eds., *America Votes: A Handbook of Contemporary American Election Statistics* (Washington: Congressional Quarterly, 1985); "Unpledged Delegates: Possible Challenges," internal Mondale campaign memo, June 21, 1984, author's files.

a. Jesse Jackson won the Louisiana primary.

were no more House or Senate caucuses to elect delegates. All Democratic senators, representatives, governors, members of the Democratic National Committee, and "distinguished leaders" such as former presidents and former party chairmen had become automatic delegates.

No one cared about the superdelegates until the 2008 primary election race. Unlike Mondale in 1984, Hillary Clinton did not have the advantage of treating the selection of superdelegates as the first primary. Since all Democratic members of Congress were now delegates, their selection did not constitute a discrete event—the way it had in 1984. She also no longer had the advantage of loophole primaries in some of the northern industrial states where she was strong (as discussed in chapter 5). Thus by the middle of February 2008, when 70 percent of the delegates needed for the nomination had been awarded to one or the other candidate, it became apparent that the distance between Obama and Clinton in the delegate count was razor thin. It didn't take long for the campaigns and the press to realize that, if this contest went all the way, the 796 or so superdelegates would decide the race for the nomination.

Counting superdelegates is tough because they are not obligated to stick with their initial choice. But beginning in the winter of 2008, various news organizations called the superdelegates as often as they could in order to try to get a count. Six days after Super Tuesday, the Associated Press counted 243 superdelegates for Hillary Clinton and 156 for Barack Obama. On February 13, 2008, eight days after Super Tuesday, CNN gave Clinton 234 and Obama 156, while CBS gave Clinton 210 and Obama 141.[20] Moreover, these news organizations kept separate counts of superdelegates and ordinary delegates, making it more difficult for Clinton to use her superdelegate advantage to mask her campaign's weakness in the elected delegate count.

On February 16, 2008, Harold Ickes, a top Hillary Clinton supporter (and ironically, a former adviser to Jesse Jackson and party reformer who had always opposed the notion of superdelegates) predicted that Clinton would win the convention because the superdelegates would vote for her as the strongest general election candidate. The Obama campaign saw an opening and took it. As Fox News reported, "Obama Campaign Manager David Plouffe on Saturday blasted Clinton. . . . 'The Clinton campaign just said they have two options for trying to win the nomination—attempting to have super-delegates overturn the will of the Democratic voters or change the rules they agreed to at the eleventh hour in order to seat non-existent delegates from Florida and Michigan,' he said in a statement."[21]

Obama's advisers realized that by convincing the superdelegates to follow the pledged delegates, they could make it very difficult for Clinton to catch up in the delegate count. They got a significant boost toward this goal from the liberal blogosphere, which boiled over with outrage at the possibility that superdelegates could deny Obama the nomination. Super-blogger Markos Moulitsas, founder of the Daily Kos, claimed that Clinton was seeking to win the nomination in "a coup by super-delegate—the overturning of the popular results by the party elite." His views were echoed by "Big Tent Democrat" who responded, "If Obama is the pledged delegate leader and the popular vote leader then any action by the super-delegates to subvert such a result would be outrageous and wrong."[22]

While Hillary Clinton's campaign kept up a steady stream of arguments designed to convince the still uncommitted superdelegates to support her,

Barack Obama's campaign pursued a two-track strategy. On the one hand, they stoked the anger people felt at the prospect that superdelegates could reverse "the will of the people" and encouraged superdelegates to vote as the voters had voted; on the other hand, they courted superdelegates. They realized what many experienced Democrats had understood: Hillary Clinton's long engagement with the Democratic Party meant that the superdelegates who were going to be for her were for her early on. "After Iowa," said Jeff Berman, Obama's director of delegate selection, "you're left with all those who didn't sign on when she [Hillary] was at her peak. Those who were still uncommitted as a whole leaned heavily to Barack."[23]

Stunned by her string of defeats in caucus states, Clinton planned for a March 4 comeback. Her hope was to win Ohio and Texas, the two big states on that day, decisively enough to halt Obama's momentum. But it didn't happen. Her win in Ohio, while substantial, did not erase the delegate gap, and her win in Texas ended up, because of the bizarre rules there, in a delegate loss. Thus by March the Clinton campaign was forced to play the superdelegate card even more overtly. On April 13, 2008, in the run-up to the critical Pennsylvania primary, Hillary Clinton told reporters: "I believe that the super-delegates should do the same as any other delegate or voter, which is to determine who they believe will be the best President."[24]

Clinton had a very strong finish to the campaign, winning key big states like Ohio, Texas, Pennsylvania, and Indiana. But proportional representation kept her from closing the pledged delegate gap with Obama. And along the way, Obama began to pick up superdelegates. By May 9, 2008, ABC News and the *New York Times* were reporting that he had gained more superdelegates than Clinton. On that day the Obama campaign announced that New Jersey representative Donald Payne had switched from Clinton to Obama and that Oregon representative Peter DeFazio had endorsed Clinton, giving Obama a 267–266 lead over Clinton among superdelegates. And on May 10 the Associated Press was running the following lead: "Obama Overtakes Clinton in Democratic Superdelegates."[25]

But Obama still did not have the magic number, and in the meantime Clinton had one more tactic to use in her attempt to regain momentum: that was to try to get Florida and Michigan back in the game. Since the DNC had stripped both states of their delegates in the late summer of 2007, neither state's delegates factored into the delegate counts. Yet Clinton had won both states, outpolling Obama in Florida and "uncommitted" in Michigan. If the DNC reinstated the delegates from Florida and Michigan, Clinton strategist Mark Penn argued, that could "move the delegate count close enough to win with super delegates if they became convinced that Barack Obama could not win the presidency."[26]

And so the Clinton campaign began an intensive lobbying effort to get Florida and Michigan included in the delegate count. The campaign tried to get "do-overs" in both states, something that the Obama people in Michigan opposed and a suggestion that died in the end because it raised too many practical problems. Hillary Clinton traveled to Florida, where she likened the situation to the disenfranchisement many believed they had suffered in the 2000 presidential election. The true prize at stake, though, was not the pledged delegates, but the superdelegates. Including Florida and Michigan would not have given Clinton a delegate lead, although it would have closed the gap considerably. But by getting Florida and Michigan counted, what the Clinton campaign hoped to do was to convince the superdelegates that their candidate was still in the game.

On May 31, 2008, the party's Rules and By-Laws Committee finally resolved the Michigan and Florida challenges by reinstating half their delegates and awarding Obama four more votes in Michigan than he would have won had "uncommitted" been treated under proportional rules. (Instead of giving four delegates to "uncommitted," the Obama campaign argued that since he had, in good faith, taken his name off the Michigan ballot his supporters had voted for "uncommitted" and that these four delegates belonged to him. The Rules Committee eventually agreed.) The Obama campaign now knew the magic number it needed to get to the nomination. Like Walter Mondale almost exactly 24 years earlier, Barack Obama set out to call the still uncommitted superdelegates. In those calls he let it be known that an endorsement now, in the days between the Rules Committee decision and the final primaries on June 3, would mean a great deal because it could get him over the top.[27]

The strategy worked. On June 3, 2008, his campaign announced, and the delegate counters in the media confirmed, that Barack Obama had the magic number of delegates, 2,118, to win the Democratic nomination. Like Mondale before him, he was put over the top by superdelegates, and again like Mondale, he took pains to mask that fact by having his assertion of victory coincide with the end of the public process, the primaries in Montana and South Dakota.

Challenges to the Post-Reform System

No wonder modern conventions are so boring. Delegates are selected for their loyalty to presidential candidates, there are almost no uncommitted or favorite-son delegates by the end of the primary season, and even the superdelegates see their role as ratifying, not overturning, the will of the voters. So the typical post-reform convention is a carefully choreographed production for the benefit of television viewers. There are no surprises and no drama. And yet, with all the factors conspiring against exciting conventions, there have been three dramatic, contested conventions in the post-reform era. It is to these that we now turn.

FIGHTING TO THE FINISH

No post-reform nominating convention has rejected the presidential candidate who won pluralities in the most primaries and caucuses; but three candidates have tried to make that happen. In 1972, Maine senator Ed Muskie led the "Anybody but McGovern" forces in an attempt to deny McGovern the nomination; in 1976, California governor Ronald Reagan mounted a convention challenge to President Gerald Ford; and in 1980, Senator Ted Kennedy challenged President Jimmy Carter all the way to the convention.

So, why did the candidates in question think that they could change the outcomes of the primaries? First, in all three cases there was widespread consensus within the party and the general political class that the front-runner would lose the general election. This was clear for George McGovern, who was running sixteen points behind President Richard Nixon in June 1972.[28] It was clear for President Gerald Ford, who trailed Jimmy Carter by margins of two to one in the summer of 1976.[29] Ford had never been elected president in his own right. He ascended to the office only after Vice President Spiro Agnew had been forced to resign on corruption charges and President Richard Nixon had been forced out of office by the Watergate scandal and impeachment proceedings. Adding to Ford's problems was his pardoning of Nixon. Suffice it to say, it was not a good year for Republicans. And finally, it was clear for President Jimmy Carter, whose international standing had been crippled by the Iranian hostage crisis in the spring of 1980 and who had presided over an economy that managed to have high inflation and high unemployment at the same time. At one point in the summer of 1980, Reagan held a 27-point lead over Carter, and going into the Democratic convention, Reagan's lead varied from 14 to 20 points.[30]

Second, in all three cases the challenger waged an ideological war for the nomination—a fight for "the soul of the party." In 1972 the mainstream of the party was astonished by George McGovern's takeover and dismayed by the hordes of young hippies who flocked to his antiwar message. In 1976, Ronald Reagan waged a campaign all the way to the convention on behalf of conservatives who felt that the Republican Party had abandoned its bedrock principles by espousing détente and "giving away" the Panama Canal. And in 1980, Senator Ted Kennedy justified his fight to the convention on the grounds that Carter had abandoned the liberal Democratic orthodoxy of the New Deal and Great Society.

Third, in each case, it seemed possible that the challenger's quest could, in fact, succeed. The first post-reform convention was held in 1972. Slow to adjust to the new rules, Democratic Party regulars believed that the convention delegates would regard the results of the primaries as advisory only. In the Credentials Committee, representatives of the party establishment had managed to strip McGovern of 151 delegates. They thought, wrongly, that they could prevail on the same issue on the convention floor and use their momentum to deny McGovern a first-ballot victory.

Ronald Reagan's challenge at the 1976 Republican Convention seemed even stronger. At the end of the primaries, he was only 117 votes behind Ford, and there was enough uncertainty about the delegate count that, for all practical purposes, the two candidates were tied as they went into the convention. John Sears, Reagan's campaign manager, decided to test his candidate's strength with a vote on the newly proposed Rule 16C (part of the Republican Convention Rules), which would have required all presidential candidates to announce their vice-presidential selection before the balloting began. The substance of the rule was not important. What Sears sought was to defeat Ford's supporters over the issue and thereby turn convention momentum against the president. But in a close vote, it was the Reagan forces—and Reagan's candidacy—that went down to defeat.

In contrast to Ford, President Carter ended the 1980 primary season with a margin of several hundred delegates over his challenger, Ted Kennedy. However, Kennedy had won all the late primaries. Moreover, Carter was weakened by a scandal involving his brother Billy's ties to Libya that had erupted in July. Kennedy's backers seized the opportunity to press the fight to the convention. But like Reagan in 1976, Kennedy saw his candidacy die on a test vote involving party rules. (This vote is discussed in greater detail below.)

Thus in all three instances the challengers felt that they had a chance to restore to the convention the deliberative function it had had in pre-reform days. In each instance there was a test vote, and when the challengers lost, their chances of opening up the convention were doomed. In each instance, as expected, the nominee went on to lose the general election. However, we should be careful to get the causality straight. Contested conventions may damage the nominee of the party, but contested conventions do not happen to nominees who are not already very weak general election candidates.

The Robot Rule

At the 1980 Democratic convention, the issue that became the test vote went to the very heart of the role of delegates in the modern nominating convention. Therefore it deserves special attention here. Rule 11(H) was added to the delegate selection rules by the Winograd Commission. As drafted by Rick Hutcheson, a White House staffer who had been Carter's delegate hunter in 1976, the new rule read:

> All delegates to the National Convention shall be bound to vote for the presidential candidate whom they were elected to support for at least the first convention ballot, unless released in writing by the presidential candidate. Delegates who seek to violate this rule may be replaced with an alternate of the same presidential preference by the presidential candidate or that candidate's authorized representative(s) at any time up to and including the presidential balloting at the National Convention.

After some discussion of the significance of establishing a uniform binding law, and after some discussion to establish that this rule did not apply to nonpresidential votes, such as platform votes, the commission passed the rule unanimously.

For the first time ever, the party had formalized in a rule what had become political reality for post-reform conventions. This definition of the delegate's role as a messenger from the electorate was summed up by Commissioner Scott Lang: "When all is said and done, the individuals who are elected as delegates are elected to represent those who have sent them forward in the process and I think that requiring them, even binding them, to vote for one ballot for the candidate they were elected to serve is not unduly burdensome and prevents mischief."[31]

This was the last public discussion of Rule 11(H) before the 1980 primary season. That March, Ted Kennedy was faced with the fact that he was seriously behind Carter in the number of committed delegates. At a news conference the day after his defeat in the Illinois primary, Kennedy "hinted" at a rules change strategy, saying he would take his campaign to the convention even if Carter won a majority of delegates.[32] Discussion of a possible rules change stayed alive in the press throughout April.[33] In May, Kennedy offered to withdraw from the race if Carter would debate him and if Carter won the June 3 primaries.[34] Carter refused, and by June 3, 1980, the last day of the primary season, it was still unclear whether Kennedy would pursue a rules fight.

But by mid-June, when the Platform Committee began meeting in preparation for the convention, it was clear that the Kennedy campaign was pursuing a full-fledged convention effort aimed at winning delegates for Kennedy. Instead of compromising on platform planks, the Kennedy operatives on the Platform Committee pursued a strategy of filing as many minority reports as possible. Had the Kennedy campaign demanded full debate and a roll call vote on every one of its platform minority reports, they could have taken up the entire convention and caused it to run for five days instead of four. Thus the 25 minority reports filed on the platform served as bargaining chits for everything from extra passes for the Kennedy campaign to a primetime television spot for Kennedy's speech to the convention.

Similar conflict erupted in the Rules Committee. On July 8, 1980, the committee, which was controlled by Carter partisans, defeated an attempt to change Rule 11(H) and an attempt to delete F3(C) (the same rule) from the temporary Call to the Convention. The Kennedy campaign filed a minority report, guaranteeing a floor fight over this rule in the first session of the convention. For the next month, the Carter campaign called and recalled every one of its pledged delegates to explain the rule, the controversy, and the motives of the Kennedy campaign. The Kennedy campaign organized an equally impressive delegate tracking operation, hoping to convince delegates that they could abandon Carter and vote for him. When delegates were not being phoned, they were receiving mail; when they were not receiving mail, they were reading about the controversy in a vast array of editorials in papers across the country.

As the preconvention campaign mounted in intensity, Kennedy forces dubbed Rule F3(C) "the robot rule" —splashing the slogan "free the delegates" across posters and buttons and printing pictures of a robot with a red slash across it. The symbol was particularly appropriate, given the observation V. O. Key had made sixteen years earlier: "While the primary has modified nominating practices, it has not produced conventions of automata that mechanically record the preferences expressed by the voters at home."[35] "Mechanically record" was exactly what the 1980 delegates were being asked to do. Nonetheless, few Carter delegates seemed troubled by this proposition. An Associated Press poll in early July found that only 4 percent of the Carter delegates would vote to unbind the delegates and 7 percent were unsure what they would do. This left a whopping 89 percent of the Carter delegates loyal to the Carter campaign position.[36]

Then on July 15, 1980, the *Washington Post* reported that Carter's brother Billy had been a lobbyist for the terrorist government of Libya. "Billygate" as it became known was just one more blow for a beleaguered presidency. The Carter White House was already dealing with rampant inflation, high interest rates, the ongoing hostage crisis, and a series of difficulties ranging from a cocaine investigation of the White House chief of staff to a bungled vote at the United Nations on Israel, and now brother Billy.

In July, Carter's approval rating in the Gallup Poll hit a new low of 21 percent—the lowest rating since Gallup started measuring presidential popularity in 1938.[37] In match-up after match-up with Republican candidate Reagan, Carter lost by large margins. Kennedy did no better, and elected officials, especially junior members of Congress, began to fear the effects of a Carter candidacy (or a Kennedy candidacy) in November on their own reelection efforts. If ever a party needed a deliberative convention that could provide new options for the head of the ticket, it was the Democrats in 1980.

In late July a group of 40 House members, mostly young, many from the independent-minded class of 1974, organized an Open Convention

Committee with the goal of opening the convention to candidates other than Carter or Kennedy. Names were floated, among them Vice President Mondale, who quickly denied any interest, and Secretary of State Edmund Muskie, whose denial was somewhat less Shermanesque. With a budget of $200,000, the Open Convention Committee opened offices in Washington and New York, held press conferences, put out press releases, and recruited more elected officials, such as Governor Hugh Carey of New York, Governor Richard Lamm of Colorado, and Senator Robert Byrd of West Virginia, the Senate majority leader. Then they began to lobby delegates.

The effort was doomed from the outset. By the end of June 1980, when most of the state delegations were complete, there were 114 uncommitted and "other" delegates to the convention (out of 3,331), or 3 percent of the convention, hardly enough to begin a bandwagon for Ed Muskie or anyone else. Without a bloc of unaffiliated delegates to lobby, the open convention advocates were forced to try to persuade committed Carter and Kennedy delegates, a much more difficult task. One unnamed Democratic leader who thought the prospects of dumping Carter were dim put it this way: "My mother didn't raise me to be a Kamikaze pilot."[38]

Table 6-5 lists the 28 most prominent members of the open convention movement by state. If we assume that each member's influence was greatest on delegates from his or her own state, we can assess the efforts of the open convention advocates by looking at the vote in favor of Minority Report #5 (which would have unbound the delegates) and comparing it to the number of pledged Kennedy delegates in the state's delegation as of the end of June 1980. In state after state, the open convention movement's impact was minimal. In some cases, Open Convention members even seem to have lost votes for their cause!

Despite the efforts of the open convention advocates and the Kennedy campaign, despite Carter's incredibly low approval rating, despite Billygate— in short, despite all the signs pointing to an electoral disaster for the Democrats, on the test vote at the convention on the "robot rule" Jimmy Carter lost the votes of only 35 delegates between June and the convention. Delegates to the 1980 convention were so thoroughly bound to the presidential candidate by virtue of the rules and the expectations they produced that the party was unable to save itself from the electoral disaster that followed.

Table 6-5. *Leaders of the "Open Convention" Committee and Their Impact on the Vote, by State, 1980*

State leaders	Net impact on the convention vote[a]
California: Reps. Ron Dellums, Don Edwards, James Lloyd, Pete Stark, Henry Waxman	+4
Colorado: Gov. Richard Lamm, Reps. Patricia Schroeder, Tim Wirth	+11
Connecticut: Rep. Toby Moffett	−1
Illinois: Rep. Paul Simon	+10
Maryland: Reps. Mike Barnes, Barbara Mikulski	+1
Massachusetts: Rep. Ed Markey	+4
Michigan: Reps. Bob Carr, John Conyers	0
Minnesota: Rep. Richard Nolan[b]	+30 or −7
New York: Gov. Hugh Carey, Sen. Daniel Patrick Moynihan, Reps. Jerome Ambro, Shirley Chisholm, Thomas Downey	−1
Oregon: Rep. James Weaver	+1
Washington; Sen. Henry Jackson, Reps. Norm Dicks, Al Swift	+3
West Virginia: Sen. Robert Byrd	+3
Wisconsin: Sen. Gaylord Nelson, Rep. James Oberstar	0

Sources: Vote totals for the open convention vote can be found in *1980: The Official Report of the Proceedings of the Democratic National Convention,* August 11–14, 1980 (Washington: Democratic National Committee), pp. 204–13. Kennedy's delegate count can be found in *Congressional Quarterly Weekly Report,* June 28, 1980.

a. Net impact is calculated by comparing the "yes" vote on Minority Report #5 at the 1980 Democratic Convention with the Kennedy delegate count, as reported in *Congressional Quarterly,* June 28, 1980.

b. Minnesota is a special case. Because it was a caucus state and because it was Vice President Mondale's home state, those who wished to oppose Carter ran as uncommitted instead of as Kennedy delegates in order to avoid embarrassing Mondale. The 30 "yes" votes came from the uncommitted delegates. It looks as if the efforts of Representative Nolan picked up 30 votes for the open convention position. However, assuming that the 37 were really Kennedy supporters being polite to Mondale, the efforts of Representative Nolan probably resulted in a net loss of 7 votes.

Conclusion

The "robot rule" died a quiet death in 1982 as the Hunt Commission replaced it with a rule that pledged convention delegates to vote for the presidential candidate they were elected to represent "in all good conscience." This Democratic Party rule and the absence of a uniform rule in the Republican Party leave open the possibility that future nominating conventions could over-turn the verdict of the primaries and save a party from defeat in November. But this remains a slim possibility.

In 2008, Hillary Clinton's campaign toyed with the idea of taking the fight to the convention right up until she withdrew from the race. But the superdelegates, who would have had to lead the charge, were unconvinced by arguments that she would be the stronger nominee against McCain because she had defeated Obama in the big industrial states. As Obama won more and more primaries, Americans got more comfortable with him, and his polling numbers went up. It was hard to argue that he would do worse than Clinton in what was shaping up to be a good Democratic year.

There were other obstacles to a successful convention fight. On the issues, Clinton and Obama were not very far apart. It would be hard to turn man-dating the purchase of health insurance (one of the few sharp exchanges they had in the debates) into a struggle for the soul of the Democratic Party. Nor was it easy to make support for the Iraq War into an ideological fight when so many Senate Democrats had voted for it. Equally important, the superdelegates were worried about having the African American base of the Democratic Party, perhaps the most loyal base in modern party history, feel that the election had been stolen from them. But what probably kept the Clinton campaign from pursuing a race to the convention is the fact that, for better or for worse, by 2008 most voters didn't even know what a brokered convention was, and they didn't like what little they did know. A public that had reacted with shock and anger to the very existence of superdelegates was not likely to support a process that epitomized an old-fashioned inside game, a process in which the delegates that they had elected could exercise their own judgment.

The transformation of the nominating convention is the natural result of the modern nomination process in which the public has come to dominate and the institutional party and its leaders fit their decisions around the pub-lic's desires. Nonetheless, the nominating conventions are still the final legal authority for determining who the major party's nominees are. Their role is protected by several Supreme Court decisions granting political parties protection under the First Amendment. It is highly unlikely, but not impos-sible, that a future nominating convention will actually pick a president. As we saw in 2008, the proportional rules of the Democratic Party make it very easy for two strong candidates, evenly matched in money and influence, to accumulate approximately the same number of delegates. Had the Clinton campaign competed in caucuses and had Florida and Michigan not been out of the game, it is possible that the two candidates would have ended the 2008 race in practically a dead heat.

But short of a virtual tie, and short of extraordinary circumstances that occur in the period of time between the end of the primaries and the opening of the party conventions, the party conventions are likely to remain simply the culmination of a process in which the will of the voters dominates. It will take an extreme set of circumstances, circumstances that were not at all present in 2008, for a future nominating convention to overturn the will of the voters.

7

THE PROBLEM OF
"THE DECIDER"

There are many proposed alternatives to the modern nominating system as it has evolved. All of them are more rational and orderly than the hodge-podge of systems that voters experience today. The most popular alternative among party leaders and elected officials is some variation on the theme of the regional primary. In contrast to voters, most of whom favor a national primary, politicians tend to value the sequential nature of the nomination process but seek to make the system more fair.

The preeminent reform plan is the Regional Presidential Primaries Plan. This proposal, which was adopted by the National Association of Secretaries of State in 1999, divides the country into four regions: East, South, Midwest, and West. Following a drawing by lottery to establish the initial order of voting, the first region would hold its primaries on a single date in March, the second on a single date in April, and so on. Every four years the regions would move one position in the sequence: the region that was first would go last and the other regions would move forward.[1] In the NASS plan and the version of it introduced into Congress as the Regional Primaries Act of 2007 by Senators Amy Klobuchar (Democrat from Minnesota), Lamar Alexander (Republican from Tennessee), and Joseph Lieberman (Independent from Connecticut), Iowa and New Hampshire would be allowed to hold their contests before the first regional primaries, in order to allow lesser-known candidates a chance to create early momentum. (A slightly different version of the NASS plan was introduced to the Republican Rules Committee; this one did not include a special exemption for Iowa and New Hampshire.)

At an April 2008 conference at Harvard University's Kennedy School of Government, Todd Rokita, secretary of state of Indiana, defended the NASS plan against one of the most common criticisms: that a candidate who happened to come from the region that voted first that year would have an enormous advantage, otherwise referred to as the "regional favorite-son or -daughter issue." Rokita argued, "I think the media and the voters would see that home town advantage and certainly the media would point that out and I think that would be calculated objectively and discounted to the extent necessary for that particular candidate."[2] As we have seen, the expectations game played by the media tends to correct for a candidate's home region. Al Gore in 1988 didn't get anywhere by winning states in his home region of the South, but Michael Dukakis of Massachusetts got a huge boost from winning in Florida and Texas.

A second type of regional primary is called the Texas Plan. It was submitted to the Republican Rules Committee in 2008 by Bill Crocker, an RNC member from Texas. Like the NASS plan, it divides the country into four groups; and like the NASS plan, the order in which each group votes would rotate every four years. However, there are two important differences between this plan and the NASS proposal. The first is in the composition of the groups. Rather than group states by geographic region, the Texas plan creates four roughly comparable groups—that is, groups that as near as practicable have the same number of states, the same number of delegate votes, the same number of electoral votes, and the same ratio of Republican to Democratic states.[3] According to Crocker, "We wound up with balanced groupings of states in each of the four groups, north-south, east-west, red-blue, racially diverse."[4] The second big difference is that the Texas Plan does not require all the states in a group to hold primaries on the same date. States in the first group can have their contests at any time after the first of March, states in the second group any time after the first of April, states in the third group any time during the month of May, and states in the fourth group any time in the month of June. One criticism of the Texas Plan is that the states in each group are geographically far-flung. But Crocker maintains, "The expense of having to appeal to a diverse group of states is far better than, for instance, all of the New England states going first and producing candidates with momentum, at least, if not quasi decisions made for the parties, that appeal to that unique population."[5]

A third variation on the theme is the Ohio Plan, sponsored by Robert T. Bennett, the long-serving chairman of the Ohio Republican Party. This plan was adopted by the Republican Rules Committee on April 2, 2008. Throughout the spring and summer of 2008 it was the leading primary reform plan on the Republican side. It allows Iowa and New Hampshire to retain their traditional first-in-the-nation status. It also permits Nevada and South Carolina (which the DNC included as early states in the 2008 season) to retain their special status since those two states bring geographic and racial diversity to the early voting period. After that, however, the Ohio plan creates four pods. The first pod consists of 15 small states and territories, each with three to five electoral votes.[6] These states, which collectively hold 55 electoral votes, would be allowed to have contests starting no earlier than the third week in February. They are allowed to go early in order to guarantee a "retail politics" phase in the nomination race. Following the four early states and the flight of small states, three other groups of states would rotate through the remaining months.

The logic behind the Ohio Plan is to group states of similar electoral size together with one or two significantly larger "anchor" states. The states in the first group would conduct their contests starting the first full week of March, the second group would vote beginning in the fourth full week of March, and the final group would vote beginning in the third full week of April. Like the Texas Plan and unlike the NASS plan, the Ohio Plan would not require that states in a group hold contests simultaneously; instead it would create a window for each group.

According to its author, Bob Bennett, the Ohio plan is a hybrid of many other plans created in the past. Bennett argued its virtues as follows:

If you look at the Delaware plan [discussed below], the big states never get the opportunity to go first, never get an opportunity to make a decision. If you look at California, New York, Texas, Florida, they are going to be put in last continuously. If you look at the rotating NASS plan, the rotating regional plan, the objection that I've head from many people here is that, since one region becomes dominant four years ahead of time, a governor or a senator who is very popular in that region can work that region [well] and in effect, block out a strong candidate from another region.[7]

A fourth alternative is the Michigan Plan (also known as the Levin/Nelson Presidential Primary Reform Bill, the Fair and Representative Presidential Primaries Act of 2007, and the Anuzis-Dingell Plan, each with different sponsors). The Michigan plan is one of the most complicated proposals because it tries to solve a variety of problems. Not surprisingly, given Michigan's past opposition to the privileged position enjoyed by Iowa and New Hampshire, the plan does not preserve those states' traditional first-in-the-nation status. Instead it divides the country into six pods in order to give each state the chance to be part of the first voting group. Voting takes place starting in March and goes through June. States can hold their nominating contest at any time during or after their designated month—but not earlier.

As in the Ohio plan, each pod contains approximately the same number of electoral votes. In addition, each pod combines states from all across the country. For example, one pod contains two eastern states, Connecticut and Rhode Island; a mid-Atlantic state, West Virginia; two southern states, Arkansas and Georgia; and Oklahoma, Idaho, Nevada, and Utah, for a total of 75 electoral votes.[8] This aspect of the plan, according to Sander Levin, makes it more representative: "Trying to have a representative system . . . meant that you could not do it region by region because there are simply too many differences among the regions. To have the South go first and the Midwest go last or the Midwest go first and the South go last was not going to create a representative system."[9]

Three objections have been raised to the Michigan plan as it has been discussed in party meetings. One was that the cost of travel is enormous since each pod would require candidates to campaign all over the country. But Levin points out that the cost of travel in the current system is already enormous. The second objection is that the plan is confusing. Saul Anuzis admits, "Clearly we have the most confusing plan. . . . However, having said that, I also think it was as fair as someone is going to get; the idea here was to make it as random as possible." Third, the constant rotation of states would force state legislatures to change their primary dates every four years. Anuzis concedes, "That probably is enough to not make it work which is why there was

I think overwhelming opposition [among the Republicans] . . . even though I think it was probably the fairest [plan]."[10]

A fifth alternative, the Delaware Plan, was favored by the Republican Party's Rules Committee at the 2000 convention but defeated by last-minute opposition from George W. Bush's team. The Delaware Plan allows Iowa and New Hampshire to go first and then groups states into four pods according to population.[11] The first pod contains small states totaling 14 million people and the final one contains large states totaling 160 million people. The plan was first proposed by Robert D. Loevy in a 1992 book on the presidential nominating process.[12] Some years later it was adopted by Basil Battaglia, Republican state party chairman from Delaware, and presented to the 1999 Republican Party's Advisory Commission on the Presidential Nominating Process. It picked up adherents in the Republican Party but failed ultimately for three reasons. First, big states, coming at the end of the process, feared that their role would be minimized. Second, there was concern that the Democrats would pick a plan that would allow them to select a nominee early and use the remaining months of the Republican contest to mount a general election campaign. And finally, at the eleventh hour, the 2000 Republican nominee, George W. Bush, said no. Like presidential candidates before him, he had concluded that there was nothing wrong with a system that had nominated him. Ron Thornburgh, Kansas secretary of state, who presented the Delaware Plan before the RNC Rules Committee in 2000, recalls: "I left the room feeling good and big old Joe Allbaugh sidles up to me with the flat-top haircut and the cowboy boots and said, 'Ron, that was nice but we ain't gonna do it.' And I said, 'But Joe it was great,' and he said 'I know, but we are going to the convention and we don't want any fights over anything; this is to give our candidate a bounce.' And that's what it boiled down to."[13]

The final reform plan to win serious consideration is one that would keep the current system but move the starting date to March, with no exceptions. This proposal was the second most popular option, after the Ohio Plan, among members of the RNC's Rules Committee in 2008. The plan stipulates that states that hold contests before March would be penalized by losing 50 percent of their delegates. In 2008 the RNC applied the same penalty to the six states that set dates earlier than February 5—the opening date of the Republican window. On the Democratic side, four of the early states received exemptions from the DNC, and the two others—Michigan and Florida—were hit with a 50 percent penalty (after having been initially stripped of all their delegates). Arguing in favor of this plan, Blake Hall, general counsel to the RNC, observed: "I don't think we can entirely assume that any resolution that we have would necessarily solve the very problems that we are addressing. And that's why, quite frankly, at least a third of the Rules Committee felt like the only real problem with the process this time was the fact that we started too early and that we needed to move it back."[14]

The Constitutional Problem

Most of the ambitious plans outlined above seek to preserve the sequential nature of the nominating process while removing the biases in it—especially the biases introduced by having Iowa and New Hampshire always go first. They seek to do away with these biases by creating a particular sequence of state contests. Such a sequence would be difficult, if not impossible, to achieve through voluntary actions on the part of 50 state legislatures. Therefore most of these plans assume congressional action.

There is considerable constitutional ambiguity surrounding Congress's ability to play a role in this area. Supreme Court Justice Antonin Scalia, writing in 1981 (before he was on the Court) put the issue as follows: "There are three major legal issues bearing upon the ability of the political parties to reform the presidential nominating process. First, what restrictions does the Constitution itself place upon the parties? Second, what restrictions may the states constitutionally impose? And third, what may federal legislation do, by way of restricting either the states or the parties, or by way of facilitating the nominating process? I am sorry to report the answer to none of these questions is entirely clear."[15]

As discussed in chapter 1, for much of American history political parties and their activities were treated as private, not public, matters. Indeed the entire pre-reform-era nomination system was essentially a semi-private, if not entirely private, enterprise. As state legislatures introduced primaries at the turn of the century, spurred on by the Progressive reform movement, the result was a certain degree of regulation through statutes creating the primaries. But by and large the federal government stayed out of the business of party nominations at all levels.

Then in 1944 the Supreme Court ruled in *Smith* v. *Allwright* that political parties are state actors and cannot discriminate.[16] At the time, many southern Democratic state parties restricted participation to whites, effectively disenfranchising African Americans. By prohibiting them from voting in primary elections, the state parties, for all practical purposes, prevented African Americans from having any say in the electoral process, given the Democrats' uncontested control of the South. The Supreme Court saw a compelling interest in protecting the right to vote and intervened to prohibit all-white primaries. The Court has also intervened in the political process in several other important cases. In *Burroughs* v. *United States,* decided in 1934, the Court found the Federal Corrupt Practices Act constitutional on the grounds that Congress had the authority to protect the election process from corruption.[17] Similarly in *Buckley* v. *Valeo* (1974) the Court ruled that parts of the new campaign finance law were constitutional because they empowered Congress to prevent corruption in the nominating system.[18] And in *Oregon* v. *Mitchell* (1970) the Court ruled that states had the power to extend the right to vote to those who were 18 years old.[19] Finally, those who argue that the Court would permit Congress to determine the order of voting in the presidential nomination system point to Article II, section I, of the Constitution: "The Congress may determine the Time of chusing the Electors, and the Day on which they shall give their Votes; which Day shall be the same through the United States."

Proponents of congressional action argue that the above cases, in addition to the Constitution's directives on the Electoral College and on congressional elections, provide plenty of precedent for Congress to be able to set the calendar for presidential nomination contests. Opponents of congressional action generally point to two Court cases that support the primacy of political parties in setting their own nomination rules. In *Ray* v. *Blair* (1952) the Supreme Court ruled that it was constitutional for a state to allow a state party to make potential electors to the electoral college sign a pledge of loyalty to that party.[20] In *Cousins* v. *Wigoda* (1974), the Court ruled that political parties have the authority to set their own rules for their nomination process, including the rules that determine how delegates are seated at the national convention, and that such party rules trump state laws.[21]

Richard Hasen, a law professor, argues that "at least if it comes to ordering a primary and perhaps ordering the timing of the primaries, that might not violate the party's associational rights." He also points to Article 2 of the Constitution, which gives Congress the right to set the date for choosing presidential electors and argues that "if Congress has the power to set the date for choosing electors, it should also have the power . . . to set the date for choosing primaries."[22] On the other side of the question, political scientist William Mayer argues that, since *Cousins* v. *Wigoda:*

> the Supreme Court has quite consistently upheld the claims of political parties almost every time they have come in conflict with state law. In 1981, it overruled the Wisconsin Supreme Court's attempt to assert the supremacy of that state's "open primary" law against national Democratic rules. In 1986, the Court allowed the Connecticut Republican party to open up its primaries to independent voters, even though state law limited primaries to registered party members. In 1989, the Court invalidated California laws that dictated the organization and composition of party governing bodies and prohibited those bodies from making endorsements before a primary. In 2000, it declared that the state of California could not compel the Democratic and Republican parties to nominate their candidates through a so-called blanket primary.[23]

As this abbreviated discussion illustrates, both proponents and opponents of federal action on the presidential nomination system can find in the Supreme Court an argument for their point of view. No one will be certain of the constitutionality of this issue, however, until after Congress acts; and that too is problematic.

Congress

The constitutional ambiguity persists because Congress's authority to regulate the nominating process has never been put to the test. Over the years, lawmakers have introduced more than 300 bills in the House and Senate to transform the presidential nomination system, and not one of them has seen the light of day.[24] The reason is simple: members of Congress have no interest in putting themselves at odds with the leaders of their party, and party leaders have been reluctant to hand over the nomination process to Congress and thus to the federal government.

One reason, as Professor Thomas Patterson argues, has to do with the flexibility available under the current system: "The problem you have with congressional action is that once you do it, then it's kind of hard to change. And parties are much more flexible instruments. One advantage of federalism, whatever else we may think of it, it also allows for states to experiment with different ways of doing things."[25] Another reason is, simply, the party leaders' desire to preserve their own authority. As David Norcross of the RNC puts it, "Any time Congress begins to sniff around your yard and front door, you'd better be aware of the fact that they'll soon be inside eating your lunch."[26] This sentiment is particularly strong on the Republican side. According to Saul Anuzis, congressional action in this realm could become "a rallying cry for Republicans and [lead to] a massive challenge, state by state, of Republican Congress members even considering taking away party rights."[27] But the reluctance to surrender any power to Congress is not all on the Republicans' side. As Jim Roosevelt, chair of the DNC's Rules Committee, observes, "I don't think members of the Democratic Party would be any more interested in having Congress do this on its own than Republicans would be."[28]

Beyond opposition from the parties, there are other political obstacles to getting Congress to act on any kind of presidential primary legislation. While a few members of Congress, such as Senator Carl Levin of Michigan, are intensely interested in reforming the nominating system, most are not. Congressional action to create some form of regional primary system would most likely involve Congress in picking up the tab for those elections—a move that would probably decrease, not increase, congressional interest in the reform. Reform proposals also bring up the question of sanctions. Suppose, for instance, New Hampshire decided it did not want to be part of a congressionally mandated New England primary? What would Congress do? Cut off its highway funding? Close down the Portsmouth Naval Shipyard? Highly unlikely.

The Voters

A last reason for the lack of congressional action is the fact that there is no public clamor for an alternative to the current nominating process. Public opinion is divided on the advisability of regional primaries. In a January

2000 poll, 46 percent of respondents indicated that they preferred the current system to a system of rotating regional primaries (which was favored by 44 percent); two months later, 47 percent expressed a preference for regional primaries.[29] In contrast, a majority has consistently supported a national primary over the past fifty years, with the percentage favoring this option over the existing system ranging from 56 percent to 76 percent.[30] But support for an alternative to the current nomination system is simply not a high priority for most voters. This helps explain why Congress has never taken significant action on the issue.

The Problem of "the Decider" and the Legacy of the 2008 Elections

Let us stipulate, as the lawyers say, that every one of the alternatives outlined above, and many more that well-meaning activists and scholars have come up with over the years, is more rational and more orderly than the current system. And yet none of them has ever come close to being implemented and probably never will. Why? The answer is simple. No one is really in charge of the presidential nominating system; there is no "decider." As we've seen, Congress has failed to act on the matter. The national political parties and state political parties often do not see eye-to-eye. Nor do they always act in concert with state legislatures, which set primary dates and appropriate funding for primaries. State secretaries of state often try to collaborate on a more sensible system, only to find their plans thwarted by their own legislatures or by one or more of their state parties. In a federal system where the power to control elections has historically been vested in the states, the absence of central control has been the normal state of affairs.

Thus change in 2012 and beyond will probably come in the same way that it has come in the past: through the complex interaction of presidential hopefuls (past and present) and party politics. In the Democratic Party, the 2008 convention mandated the creation of yet another rules commission. Once Hillary Clinton had dropped out of the race, the Obama campaign felt safe enough in its control of the nomination to write to the convention's Credentials Committee and ask that all delegates from Florida and Michigan be seated and that these two states be restored to their original voting strength. The Credentials Committee voted unanimously to seat the delegates, and Jim Roosevelt, chair of the DNC Rules and By-Laws Committee and the

Convention Credentials Committee, who had presided over the loss of 100 percent, the loss of 50 percent, and the restoration of 100 percent of the two states' delegates, received kudos and hugs from all the players.

Party leaders argued that Florida and Michigan had been punished enough by having missed one of the most exciting primary fights in decades. And yet, people asked, where do we go next? And so another Democratic rules commission will be appointed. According to Jim Roosevelt, some of what the next commission does will be to go over the same old ground: who gets to move when. Consistent with the tendency of Democratic rules commissions to reflect the complaints of the most recent losing candidate, the next commission will also almost certainly take a close look at caucuses. "Some caucuses," Roosevelt says, "are well established, like Iowa, and are seen as fair—albeit idiosyncratic. Some, however, like the Texas caucuses, came out of the process viewed as illegitimate."[31] In addition, according to Roosevelt, the commission will probably consider permitting winner-take-all systems for the allocation of delegates elected later in the nominating season. As we've seen, this move would run counter to a long and powerful reform tradition in the Democratic Party.

But the biggest change for 2012 is that the Democrats will not be alone in reviewing their rules. As a result of changes adopted at the 2008 Republican Convention in Minneapolis, for the first time in history the Republican National Committee has been empowered to adopt reforms to the nomination system in between its quadrennial conventions. Previously the Republican Party could act on such issues only at the convention, making it impossible for the two parties to synchronize on reforms, such as the creation of a starting date for the primary season.

This historic change was precipitated by the last-minute failure of the Ohio Plan. This plan had been adopted in the spring of 2008 by the Rules Committee of the Republican National Committee; and its promoters, notably Bob Bennett, had gone into the convention thinking they had the votes for passage, as well as a pledge from John McCain's campaign to remain neutral on the topic. Once in Minneapolis, however, the McCain campaign signaled, through RNC chairman Mike Duncan, that it did not support the measure and, to the surprise of many, after a fairly rancorous meeting of the Convention Rules Committee, the proposal failed. Not surprisingly, Bennett felt he'd been misled, and the McCain campaign had to deal with the fact that they had a very unhappy party chair of Ohio, a critical state, on their hands. And so, after some acrimonious negotiations between Bennett and the campaign, the Republican reformers got a 15-member commission that would report to the RNC in 2010 and permission for the RNC to write the 2012 rules.

What happens now? Democrats will take a long hard look at the caucus system and apply some reforms. Even though caucus systems are very open systems, the absence of provisions for absentee voting in most caucus states means that caucuses tend to fall short of the participatory ethos that is so important to the modern presidential nomination system. Hillary Clinton's poor performance in caucuses, and the widespread feeling among her supporters that the caucus system was deeply flawed (for example, members of the military on deployment cannot participate in a caucus), will no doubt keep this issue alive, perhaps resulting in fewer caucuses or in steps that make caucuses look even more like primaries. In addition, Hillary Clinton's supporters may try and reform the proportional representation rules that so diluted her big-state wins. On the other hand, President Obama will control the Democratic National Committee and the reform commission, thus making the probability of change low.

But for both parties the really big questions will be about sequence and about the allocation of delegates. Candidates will continue to play the politics of Iowa and New Hampshire. President Obama owes a great deal to Iowa caucus voters; it is hard to imagine him abandoning them by supporting any rules changes that deprive them of their privileged place. And on the Republican side a whole new generation of presidential hopefuls is likely to discover, as have candidates before them, that it is never a good idea to anger Iowa and New Hampshire voters. If the two parties can agree on a starting date for Iowa that is somewhat later than New Year's Day and enforce it, that will in itself be a big step.

Then, what to do with everyone else? On the one hand, the drawn-out but exciting 2008 nomination season might convince states that by going later they too can get some attention. The Democrats are unlikely to see another hotly contested race for the nomination soon, but anticipation of a big race among a new generation of Republican leaders might strengthen the incentives for Republican-controlled states to hold later primaries. In addition, Republican efforts to block states from moving too early will have greater credibility. To its credit, the Republican convention stuck to its guns and cut the delegate strength of the six states that moved too early. Democrats restored the votes of Florida and Michigan, potentially sending the wrong message to future presidential candidates: campaign everywhere and worry about party rules later.

In addition, in the future, rather than rely exclusively on punishments, both parties will probably consider incentives for states to hold their primaries or caucuses later in the season. The Democrats already allocate bonus delegates to states that go late, but this may not be much of an inducement if sequence rules and the nomination is decided in the first week or two. An alternative is to allow late states to use winner-take-all primaries. Similarly, Republicans might consider trying to prohibit winner-take-all primaries early in the season as a means of forestalling a premature closure in their race and making sure that later states get a say in the nomination. In the current system, early is better; hence the importance of Iowa and New Hampshire. But everyone cannot be first, and thus both parties should look for ways to make voters in later states count. Winner-take-all rules for late states might just do it.

Whatever happens in 2012, the process will create frustration because the presidential nomination process is the result of the interplay of state and national political parties, reformers, and presidential hopefuls. For a long time, the action was on the Democratic side, as Democrats sought to end their presidential losing streak. If, as some people think, President Obama begins a long period of Democratic dominance, will the reform energy shift to the Republicans? Anything is possible in a system that is as innovative and unpredictable as the country that produced it.

NOTES

Chapter One

1. Nelson Polsby and Aaron Wildavsky, *Presidential Elections: Strategies of American Electoral Politics,* 3rd ed. (New York: Charles Scribner's Sons, 1971), p. 133.

2. W. H. Lawrence, "Rockefeller Sees President Today," *New York Times,* June 8, 1960.

3. James Reston, "Humphrey Staff Sure of Nomination," *New York Times,* June 24, 1968.

4. The Southern Manifesto, which was a document prepared in response to the Supreme Court's ruling in *Brown* v. *Board of Education,* opposed racial integration in public schools.

5. *Congressional Quarterly,* July 10, 1959, p. 941; and August 28, 1959, p. 1170.

6. Theodore H. White, *The Making of the President, 1960* (New York: New American Library, 1961), p. 113.

7. Stephen Shaddag, *What Happened to Goldwater? The Inside Story of the 1964 Republican Campaign* (New York: Holt, Rinehart, and Winston, 1965), p. 92.

8. John Kessel, *The Goldwater Coalition: Republican Strategies in 1964* (Indianapolis: Bobbs-Merrill, 1968), p. 41.

9. Robert Novak, *The Agony of the GOP, 1964* (New York: Macmillan, 1965), p. 345.

10. Theodore H. White, *The Making of the President, 1964* (New York: New American Library, 1965), pp. 166, 170.

11. *Newsweek,* May 18, 1964.

12. Interview with David Plouffe, December 12, 2008.

13. Peter Wallsten and Peter Nicholas, "Role of 'Superdelegates' Debated; Should They Vote as Their Constituencies Did? Go with Their Personal Preference? Or Throw in with Whoever Leads?" *Los Angeles Times*, February 13, 2008.

14. Frederic J. Fromer, "Kind Calls on Democrats to Scrap Superdelegates," Associated Press, February 13, 2008.

15. Quoted in Nelson Polsby, *Consequences of Party Reform* (New York: Oxford University Press, 1983), p. 14. Originally quoted in White, *Making of the President, 1960,* p. 104.

16. Byron E. Shafer, *Quiet Revolution: The Struggle for the Democratic Party and the Shaping of Post-Reform Politics* (New York: Russell Sage Foundation, 1983), p. 525.

17. Nelson W. Polsby, "The Democratic Nomination," in *The American Elections of 1980,* edited by Austin Ranney (Washington: American Enterprise Institute, 1981).

18. Caucuses are party meetings, often at the precinct level, to elect delegates to county-level or state-level conventions, which in turn elect delegates to the national convention.

19. Shafer, *Quiet Revolution,* p. 387.

20. See, for example, Thomas Marshall, *Presidential Nominations in a Reform Age* (New York: Praeger, 1981), p. 140.

21. Jack W. Germond and Jules Witcover, *Blue Smoke and Mirrors: How Reagan Won and Why Carter Lost the Election of 1980* (New York: Viking, 1981), p. 96.

22. Frank Lynn, "McGovern Victory Expected in Vote in State Tuesday," *New York Times,* June 18, 1972, p. 1.

23. Interview with Peter Kyros, Mondale political aide, March 14, 1985.

24. Jules Witcover, *Marathon: The Pursuit of the Presidency 1972–1976* (New York: Viking, 1977), p. 200.

25. See Commission on Presidential Nomination and Party Structure, Transcript, August 11, 1977, pp. 5–16, available at the National Archives or through the Office of the Secretary, Democratic National Committee.

26. Ibid.

27. David Price, *Bringing Back the Parties* (Washington: CQ Press, 1984), pp. 156–59.

28. Early reform efforts revolved around the attempt, by Democratic Party reformers, to make sure that women and minorities were represented as convention delegates. But fights over affirmative action and quotas diminished in importance as it became clear that convention delegates in the reformed system did not have the same power as they did in the pre-reform system.

29. Witcover, *Marathon.*

30. Interview with former Iowa Republican national committeewoman Marge Askew, April 15, 1985.

31. Primary dates are usually set by state legislatures that enact the date and fund the primary. Since 1980, however, the dates within which states could hold their primaries have been set by national Democratic Party rules, and this has meant that state legislatures and state parties and the Democratic National Committee have sometimes engaged in complex negotiations over when to hold a primary. Nonetheless, the most popular day has been the first "official date" set by party rules.

32. See also David Price, *Bringing Back the Parties,* pp. 224–28; William Crotty and John S. Jackson III, *Presidential Primaries and Nominations* (Washington: Congressional Quarterly, 1985), pp. 65–66; and Andrew E. Busch and William G. Mayer, *The Frontloading Problem in Presidential Elections* (Brookings, 2003).

33. See Polsby, *Consequences of Party Reform,* pp. 173–80.

34. Andrew E. Busch, "In Defense of the 'Mixed System': The Goldwater Campaign and the Role of Popular Movements in the Pre-Reform Presidential Nominating Process," *Polity* 24, 4 (Summer 1992): 527–49.

35. Austin Ranney, *Curing the Mischiefs of Faction: Party Reform in America* (University of California Press, 1975).

36. Ibid.; James W. Ceaser, *Presidential Selection: Theory and Development* (Princeton University Press, 1979).

37. Kenneth Baer, "A Democratic Primary: It's Time to Give All Voters a Voice and Have a National Primary," *Democracy,* no. 7 (Winter 2008): pp. 122–26.

Chapter Two

1. Interview with Jody Powell, December 5, 2008.

2. Jules Witcover, *Marathon: The Pursuit of the Presidency 1972–1976* (New York: Viking, 1977), 203–05.

3. Interview with Phil Wise, former appointments secretary to President Carter, March 28, 1985.

4. The author was executive director of the Compliance Review Commission in the Carter administration.

5. See Nelson W. Polsby, "The Democratic Nomination," in *The American Elections of 1980,* edited by Austin Ranney (Washington: American Enterprise Institute, 1981), pp. 47–48, for a quote from this memo and a description of this strategy.

6. Ibid., p. 48.

7. See Richard Fenno, *The Presidential Odyssey of John Glenn* (Washington: Congressional Quarterly, 1990).

8. Because Mondale had been a sitting vice president, he enjoyed the support of much of the Democratic Party's hierarchy, and because of that he expected to do well in caucuses, reasoning that his superior organization and ties to the establishment would help him defeat any challengers. Because the Wisconsin primary law permitted Republicans to vote in the Democratic primary, the law was in violation of party rules, and thus Wisconsin adopted a caucus system instead of a primary system for the selection of delegates.

9. The cost of running a primary election in the state of California is substantial. Traditionally the primary for president was on the same day as the primary for all other statewide offices, and local and statewide elected officials were resistant to moving all their primaries up to March just to have a once-every-four-years shot at dominating the presidential campaign. In recent years, however, they have held an early presidential primary and kept the primary for all other offices in June.

10. Although the term "Super Tuesday" did not come into widespread use until 1988, its origins lie in the 1980 presidential campaign when, for the first time ever, as we will see in chapter 3, the Democratic Party declared a starting date for the nomination season. The effect was to create, in every season since then, a day on which the largest number of delegates are selected and a day whose contests would be very attractive to presidential candidates.

11. Interview with Tad Devine, May 13, 2008.

12. Interview with Dan Ross, former Republican state chair, June 9, 1986.

13. It was in South Carolina that Connally won his one, very expensive delegate to the 1980 Republican convention.

14. Michael Kramer, "Dubya's Firewall Could Melt," *Daily News* (New York), January 30, 2000.

15. Interview with John Sasso, December 11, 2008.

16. David S. Broder, "No More Super Tuesdays," *Washington Post,* March 2, 1988.

17. Brent Seaborn, at the Campaign Managers Conference, Cambridge, Massachusetts, December 11, 2008.

18. Marc Ambinder, "Rudy's February 5 Gamble," *National Journal,* May 26, 2007.

19. "Giuliani Falls Far Behind in Florida," *Washington Times,* January 28, 2008.

20. Deborah Howlett, "Giuliani Eyes Winner-Take-All Primaries," Newhouse News Service, December 24, 2007.

21. Ambinder, "Rudy's February 5 Gamble."

22. The southern Super Tuesday had fractured somewhat by 1992, with Arkansas, Kentucky, and Virginia moving to new dates.

23. "The 1992 Campaign: Media: One Campaign That Stumbles to Success, Another That Seldom Stumbles," *New York Times,* March 10, 1992.

24. "Bush Opens 11-Point Gap over Clinton in Time Magazine Poll," Associated Press, April 11, 1992; "Poll Shows Bush Leading Perot, Clinton," Associated Press, May 20, 1992; "Times-CBS Poll: Bush, Clinton Sage: Perot Getting Closer Eye," United Press International, June 3, 1992.

25. William Schneider, "Democrats' Strategy Is Ready to Backfire," *St. Petersburg Times,* February 15, 1992.

26. Interview with Jeff Berman, November 24, 2008.

27. David Plouffe, appearance at the Forum, Harvard University, Kennedy School of Government, December 11, 2008, author's notes.

28. Interview with Guy Cecil, December 12, 2008.

29. Quoted from David Plouffe's appearance at the Forum, Harvard University, Kennedy School of Government, April 15, 2009, author's notes.

30. Kevin McDermott, "Earlier Illinois Primary in Wind; Move Is Intended to Help Obama Should He Run for President," *St. Louis Post-Dispatch* (Springfield Bureau), January 11, 2007.

31. Interview with David Plouffe, December 11, 2008.

32. Plouffe, Kennedy School of Government Forum, April 15, 2009.

33. Interview with Jeff Berman, November 24, 2008.

34. Ibid.

35. Ibid.

36. Memo from Harold Ickes, March 29, 2007, in Joshua Green, "The Front-Runner's Fall," *Atlantic Monthly,* September 2008, pp. 64–74 (www.theatlantic.com/doc/200808u/clinton-memos [March 20, 2009]).

37. In a February 4, 2008, memo, Harold Ickes states, "Given the lack of polling information, for post 5 Feb states, these projections are based on best estimates." The memo was cited in Green, *The Front-Runner's Fall.*

38. "Strategy Session Overview—Sunday, March 30, 2008," ibid.

39. Between March 9 and 19, 2008, there were the following Democratic contests: Louisiana primary, Nebraska caucus, Washington State caucuses, Maine caucus, D.C. primary, Maryland primary, Virginia primary, Hawaii caucus, Wisconsin primary.

40. The FEC loosened some regulations in the early 1990s, but by the 2008 campaign the expenditure limits of $1,532,000 in Iowa and $841,000 in New Hampshire had become laughable. See www.fec.gov/pages/brochures/pubfund_limits_2008.shtml [April 26, 2009].

41. Don Van Natta and John M. Broder, "The 2000 Campaign: The Money: With a Still Ample Treasury Bush Builds a Green 'Fire Wall' against McCain," *New York Times,* February 21, 2000.

42. See www.fec.gov [March 19, 2009].

43. Brian C. Mooney, "After Spending in N.H., Iowa, Money May Be Tight," *Boston Globe,* January 6, 2008.

Chapter Three

1. The New Hampshire Political Library, at www.politicallibrary.org/Past-Primary/History.aspx [April 22, 2009].

2. "Eisenhower Defeats Taft, Kefauver Wins over Truman in New Hampshire Primary," *New York Times,* March 12, 1952.

3. Democratic National Committee, Commission on Presidential Nomination and Party Structure, Transcript, May 9, 1977, p. 11, available from the National Archives or through the Office of the Secretary of the Democratic National Committee, Washington.

4. Ibid., p.145.

5. DNC, Commission on Presidential Nomination and Party Structure, Transcript, May 9, 1977, pp. 152–53.

6. Ibid., January 21, 1978, pp. 112–13.

7. Ibid., p. 52.

8. The New Hampshire hearing was held on October 26, 1977, and the Iowa hearing on December 3, 1977. Hearing summaries can be found in files of the Commission on Presidential Nomination and Party Structure at the Democratic National Committee.

9. DNC, Commission on Presidential Nomination and Party Structure, Transcript, August 11, 1977, p. 120.

10. DNC, Commission on Presidential Nomination and Party Structure, Transcript, January 21, 1978, p. 122.

11. Adam Clymer, "Carter Aides Spur Drive to End Early Caucuses," *New York Times,* January 22, 1978.

12. See *New Republic,* May 27, 1978; Connie Stewart in the *Des Moines Register,* September 29, 1977; *Washington Post,* March 3,1978.

13. DNC, Commission on Presidential Nomination and Party Structure, Transcript, January 21, 1978, p. 139.

14. DNC, Delegate Selection Rules for the 1980 Democratic Convention, adopted by the Democratic National Committee 1978, p. 10.

15. *Manchester Union Leader,* April 27, 1979.

16. DNC, Commission on Presidential Nominations (Hunt Commission), Transcript, August 20, 1981, p. 63.

17. Ibid., August 21, 1981, p. 13.

18. Quoted in *The Baron Report,* edited by Alan Baron, October 11, 1981, p. 1.

19. DNC, Commission on Presidential Nominations, Transcript, January 15, 1982, 71.

20. U.S. Representative Norman D'Amours (D-N.H.), quoted in the testimony of William G. Mayer to the Hunt Commission, Transcript, November 6, 1981.

21. Ibid., p. 7.

22. Interview with John Rendon, political consultant to Governor Gallen and New Hampshire's state Democratic Party, March 14, 1985.

23. See *Cousins* v. *Wigoda*, 419 U.S. 477 (1975); and *Democratic Party of the United States* v. *Wisconsin*, 450 U.S. 107 (1981).

24. DNC, Commission on Presidential Nominations, Transcript, November 6, 1981, pp. 215–17.

25. The author was a member of the Technical Advisory Committee.

26. DNC, Commission on Presidential Nominations, Transcript, January 15, 1982, p. 64.

27. This decision was made in a meeting of senior Mondale advisers at Mondale's law firm on January 9, 1982, which the author attended.

28. DNC, Commission on Presidential Nominations, Transcript, January 15, 1982, p. 12.

29. Ibid., p. 11.

30. Ibid., p. 95.

31. DNC, Commission on Presidential Nominations, Transcript, February 5, 1982, p. 5.

32. See Title LXIII, Election of Officers and Delegates, Chapter 653:9 (www.gen court.state.nh.us/rsa/html/lxiii/653/653-9.htm [March 19, 2009]).

33. See David Yepson, "Branstad Threatens to Keep Democratic Caucuses Early," *Des Moines Register,* March 29, 1983.

34. Ibid.

35. See Fred Barnes, "New Hampshire Fights to Keep Its Primary First," *Baltimore Sun,* April 18, 1983.

36. See Paul Taylor, "Who's on First? Rears Its Ugly Head in National Primaries," *Washington Post,* April 27, 1983. See also Curtis Wilke, "Democrats in Disorder over Primary Schedule," *Boston Globe,* April 28, 1983.

37. See Democratic National Committee, Delegate Selection Rules for the 1984 Democratic National Convention, 1982, Rule 19C.

38. Quoted in Barnes, "New Hampshire Fights."

39. See Joseph Mianomany, United Press International, May 3, 1983.

40. See Senate File 552 amending Section 43.92 of the Iowa Code. See also Roger Munns, "Iowa Caucus Stays First-in-the-Nation," *Des Moines Register,* May 12, 1983.

41. "New Hampshire Resubmission Evaluation," passed by the CRC, October 14, 1983, files of the Compliance Review Commission, Washington.

42. Interview with Charles Campion, New Hampshire state coordinator, Mondale for President campaign, March 14, 1985.

43. Letter to Walter Mondale from Alan Cranston, November 23, 1983, author's files.

44. See "Harkin Supports Feb. 27 as a Date for the Iowa Caucus," *Des Moines Register,* November 17, 1983.

45. Jonathan Moore, ed., *Campaign for President: The Managers Look at 1984* (Dover, Mass.: Auburn, 1986.)

46. See *Campbell et al.* v. *Iowa State Central Committee,* #83-115-w, filed December 13, 1983, U.S. District Court, Southern District of Iowa, Western Division.

47. Ibid.

48. "GOP Alters Nominating Process," Political Report, *1996 Congressional Quarterly Almanac* (Washington: Congressional Quarterly, 1996), pp. 11–18.

49. "Dean Tapes: Nucks, Gibes and Videotape," *The Hotline,* January 9, 2004.

50. Mike Glover, "Dean Tries to Stem Fallout from Comments about Caucuses," Associated Press, January 9, 2004.

51. Quoted in States News Service, September 6, 2007.

52. Ron Walters, testimony before the Commission on Presidential Timing and Scheduling, Transcript, March 12, 2005, p. 97, available through the Office of the Secretary of the Democratic National Committee, Washington.

53. Ibid., p. 135.

54. E. J. Dionne, "Democrats Revisit Party Reform," *Washington Post,* February 26, 2005.

55. "Primary Calendar: MI Wants Fairness, Yes They Do," *The Hotline,* November 7, 2005, section: White House 2008.

56. DeWayne Wickham, "Democrats Must Fold Diversity into Party Primaries, Caucuses," *USA Today,* December 13, 2005.

57. "New Hampshire Secretary of State Says New Hampshire Primary Could Be in 2007," PR Newswire, May 29, 2007.

58. Robert A. Dahl, *A Preface to Democratic Theory* (University of Chicago Press, 1963), p. 90.

Chapter Four

1. See Barbara Norrander, *Super Tuesday* (University of Kentucky Press, 1992), p. 43; and Elaine C. Kamarck, "Delegate Allocation Rules in Presidential Nomination Systems: A Comparison between the Democrats and the Republicans," *Journal of Law and Politics* 4 (1987): 275–310.

2. David Price, *Bringing Back the Parties* (Washington: Congressional Quarterly Press, 1984), p. 219.

3. Interview with Frank Fahrenkopf, November 30, 2008.

4. For a good discussion of this, see Paul T. David and James W. Ceaser, *Proportional Representation in Presidential Nominating Politics* (University of Virginia Press, 1980), chap. 5.

5. Commission on Party Structure and Delegate Selection, 1970, p. 32. Commission files and transcripts are available from the National Archives or through the Office of the Secretary of the Democratic National Committee, Washington.

6. Ibid., guideline B-6.

7. For a longer description of this fight, see Theodore H. White, *The Making of the President, 1972* (New York: Bantam Books, 1973), chap. 7; and Bruce Miroff, *The Liberals' Moment: The McGovern Insurgency and the Identity Crisis of the Democratic Party* (University of Kansas Press, 2007), chap. 4.

8. Transcripts of the Credentials Committee for the 1972 Democratic Convention, June 29, 1972, p. 594, Available from the National Archives or through the Office of the Secretary of the Democratic National Committee, Washington.

9. Transcripts of the Rules Committee for the 1972 Democratic Convention, p. 3, available from the National Archives or through the Office of the Secretary of the Democratic National Committee, Washington.

10. Rules Committee Report to the 1972 Democratic Convention, p. 12, available from the National Archives or through the Office of the Secretary of the Democratic National Committee, Washington.

11. Quoted in Philip A. Klinker, *The Losing Parties: Out-Party National Committees* (Yale University Press, 1994), p. 106.

12. Commission on Delegate Selection and Party Structure (not the same as the similarly named commission cited in note 5 and elsewhere), April 28, 1973, transcript of remarks by Barbara Mikulski, p. 7.

13. Interview with Don Fowler, June 10, 1985.

14. Interview with Ken Bode, June 6, 1985.

15. It is interesting to note that the leaders of the CDM went on to become the leaders of the neoconservative movement in the 1980s and later: among them were Ben Wattenberg, Max Kampelman, Jeane Kirkpatrick, Nathan Glazer, Seymour Martin Lipset, Michael Novak, Norman Podhoretz, and Midge Decter. See Klinker, *The Losing Parties*, p. 110.

16. Ibid., chap. 6.

17. Interview with Ken Bode, June 6, 1985.

18. Commission on Delegate Selection and Party Structure, 1973.

19. Michael Malbin, "Political Controversy over Charter Reflects Democratic Party Division," *National Journal*, September 21, 1974, p. 1409.

20. Ibid., p. 1414.

21. Ibid.

22. Interview with Mark Siegel, December 2, 1986.

23. *Charter of the Democratic Party of the United States* (Washington: Democratic National Committee), Article II, section 4.

24. Interview with John Perkins of the AFL-CIO, December 9, 1985.

25. Report of the Rules Committee to the 1976 Convention, pp. 18–19. Office of the Secretary of the Democratic National Committee, Washington.

26. Interview with Morley Winograd, November 15, 1985.

27. Statement of Mildred Nichols, Democratic national committeewoman from Rhode Island, *Official Proceedings of the 1976 Democratic National Convention,* p. 350; and statement of Carrin Patman, Mikulski Commission member from Texas, p. 349, available from the Office of the Secretary of the Democratic National Committee, Washington.

28. Commission on Presidential Nomination and Party Structure, Transcript, September 9, 1977, p. 435.

29. Ibid., p. 437.

30. Commission on Presidential Nomination and Party Structure, Transcript, January 21, 1978, p. 105.

31. Ibid., p. 107.

32. Ibid.

33. Adam Clymer, "Carter Aides Spur Drive to End Early Caucuses," *New York Times,* January 22, 1978.

34. Editorial, *Washington Post,* January 31, 1978.

35. "Overdog's Charter," *The Economist,* February 4, 1978, pp. 42–43.

36. Dan Mcleod, Associated Press Wire, February 8, 1976.

37. Letter from Senator George McGovern to "Fellow Democrats," May 3, 1978, author's files.

38. See, for example, Terrence Smith, "It's Carter Folk vs. Regular Democrats," *New York Times,* December 11, 1977.

39. Memorandum to President Jimmy Carter from John White and Hamilton Jordan, May 9, 1978, author's files.

40. *Delegate Selection Rules for the 1980 Democratic Convention* (Washington: Democratic National Committee, 1978), p. 12.

41. Ken Bode, "Sliding Windows to Floating Thresholds Restacking the Deck," *New Republic,* May 27, 1978.

42. David Broder, "Democrats Tighten Rules in '80 Nominating Process," *Washington Post,* June 10, 1978, p. 2.

43. See John Scotzin, "Complex Delegate Setup May Bump 'Winners,'" *Harrisburg*

Patriot, January 22, 1979; and comments by Dorothy Zug, Commission on Presidential Nomination, Transcript, November 6, 1981, pp. 90–91.

44. "Chicago Mayor Byrne Apparently Supports Carter for Re-Election," *Washington Post,* October 9, 1979; "Chicago Mayor Clarifies Comment on Support of Carter," *Washington Post,* October 10, 1979; "Chicago Mayor Continues to Be Evasive on Backing President Carter," *Washington Post,* October 16, 1979; "Chicago Mayor Says She Will Support Kennedy for President," *Washington Post,* October 28, 1979.

45. The poll was conducted by Market Share Corp. on October 10, 1979, and reported by UPI at the time and on January 3, 1980.

46. See Legal Advisory Board memo to the CRC, November 16, 1979, files of the Democratic National Committee and author's files.

47. *Delegate Selection Rules for the 1980 Democratic Convention,* p. 13.

48. DNC, Regulations of the Compliance Review Commission, adopted February 23, 1979.

49. Letter from Robert Walling, counsel, Georgia Democratic Party, to Rick Hutcheson, White House, July 30, 1979, author's files.

50. See DNC, complaint before the Judicial Council of the Democratic Party, Appendixes B and C, CRC response to Libby Moroff et al., January, 1980.

51. Regulations of the Compliance Review Commission, as amended, September 7, 1979.

52. The complainants were Libby Moroff, New York; Jo Baer, New York; Don Fraser, Minn.; John Isaacs, D.C.; and Louis Maisel, Maine.

53. Letter from Libby Moroff et al. to the Honorable James O'Hara, chair of the DNC Judicial Council, October 4, 1979.

54. See Commission on Presidential Nomination, Transcript, November 7, 1981.

55. Commission on Presidential Nomination, Transcript, January 14, 1982, p. 243.

56. The "at-large" portion of a delegation is that portion that is elected statewide, usually at a state convention, as opposed to at the congressional district level.

57. Commission on Presidential Nominations, Transcript, January 15, 1982, pp. 125–26.

58. Ibid., p. 150.

59. Ibid., p. 152.

60. William Raspberry, "Jesse Jackson—Independent?" *Washington Post,* August 12, 1983.

61. United Press International, Monday PM Cycle, Washington News, March 23, 1983.

62. See Dan Balz, "Mondale and Jackson Camps Engaged in Unusual Dialogue," *Washington Post,* July 23, 1983.

63. Interview with Tom Donilon, February 5, 1986.

64. See "Jackson Attacks Democratic Party's Presidential Nominating Process, Saying It Locks Out Poor and Minorities," *Washington Post*, November 10, 1983.

65. Letter from Jesse Jackson to Charles T. Mannatt, December 20, 1983, author's files; and Howell Raines, "Democrats Reach Accord in Dispute on Delegates," *New York Times*, December 20, 1983.

66. Jack W. Germond and Jules Witcover, *Wake Me When It's Over: Presidential Politics of 1984* (New York: Macmillan, 1985), p. 346.

67. Testimony of U.S. Representative John Conyers Jr. before the Fairness Commission of the Democratic National Committee, Southern Regional Hearing, New Orleans, Louisiana, August 23, 1985, files of the Fairness Commission, Office of the Secretary of the Democratic National Committee and National Archives, Washington.

68. Statement of Jesse Jackson of the National Rainbow Coalition, August 23, 1985, in ibid.

69. The debate over the Rules Committee Report at the 1984 Convention contained heated language against loophole primaries, and yet the party in its subsequent actions ignored the convention debate.

70. Letter from Jesse Jackson to Paul Kirk, October 21, 1985, files of the Fairness Commission, Office of the Secretary of the Democratic National Committee and National Archives, Washington.

71. See Barbara Norrander, *Super Tuesday: Regional Politics and Presidential Primaries* (University of Kentucky Press, 1992), p. 83.

72. Jackson missed filing 37 delegates in Pennsylvania and failed to get on the ballot in three congressional districts in Ohio. Evans Witt, "The Road Is Long with Many a Winding Turn," Associated Press, April 20, 1988.

73. Richard E. Berke, "Jackson Renews Complaint over His Share of the Delegates," *New York Times*, May 6, 1988.

74. "Harmony's Price," *Washington Post*, Editorial, June 29, 1988.

75. Official Proceedings of the Democratic National Convention, Report of the Rules Committee to the 1988 Democratic National Convention, Resolution 2, July 18, 1988, p. 7.

76. Ibid., p. 192.

Chapter Five

1. See Paul T. David and James W. Ceaser, *Proportional Representation in Presidential Nominating Politics* (University of Virginia Press, 1980), p. 114.

2. Lou Cannon, "Bill to Alter Calif. Primary Fails; Reagan Benefited," *Washington Post*, January 24, 1980.

3. See Joseph Scott, *The Political Animal,* a newsletter published in Los Angeles by Scott, January 7, 1980.

4. "Election Notes," *Congressional Quarterly Weekly Report,* May 3, 1980, p. 1203.

5. See "Delegate Selection Rules to the 1984 Democratic Convention," Democratic National Committee, Office of the Secretary, Washington, D.C.

6. See Gene Jordan, "Dems Adopt Plan to Give Glenn All of Ohio's Delegates," *Columbus Dispatch,* June 14, 1983.

7. See Brent Larkin, "Ohio Democrats Seek Bonus Delegate System," *Plain Dealer* (Cleveland), November 18, 1983.

8. Dale Leach, Associated Press, AM Cycle, May 9, 1984.

9. Interview with David Von Savage, September 18, 2008.

10. Marc Ambinder, "The Giuliani Strategy Encapsulated," *Atlantic Monthly* blog on politics, November 12, 2007 (http://marcambinder.theatlantic.com/archives/2007/11/the_giuliani_strategy_encapsul.php [April 23, 2009]).

11. Comments of Steve Grubbs, campaign manager for Tommy Thompson, at "Campaign for President: The Managers Look at 2008," at the John F. Kennedy School of Government, Harvard University, December 11, 2008.

12. Charles J. Dean, "Arkansan Espouses America's Promise, Good Fortunes; Huckabee Embraces Dreams, Traditions," *Birmingham News,* January 27, 2008.

13. Bill Peterson and Robert Kaiser, "The Eagle's Nose Dive: Bush Plummeting in a Campaign Tailspin," *Washington Post,* March 22, 1980.

14. See *Congressional Quarterly Weekly Report,* March 29, 1980, p. 851.

15. David S. Broder, "Bush Tops Reagan in Conn. Primary; Kennedy Upsets President; Bush Wins in Connecticut; Reagan Adds to Total in N.Y.," *Washington Post,* March 26, 1980.

16. David Broder, "Mathematics Worked against Kennedy and Bush," *Washington Post,* March 27, 1980.

17. "In Sharp Reversal from '76, Reagan Wins Battle for Delegates," Associated Press, March 25, 1980; Lou Cannon, "Reagan Woos Northeast, the Key to His Nomination Strategy," *Washington Post,* January 20, 1980; Walter R. Mears, "An AP News Analysis," Associated Press, March 24, 1980.

18. *Federal Election Commission Reports on Financial Activity, 1979–1980* (Washington: Federal Election Commission, 1981), p. 13.

19. David S. Broder, "Bush Wins Pa.; Democratic Race Tight; Reagan Builds Delegate Total; Bush Beats Reagan Pa. GOP Voting," *Washington Post,* April 23, 1980.

20. David S. Broder and Bill Peterson, "Bush, Reagan Campaigns Crisscross Pennsylvania in Final Pitch for Votes," *Washington Post,* April 22, 1980.

21. Ibid.

22. Broder, "Bush Wins Pa."

23. Interview with Susan Morrison, Bush campaign deputy press secretary, March 26, 1986.

24. See Jack W. Germond and Jules Witcover, *Wake Me When It's Over: Presidential Politics of 1984* (New York: Macmillan, 1985), pp. 182–83.

25. Ibid., p. 197.

26. Ibid.

27. See, for instance, Hedrick Smith, "How Mondale's Flagging Campaign Was Revived," *New York Times*, March 15, 1984; Tom Wicker, "Balance on Tuesday," *New York Times*, March 16, 1984.

28. Author's files.

29. On February 18, 2008, I appeared with Senator Hart on "All Things Considered" on National Public Radio, where he called himself the first "victim" of superdelegates.

30. Evans Witt, "Hart Faces Uphill Battle to Win Delegates," Associated Press, March 1, 1984. Florida's pledged delegates consisted of 84 delegates elected directly on the primary ballot and 39 at-large delegates apportioned to candidates according to the proportion of the vote the presidential candidate won at the district level.

31. Ibid. See also James I. Lengle, "Democratic Party Reforms: The Past a Prologue to the 1988 Campaign," *Journal of Law and Politics* 4 (1987): 233–74.

32. "Hart Challenging Florida At-Large Delegate Selection," Associated Press, March 21, 1984.

33. See "Democratic Delegate Count," *Washington Post*, March 11, 1984.

34. Ibid.

35. Those who remained uncommitted did so to preserve their options at the convention.

36. See also "Mondale's 'Winner-Take-All' Edge," *Congressional Quarterly*, May 12, 1984, p. 1085, for a chart of how Mondale's wins in key loophole states contributed to his edge over Hart.

37. James I. Lengle and Byron E. Shafer, "Primary Rules, Political Power and Social Change," in *Presidential Politics: Readings on Nominations and Elections*, edited by Lengle and Shafer (New York: St. Martin's Press, 1980).

38. Ibid., p. 228.

39. *Congressional Quarterly Weekly Report*, July 5, 1980.

40. Interview with John Rendon, Carter's Pennsylvania field director, and Paul Tully, Kennedy's field director, March 14, 1985.

41. Off-the-record interviews with the author.

42. Memo from Harold Ickes to Clinton campaign staff, Monday, February 4, 2008, from *Atlantic Monthly*, September 2008, pp. 64–74 (www.theatlantic.com/doc/200808u/clinton-memos [March 23, 2009]).

Chapter Six

1. "Presidential Nominating Conventions: Past, Present and Future," *The Forum* 5, no. 4 (2008), Article 6.

2. James W. Ceaser, *Presidential Selection: Theory and Development* (Princeton University Press, 1979), p. 236.

3. Interview with Morley Winograd, June 11, 2008.

4. David Price, *Bringing Back the Parties* (Washington: Congressional Quarterly Press, 1984), p. 214.

5. Nelson W. Polsby, *Consequences of Party Reform* (New York: Oxford University Press, 1983), p. 161.

6. Barbara Farah, "Convention Delegates: Party Reform and the Representativeness of Party Elites—1972–1980," paper presented at the Annual Meeting of the American Political Science Association, New York, September 1981.

7. Warren Mitofsky and Martin Plissner, "The Making of the Delegates, 1968–1980," *Public Opinion Magazine,* October/November 1980, p. 43.

8. In contrast, in the first years of the post-reform era, delegates were elected either on the ballot or in some sort of pre-primary meeting. As the years wore on, party leaders realized that it made more sense to elect delegates after the primary had occurred. This removed the uncomfortable necessity of having to guess correctly which presidential candidate would win in your district or state.

9. Off-the-record conversation with the author, June 11, 2008.

10. Paul T. David and James W. Ceaser, *Proportional Representation in Presidential Nominating Politics* (University of Virginia Press, 1980), p. 38.

11. Arthur Krock, "G.O.P. Choice May Hinge on Delegate Contests," *New York Times,* June 22, 1952.

12. Testimony of Representative Gillis W. Long, Democrat of Louisiana, November 6, 1981, files of the Hunt Commission, Democratic National Committee, National Archives.

13. Remarks, Governor James B. Hunt Jr., Conference on the Parties and the Nominating Process, Institute of Politics, JFK School of Government, Harvard University, December 5, 1981, author's files.

14. See Susan Estrich, "Unintended Consequence," memorandum to the Hunt Commission, September 9, 1981, author's files.

15. See Price, *Bringing Back the Parties,* pp. 69–71.

16. At-large delegates are elected in statewide meetings after delegates are elected in congressional districts. In the Democratic Party the purpose of the at-large delegation is to make sure that the whole delegation is equally divided between men and women and that there are representative numbers of minorities in the delegation.

17. Jack W. Germond and Jules Witcover, *Wake Me When It's Over: Presidential Politics of 1984* (New York: Macmillan, 1985), p. 311.

18. Ibid., p. 320.

19. Author's files, internal Mondale campaign delegate count.

20. See Stephen Ohlemacher, "AP Exclusive: Clinton Leads with Party Insiders," Associated Press, February 10, 2008. See also Sean Mussenden, "Count of Delegates Varies by Source; News Organizations Have Different Ways to Arrive at Tallies," *Richmond Times-Dispatch*, February 13, 2008.

21. "Top Clinton Adviser Says Superdelegates Will Decide Election, Obama's Victories 'Irrelevant,'" Foxnews.com, February 16, 2008 (www.foxnews.com/politics/elections/2008/02/16/top-clinton-adviser-says-superdelegates-will-decide-election-obamas-victories-irrelevant/ [April 2, 2009]).

22. "Blogometer: Pinned Down by Blogger Fire," *The Hotline*, February 26, 2008.

23. Interview with Jeff Berman, November 24, 2008.

24. Salena Zito, "Burden of Proof," *Pittsburgh Tribune-Review*, April 13, 2008 (www.freerepublic.com/focus/f-news/2000916/posts [April 27, 2009]).

25. Jake Tapper, "Obama Takes Lead in Super-Delegate Tally," abcnews.com, May 9, 2008; Stephen Ohlemacher, Associated Press, May 10, 2008.

26. Mark Penn memo in Joshua Green, "The Front-Runner's Fall," *Atlantic Monthly*, September 2008, pp. 64–74 (www.theatlantic.com/doc/200808u/clinton-memos [April 2, 2009]).

27. Off-the-record conversation with the author, June 1, 2008.

28. Gallup Poll conducted June 16–19, 1972, and reported in "Gallup Finds Nixon Continues to Lead Top 2 Democrats," *New York Times*, July 3, 1972.

29. "Carter Leads Ford or Reagan by 2–1," Facts on File World News Digest, August 7, 1976.

30. Barry Sussman, "New Polls Show Closer '80 Race; New Polls Suggest Carter–Reagan Race Getting Tighter," *Washington Post*, August 10, 1980.

31. Commission on Presidential Nomination and Party Structure, Transcript, January 21, 1978, p. 34.

32. Edward Walsh and T. R. Reid, "Carter Aides Feel Kennedy Is Whipped, Turn Attention to Battle with Reagan," *Washington Post*, March 19, 1980.

33. See "Kennedy Camp Dreams of Convention Floor Fight," *Washington Post*, April 16, 1980.

34. Lou Cannon, "Kennedy Will Withdraw if . . . : Kennedy Raises the Stakes for Debate," *Washington Post*, May 16, 1980.

35. V. O. Key, *Politics, Parties and Pressure Groups* (New York: Thomas Y. Crowell, 1964), p. 411.

36. See remarks of Evans Witt of the Associated Press on the *MacNeil/Lehrer Report,* July 7, 1980.

37. *Gallup Opinion Index,* Report 180 (Princeton, N.J.: Gallup Poll, August 1980).

38. Joseph Kraft, "The Revolt of the 40," *Washington Post,* July 29, 1980.

Chapter Seven

1. Eastern Region: Connecticut, Delaware, Maine, Maryland, Massachusetts, New Jersey, New York, Pennsylvania, Rhode Island, Vermont, West Virginia, and the District of Columbia. Southern Region: Alabama, Arkansas, Florida, Georgia, Kentucky, Louisiana, Mississippi, North Carolina, Oklahoma, South Carolina, Tennessee, Texas, Virginia, Puerto Rico and the Virgin Islands. Midwestern Region: Illinois, Indiana, Kansas, Michigan, Minnesota, Missouri, Nebraska, North Dakota, Ohio, South Dakota and Wisconsin. Western Region: Alaska, Arizona, California, Colorado, Hawaii, Idaho, Montana, Nevada, New Mexico, Oregon, Utah, Washington, Wyoming, and Guam.

2. Comment at the Symposium on the Future of Presidential Primaries, Harvard University, Kennedy School of Government, Institute of Politics, April 29, 2008. Proceedings available at www.iop.harvard.edu/var/ezp_site/storage/fckeditor/file/Presidential%20Primaries%20Symposium [April 27, 2009].

3. Group 1: American Samoa, Arizona, California, Colorado, Delaware, Guam, Hawaii, Kansas, Maryland, Nevada, New Mexico, New York, the Northern Mariana Islands, Pennsylvania, Utah. Group 2: Alaska, Alabama, Florida, Georgia, Idaho, Mississippi, North Carolina, Oregon, Puerto Rico, South Carolina, Tennessee, the Virgin Islands, Washington. Group 3: Arkansas, Illinois, Indiana, Louisiana, Michigan, Ohio, Oklahoma, Texas, Wisconsin. Group 4: Connecticut, the District of Columbia, Iowa, Kentucky, Maine, Massachusetts, Minnesota, Missouri, Montana, Nebraska, New Hampshire, New Jersey, North Dakota, Rhode Island, South Dakota, Vermont, Virginia, West Virginia, Wyoming.

4. Kennedy School Symposium on the Future of Presidential Primaries.

5. Ibid.

6. Alaska, Delaware, District of Columbia, Hawaii, Idaho, Maine, Montana, Nebraska, New Mexico, North Dakota, Rhode Island, South Dakota, Vermont, West Virginia, Wyoming (plus the territories).

7. Kennedy School Symposium on the Future of Presidential Primaries.

8. The second pod contains New York, Kentucky, Ohio, Colorado, Mississippi, Alabama, and Washington. The third pod: Maine, New Hampshire, Vermont, Missouri, Minnesota, Arizona, New Mexico, Virginia, California. The fourth pod:

Massachusetts, Tennessee, Iowa, Texas, Florida, Hawaii, and Alaska. The fifth pod: Delaware, New Jersey, Maryland, Illinois, North Carolina, Louisiana, Oregon. The sixth pod: Pennsylvania, Indiana, Wisconsin, South Carolina, Kansas, Nebraska, Montana, Wyoming, North Dakota, and South Dakota.

9. Kennedy School Symposium on the Future of Presidential Primaries.

10. Ibid.

11. Pod 1: American Samoa, Virgin Islands, Guam, Wyoming, District of Columbia, Vermont, Alaska, North Dakota, South Dakota, Delaware, Montana, Rhode Island, New Hampshire, Hawaii, Idaho, Maine, and Puerto Rico. Population total: 14.8 million.

Pod 2: Nebraska, New Mexico, Nevada, West Virginia, Utah, Arkansas, Kansas, Mississippi, Iowa, Connecticut, Oregon, Oklahoma, and South Carolina. Population total: 33.5 million.

Pod 3: Kentucky, Colorado, Alabama, Louisiana, Arizona, Minnesota, Maryland, Wisconsin, Tennessee, Missouri, Washington, Indiana, and Massachusetts. Population total: 64.9 million.

Pod 4: Virginia, North Carolina, Georgia, New Jersey, Michigan, Ohio, Pennsylvania, Illinois, Florida, New York, Texas, and California. Population total: 160.6 million.

12. See Robert D. Loevy, *The Flawed Path to the Presidency: Unfairness and Inequality in the Presidential Selection Process* (State University of New York Press, 1992).

13. Comment at the Kennedy School Symposium on the Future of Presidential Primaries.

14. Ibid.

15. Antonin Scalia, "The Legal Framework for Reform," *Commonsense* 4, no. 2 (1981): 40.

16. *Smith* v. *Allwright,* 321 U.S. 649, 1944.

17. *Burroughs* v. *United States,* 290 U.S. 534 (1934).

18. *Buckley* v. *Valeo,* 424 U.S. 1 (1976).

19. *Oregon* v. *Mitchell,* 400 U.S. 112 (1970).

20. *Ray* v. *Blair,* 343 U.S. 214 (1952).

21. *Cousins* v. *Wigoda,* 419, U.S. 477 (1974).

22. Kennedy School Symposium on the Future of Presidential Primaries.

23. William G. Mayer, "Written Statement on Federal Primary Legislation, Submitted to the Senate Rules Committee," September 19, 2007. See www.iop.harvard.edu/var/ezp_site/storage/fckeditor/file/Presidential%20Primaries%20Symposium.

24. Kevin Coleman, "Presidential Nominating Process: Current Issues and Legislation in the 106th Congress," Congressional Research Service Report for Congress, March 21, 2000, reprinted in Advisory Commission on the Presidential

Nominating Process, *Nominating Future Presidents: A Review of the Republican Process* (Washington: Republican National Committee, May 2000), pp. 101–06.

25. Kennedy School Symposium on the Future of Presidential Primaries.

26. Ibid.

27. Ibid.

28. Ibid.

29. Costas Panagopoulos, "The Polls-Trends: Electoral Reform," *Public Opinion Quarterly* (Winter 2004): 623.

30. Ibid.; *New York Times*/CBS polls cited at: http://graphics.nytimes.com/packages/pdf/politics/20070718_poll_results.pdf [April 27, 2009].

31. Interview with Jim Roosevelt, December 19, 2008.

INDEX

Abrams, Nancy, 99
Affirmative action, 89, 92, 106
AFL-CIO, 58, 60, 61, 88–89, 108–09, 156
Agnew, Spiro, 94, 165
Alexander, Lamar, 174
Allbaugh, Joe, 73
Americans for Democratic Action, 99
Anuzis, Saul, 177, 182
Anuzis-Dingell Plan, 177
Ariyoshi, George, 155
Askew, Marge, 22
Askew, Reubin, 28, 68, 133, 134
Atwater, Lee, 36, 37
Automatic delegates, Republican Party, 20–21

Baer, Ken, 25
Baker, Howard, 15
Baron, Alan, 90
Barry, Marion, 118
Battaglia, Basil, 178
Bayh, Birch, 65
Beauty contests, 19, 64, 65
Beckel, Bob, 33, 114

Bennett, Robert, 176–77, 184–85
Bentsen, Lloyd, 94
Berman, Jeff, 43–44, 45–46, 133, 163
Biden, Joseph, 78
Bode, Ken, 55–56, 87, 90–91, 101, 107
Bond, Julian, 112
Boyer, Richard, 66
Bradley, Bill, 35
Brazile, Donna, 12
Brennan, Joseph, 16
Bringing Back the Parties (Price), 82–84, 149
Broder, David, 56, 128
Brokaw, Tom, 131
Brown, Jerry, 29, 93
Brown, Ron, 117
Brown, William, 92
Bruno, George, 68
Buchanan, Pat, 37, 71–72
Buckley v. *Valeo*, 180
Burroughs v. *United States*, 180
Busch, Andrew E., 24–25
Bush, George H. W.: election of *1988*, 37, 39. *See also* Election and primaries of *1980*

Bush, George W. *See* Election and primaries of *2000;* Election and primaries of *2004*

Byrne, Jane, 104, 112

Caddell, Pat, 61, 96, 98
Campbell, Carroll, 36
Campbell, Ed, 65, 69
Carroll, Tom, 92
Carter, Billy, 169
Carter, Jimmy: outcomes of reforms in presidency of, 24; relations with Democratic Party, 99–100. *See also* Election and primaries of *1976;* Election and primaries of *1980*
Casey, Carol, 107
Caucuses: future prospects, 185; McGovern-Fraser reforms, 14–15, 18; Obama *2008* campaign strategy, 45, 46, 142–45; party preference for primaries, 17–19, 21; representativeness rules, 18–19; requirement for simultaneous scheduling, 16–17; success of outsider candidates in, 15, 16. *See also* Iowa caucuses
Ceasar, James, 148
Cecil, Guy, 44
Charter Commission, 88, 89, 90, 91–92
Clinton, Bill, 1, 141; primaries of *1992* election, 41–43
Clinton, Hillary. *See* Election and primaries of *2008*
Coalition for a Democratic Majority, 91, 92
Collins, Martha Layne, 155
Commission on Delegate Selection (Mikulski Commission), 88–89, 90, 91, 92
Commission on Presidential Nominations, 58
Commission on Presidential Nomination Timing and Scheduling, 75–77

Commission on the Role and Future of Presidential Primaries, 96
Compliance Review Commission, Democratic Party, 29, 30, 56, 64, 67–68, 102, 103–05, 106, 122–23
Connally, John B., 36–37
Consequences of Party Reform (Polsby), 24
Constitutional law on congressional authority over nominating process, 179–81
Conventions. *See* Nominating conventions
Conyers, John, Jr., 115–16
Cousins v. *Wigoda,* 180
Cranston, Alan, 66, 69
Credentials challenges, 88–89, 94
Credentials Committee, Democratic Party, 86–87, 183–84
Crocker, Bill, 175–76
Crump, Edward, 9
Curtis, Ken, 99–100

Dahl, Robert, 80
Daley, Richard, 13, 89, 112
D'Amours, Norman, 66
Davis, Arturo, 45
Dean, Howard, 48–59, 74
DeFazio, Peter, 163
Delaware Plan for regional primaries, 178
Delegate counts: course of *1984* Democratic election, 129–34; course of *1980* Republican election, 127–29; incentives for later primary schedule, 73, 186; momentum and, 127–34; Obama *2008* strategy, 43, 44–45, 46; strategic significance, 4, 81, 119–21, 146
Delegate selection and allocation: bonus delegates, 73, 82, 111, 186; candidate right of approval, 149–50; Democratic *1968* convention, 14,

85; evolution of New Hampshire rules, 51–52; future prospects, 185; Hunt Commission changes, 59; Jackson challenges to *1984* rules, 112–16; McGovern-Fraser reforms, 15; New Hampshire *1984* conflict with Democratic Party, 65–66; party control over state rules for, 60–61, 69–71; party differences, 82–85; pledged status, 152–55, 167, 171; pre-reform nominating system, 8; robot rule, 168–70, 171; sequencing of *2008* primaries and, 123–27; strategic manipulation of rules, 121–27; strategic significance, 146; winner-take-all primaries, 82, 104–06, 125–27, 142. *See also* Delegate counts; Proportional representation

Democratic Conference, 99

Devine, Tad, 35, 159

Dingell, Debbie, 76, 77

Dionne, E. J., 76

Direct election of president, 25

Dodd, Christopher, 78

Dole, Bob, 37, 48, 71–73

Donilon, Tom, 104, 113, 114

Duhaime, Mike, 124

Dukakis, Michael. *See* Election and primaries of *1988*

Duncan, Mike, 184

Dutton, Fred, 86

Eisenhower, Dwight D., 52

Election and primaries of *1912,* 147–48

Election and primaries of *1952,* 9–10

Election and primaries of *1960,* 10–11

Election and primaries of *1964,* 11–12

Election and primaries of *1968:* Democratic convention voting rules, 85; motivation for nomination process reform, 13–14

Election and primaries of *1972:* Democratic convention, 148–50, 165, 166; Democratic delegate allocation rules, 86–87; Democratic primaries, 15–16; Iowa caucuses, 17

Election and primaries of *1976:* Carter campaign strategy, 27–28, 50, 53, 55–56; delegate allocation rules, 121; delegate counts, 94; Democratic convention, 93–96; media coverage, 21; Republican convention, 165, 166

Election and primaries of *1980:* delegate allocation rules, 96–106, 121–22; Democratic candidates' strategies and outcomes, 137–40; Democratic convention, 165–66, 167–70; Democratic Party's perception of, 106–07, 156; Republican strategies and outcomes, 36–37, 127–29; sequencing of primary contests, 28–31, 36–37, 55–56

Election and primaries of *1984:* delegate rules development for, 107–15, 122–23, 156–58; Democratic nomination reforms for, 58–63; Democratic superdelegates in, 158–60; effect of delegate selection rules, 115; Jackson candidacy, 112–16; Mondale strategy, 66, 68–69; sequencing of primary contests, 31–34, 70; strategies and outcomes, 16, 129–34

Election and primaries of *1988:* delegate selection rules, 117–18; favorite-son effects, 175; influence of sequencing on primary campaign strategies, 38–39; Jackson candidacy, 116–17; Republican campaign, 37; Super Tuesday, 38

Election and primaries of *1992,* 41

Election and primaries of *1996,* 37, 71–73

Election and primaries of *2000:* bipartisan attempt to coordinate primary schedule, 73; campaign financing, 48; Republican campaign, 37; sequencing of primary contests, 34–35

Election and primaries of *2004:* campaign financing, 48–49; Dean candidacy, 74; Republican Party schedule reform, 178

Election and primaries of *2008,* 16; campaign financing, 49, 141; delegate counts, 82, 119, 120; Democratic candidates' strategies and outcomes, 140–45; Democratic convention, 172; Democratic superdelegates in, 160–65; earliest primary contests, 22–23, 141; hypothetical winner-take-all primary scenario, 142; Super Tuesday, 45. *See also* Giuliani presidential campaign (*2008*); McCain *2008* campaign; Michigan/Florida controversy; Obama campaign (*2008*)

Election and primaries of *2012,* 183–84

Estrich, Susan, 157

Expectations, 30

Fahrenkopf, Frank, 85

Fair and Representative Presidential Primaries Act, 177

Farah, Barbara, 149

Favorite-son candidates, 153–54, 175

Federal Corrupt Practices Act, 180

Feminist politicians, 109, 157

Ferraro, Geraldine, 109, 157

Financing: Clinton *2008* campaign, 46, 141; course of *1980* Republican election, 127, 128; federal matching funds, 48–49; Internet fund raising, 48–59; public financing of primaries, 47–49

Firestone, Leonard K., 122

Firewall strategy, 37, 72

Florida. *See* Michigan/Florida controversy

Ford, Gerald. *See* Election and primaries of *1976*

Fowler, Carol, 78

Fowler, Don, 34–35, 38, 90, 97, 111, 115

Fraser, Donald, 94, 95, 107, 110. *See also* McGovern-Fraser Commission

Fraser, Douglas, 58

Friebert, Robert, 109

Fringe candidates, 105

From, Al, 109

Frontloading: cause of, 22; Clinton *1992* campaign, 42; Gore *2000* campaign, 34–35; Mondale *1984* campaign, 31–34; party attempts to reduce, 61–62; Republican response after *1996* election, 71–73; strategic implications, 22, 31, 34; trends, 22, 57, 71. *See also* Iowa and New Hampshire; Sequencing of state primaries

Front-runners, 43

Gallen, Hugh, 60, 63

Gardner, William, 64, 79

Gephardt, Dick, 117

Germond, Jack, 130–31, 159

Gifford, Charles, 69

Giuliani presidential campaign (*2008*): early primary contests, 22; financing, 49; primary strategy, 39–41, 123–24

Glenn, John, 32–33, 43, 66, 69, 70, 112–13, 122–23, 130, 133

Godwin, Lamond, 113

Goldwater, Barry, 11

Gore, Al: primary campaign *1988,* 38, 117. *See also* Election and primaries of *2000*

Governance, effects of nominating process, 24–25, 58, 59–60

Hagan, Tim, 122–23
Hall, Blake, 179
Harkin, Tom, 41, 67
Hart, Gary, *See* Election and primaries
   of *1984*
Hart, Peter, 69
Hasen, Richard, 180–81
Hatcher, Richard, 114
Haugland, Jean, 69
Henry, Mike, 46
Herman, Alexis, 3, 75–76
Hildebrand, Steve, 45
Hoffman, Harold G., 10
Huckabee, Mike, 40, 119, 125–27
Humphrey, Hubert, 13–14, 15
Hunt, Jim, 58, 156
Hunt Commission, 58–63, 107,
   108–11, 156, 158
Hutcheson, Rick, 29–30, 96, 167

Ickes, Harold, 46, 117, 141, 162
Ickes, Harold, Jr., 107
Internet, 48–59
Iowa and New Hampshire, 4; Carter
   1976 campaign, 27–28, 53–54;
   Carter *1980* campaign, 29–30, 31;
   challenges to Hunt Commission
   reforms, 63–69; competition
   between parties for earliest primary,
   21–22, 73; criticisms of electoral significance of, 54–55, 57–60; Democratic *1992* primary strategies, 39–40;
   failure of window rule, 69–71; Gore
   2000 campaign, 35; Gore *1988* strategy, 38; Hunt Commission reforms,
   58–63; media coverage, 16–17,
   21–22, 22, 59, 70–71;
   Michigan/Florida controversy and,
   74–77, 79; Mondale's *1984* strategy,
   32, 58–59; Obama *2008* strategy, 44;
   public financing of primaries and,
   48; reform efforts after *1976* election, 53–57; reform efforts after

2000 election, 73–74; regional primary proposals, 174–75, 176, 178;
   Republican *2008* primary contests,
   39–40; Republican reform efforts
   after *1996* election, 71–73; Republican sequencing strategies, 37;
   resistance to change in primary
   sequencing, 79–80; strategic significance, 22–23, 27–28, 52–53, 70–71,
   81; turnout trends, 16; window rule
   exemptions, 56–58, 60–63

Jackson, Henry S., 54
Jackson, Jesse, 38–39, 89, 112–18, 133,
   160
Jackson, John S., 150
Johnson, James, 158
Johnson, Jim, 33
Johnson, Lyndon, 13, 52
Jordan, Hamilton, 27–28, 29, 53, 100
Junkins, Lowell, 67

Kaiser, Robert, 127
Kaplan, Marty, 130–31, 159
Kefauver, Estes, 9–10
Kennedy, John F., 10–11, 112
Kennedy, Robert, 13
Kennedy, Ted, 30, 32, 62, 107, 137–39,
   157
Kerry, John, 49
Kessel, John, 11
Key, V. O., 169
Kind, Ron, 12
Kirbo, Charles, 28
Kirkland, Lane, 58
Klobuchar, Amy, 174
Kramer, Michael, 37

Labor movement, 58, 60, 61, 62, 91, 93,
   94–95, 107. *See also* AFL–CIO
Lance, Bert, 32
Lang, Scott, 55, 56, 98, 107, 168
Law, John, 61, 67

Lawrence, W. H., 9
Lawsky, David, 159
Lengle, James, 135
Levin, Carl, 34–35, 75, 76, 77, 182
Levin, Sander, 177
Levin/Nelson Presidential Primary Reform Bill, 177
Lewis, Drew, 129
Lieberman, Joseph, 174
Loevy, Robert D., 178
Long, Gillis, 109, 156, 157
Loophole primaries, 102, 103, 104, 122; after election of *1976*, 96–97; after election of *1984*, 132–33; in election of *1976*, 90–91, 94–96; reinstatement after *1980* election, 108–09, 110
Lucas, Scott, 10

Madigan, Michael, 45
Madison, James, 25
Maisel, Louis, 54
The Making of the President (White), 10
Malbin, Michael, 92
Mannatt, Charles, 65, 66, 68, 114, 157
Mayer, William, 59–60, 181
McAuliffe, Terry, 75
McCain, John, 37, 40–41, 48, 125
McCarthy, Eugene, 13
McCloskey, Peter, 122
McCollum, Bill, 40
McGovern, George, 14, 15–16, 17, 99, 165. *See also* McGovern-Fraser Commission
McGovern-Fraser Commission, 14–15, 18–19, 86–88, 89
Media coverage: campaign spending, 49; Carter *1976* campaign, 28; significance of earliest primary contests, 16–17, 21–22, 59, 70–71, 73; superdelegate count, 159–60, 162; Super Tuesday *1984* Democratic primary, 130–31

Michigan/Florida controversy: Clinton campaign strategy, 1–3, 163–64; course of Democratic primary contests, 44, 78–79; origins, 74–78; outcome, 3; resolution, 164, 183–84; superdelegate allocation, 163–64
Michigan Plan for regional primaries, 177–78
Mikulski, Barbara, 88, 90. *See also* Commission on Delegate Selection
Mitofsky, Warren, 149–50
Moe, Dick, 132
Momentum: *1976* primaries, 27–28; *1980* primaries, 127–29; *1984* primaries, 129–34; *1992* primaries, 42; *2008* primaries, 40, 44–45; proportional representation rules and, 136; strategic significance, 27–28, 47
Mondale, Walter, 16, 63, 112. *See also* Election and primaries of *1984*
Morrison, Toni, 1
Moulitsas, Markos, 162
Muskie, Edmund, 16, 17, 165

Nagle, Dave, 67, 68
National Association of Secretaries of State, 174
National Education Association, 95, 96
National primary proposal, 25, 61
New Hampshire: campaign spending on media, 49; evolution of primary process in, 51–52; significance of, for Massachusetts politicians, 62. *See also* Iowa and New Hampshire
Nixon, Richard, 94, 165
Nominating conventions: contested conventions of post-reform era, 165–67; delegate robot rule, 168–70, 171; Democrats' *1968* convention, 14–15, 85; Democrats' *1972* convention, 86–87, 148–50; Democrats' *1976* convention, 87–96; Democrats'

1980 convention, 167–70; Democrats' *2008* convention, 172; future of, 172–73; historical evolution, 147–48; presence of party notables in, 150–52; presence of uncommitted delegates in, 153–55; quota system of delegation composition, 89; Republican *2000* convention, 178; Republican *2008* convention, 184–85; Republican rule change rules, 19–20; significance of, in election process, 4–5

Nomination process, generally: congressional authority to change, 6–7; criticism of wider public participation in, 23–25; future prospects, 183–86; modern evolution, 6–7; motivation for Democratic reforms, 13–19; obstacles to congressional intervention, 179–82; pre-reform era, 7–12; rules evolution, 3–4; salient issues of modern era, 4–5; ultimate authority or oversight, 183

Norton, Eleanor Holmes, 117

Novak, Robert, 11

Obama campaign (*2008*): superdelegate strategy, 12, 162–63, 164–65; winning strategy, 43–47. *See also* Election and primaries of *2008*

O'Dwyer, William, 10

Ohio Plan for regional primaries, 176–77

Oregon v. *Mitchell*, 180

Ostro, Justin, 58

Panagopoulos, Costas, 147

Party leadership: arguments for increased role in nomination process, 24–25; control over state nomination rules, 60–61, 69–71; independence of caucus system from, 15, 16; influence in pre- reform nominating system, 8, 9–10; McGovern-Fraser reforms, 15; preference for primaries over caucuses, 17–19, 21; presence in nominating conventions, 150–52; quota system for convention representation, 89; response to Carter presidency, 58; scheduling primaries, 35; superdelegate purpose, 12–13

Patman, Carrin, 99, 107, 110, 111

Patterson, Thomas, 182

Payne, David, 163

Pelosi, Nancy, 65, 66, 68

Penn, Mark, 164

Perkins, John, 92, 108–09

Peterson, Bill, 127

Plissner, Martin, 149–50

Plouffe, David, 12, 43, 44, 45, 162

Polsby, Nelson, 8–9, 24, 31, 149

Powell, Jody, 28, 53

Presidential Elections (Polsby, Wildavsky), 8–9

Price, David, 75, 82–84, 149

Primaries: origins, 8; party preference for, versus caucuses, 17–19, 21; in pre-reform era, 8–9, 10–12; purpose, 8; reform attempts following *1976* election, 53. *See also* Iowa and New Hampshire; Sequencing of state primaries; *specific election year*

Proportional representation in delegate allocation: charges of discrimination in *1984* election rules, 113–15; Democratic *1980* contests, 137–40; Democratic *2008* contests, 140–45; election of *1976* and, 88–96; election of *1980* and, 96–106; election of *1988* and, 118; Fairness Commission reforms, 115–16; fair reflection and, 86, 89–90, 92–93, 110–11; fringe candidates and, 105; Hunt Commission reforms, 107–11, 116; mathematics, 136–37; McGovern-Fraser reforms, 86–87; origins, 85; outcomes in industrial states, 107, 108; party differences, 81–82; perceived as affirmative action plan, 106; perception of, after *1980* election, 106–07; Republican Party rules, 82–85, 121–22; sliding window rule, 97–98, 100–01; strategic implications, 82, 97, 98–99, 120, 135–36; threshold rules, 97, 98, 99, 100–01, 110, 116

Public financing of primaries: declining significance of, 47–49; sequencing strategies and, 47–48; state spending limits, 47, 48

Public opinion: national primary, 25; party role in nomination process, 25; pressure for nomination process reform, 182–83

Quiet Revolution (Shafer), 14

Ranney, Austin, 25
Ray v. Blair, 180
Reagan, Ronald, 36, 94. *See also* Election and primaries of *1976;* Election and primaries of *1980*
Reform of nominating system, 5
Regional Presidential Primaries Plan, 174–75
Regional Primaries Act, 174–75
Regional primary proposals: congressional authority to implement, 179–81; Delaware Plan, 178; Michigan Plan, 177–78; National Association of Secretaries of State's plan, 174–75; Ohio Plan, 176–77; public opinion, 182–83; Texas Plan, 175–76
Reilly, John, 111
Reilly, Richard, 155
Rendon, John, 30
Republican Party: caucus reforms to increase media coverage, 21–22;

delegate allocation system, 81–85, 120, 121–22, 125–27; DO committee reforms, 20–21; election of *1964,* 11–12; election of *1980,* 127–29; election of *2008,* 119, 125–27; future of nominating process, 184–85; party leadership presence in nominating conventions, 150–51; regional primary proposals, 175–79; restraints on nomination process reform, 19–20; sequencing of primary contests, 36–37; superdelegates, 158

Reston, J., 9
Richardson, Bill, 1, 78
Robb, Rick, 129
Robertson, Pat, 37
Rock, Phil, 104
Rokita, Todd, 175
Romney presidential campaign (*2008*), 39–40, 41, 49
Rookie candidates, 43
Roosevelt, James, 3
Roosevelt, Jim, 182, 183–84
Ross, Dan, 36–37
Rove, Karl, 73
Rules and By-Laws Committee, Democratic Party, 34–35, 77, 78, 87, 94, 95; convention of *1980,* 168–69; Michigan/Florida *2008* controversy, 2–3

Sabato, Larry, 40
Sanford, Terry, 93
Savage, David Von, 124
Scalia, Antoni, 179
Schmitz, John, 122
Schneider, William, 43
Seaborn, Brent, 39–40
Sebelius, Kathleen, 45
Segal, Eli, 107
Sequencing of state primaries: advantages of incumbency in influencing,

33; bipartisan attempt to coordinate, 73; Carter *1976* campaign, 27–28; Carter *1980* campaign, 29–30; challenges to manipulating, 35–36; competition between parties for media attention, 21–22, 73; congressional authority to set, 179–81; delegate selection rules in *2008* and, 123–27; diversity goals and, 75–76; future prospects, 185–86; implications for governance, 24–25, 58, 59–60; implications for public financing of primaries, 47–48; influence on campaign strategy, 38–39; Michigan/Florida controversy, 1–2; Obama *2008* strategy, 43–47; political restraints to congressional intervention, 181–82; Reagan *1980* campaign, 36–37; strategic significance, 4, 27, 37, 47; trend, 71. *See also* Frontloading; Iowa and New Hampshire; Regional primary proposals
Shadegg, Stephen, 11
Shafer, Byron, 14, 15, 135
Siegel, Mark, 92, 93, 96, 100
Singer, William, 89
Slagle, Robert, 114
Slating process, 128
Sliding window rule, 97–98, 100–01
Smith, Greg, 67
Smith v. *Allwright,* 180
South Carolina, Republican firewall strategy, 36–37
Special interests, 34
Spirou, Chris, 66
State rules: ability of party leadership to control, 60–61, 69–71; competition for earliest primaries, 54; New Hampshire's primary, 51–52; origins of primary system, 8; qualifications for ballot placement, 154; Republican Party delegate allocation rules, 82–85; scheduling primaries,

35; strategic manipulation of delegate allocation rules, 121–27; transition to primaries from caucuses, 21
Steiger, William A., 84
Stevenson, Adlai, 9
Strauss, Robert, 91, 93, 95, 96
Straw polls, 31–32
Superdelegates: election of *1984,* 158–60; election of *2008,* 12, 145, 160–65; Hunt Commission reforms for *1984* convention, 109; independence of, pledged status and, 12–13, 109, 162; origins, 59, 109–10, 156–58; public awareness, 12; rationale, 155–56; Republican, 158; resistance to concept of, 109, 116, 157; selection and number, 157, 158
Super Tuesday: Carter *1980* campaign, 29–30, 137; Clinton *2008* strategy, 145; Giuliani *2008* strategy, 123; Gore *1988* strategy, 38–39; Mondale *1984* campaign, 130–34; Obama *2008* strategy, 44–45, 46, 141

Texas Plan for regional primaries, 175–76
Thornburgh, Ron, 178
Thurmond, Strom, 36
Torricelli, Bob, 110–11
Touhy, Jack, 103, 104
Truman, Harry, 9, 52
Tsongas, Paul, 41–42
Tucker, Dan, 28

Udall, Mo, 28, 54–55, 94
Uncommitted delegates, 109, 152–55
United Auto Workers, 95, 96
Unit rule, 85, 87
Upton, Richard E., 51

Vance, Bob, 90
Vick, Kathy, 114
Voting Rights Act, 75–76

Wallace, George, 87, 90, 148–49
Walters, Ron, 75–76
Washington, Harold, 112
Waters, Maxine, 59
Wayne, Stephen, 40
Wexler, Anne, 96
White, Cliff, 11
White, John, 100, 103, 104
White, Theodore, 10, 11
Whitney, Tom, 56
Wildavsky, Aaron, 8–9
Wilson, Woodrow, 147–48

Window rule: challenges to Hunt Commission reforms, 63–69; exceptions, 29–30, 56–58, 60–63; failure of, 69–71; origins, 55–56
Winograd, Morley, 53. *See also* Winograd Commission
Winograd Commission, 94, 95, 96–97, 98–99, 102, 149
Witcover, Jules, 17, 21, 130–31, 159
Witt, Evan, 133

Zogby, John, 40